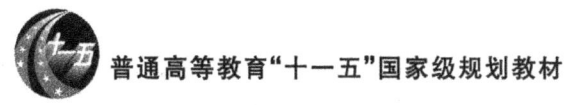

普通高等教育"十一五"国家级规划教材

美英报刊文章阅读
（精选本）学习辅导
（第五版）

主　编　周学艺　赵　林
副主编　刘满贵　张慧宇

编委　袁宪军　杨小凤　艾久红　陈文玉　丁剑仪
　　　高天增　葛　红　郭丽萍　李素杰　李　欣
　　　刘满贵　刘雪燕　罗国华　马　兴　石　芸
　　　汪学磊　韦毅民　徐　威　杨　博　叶慧瑛
　　　张慧宇　赵　林　周建萍　周学艺　左　进

图书在版编目(CIP)数据

美英报刊文章阅读.精选本.学习辅导/周学艺,赵林主编.—5版.—北京:北京大学出版社,2014.5
(大学美英报刊教材系列)
ISBN 978-7-301-24234-6

Ⅰ.①美… Ⅱ.①周…②赵… Ⅲ.①英语—阅读教学—高等学校—自学参考资料 Ⅳ.H319.4

中国版本图书馆 CIP 数据核字(2014)第 096126 号

书　　　　名：	美英报刊文章阅读(精选本)学习辅导(第五版)
著作责任者：	周学艺　赵　林　主编
责 任 编 辑：	李　颖
标 准 书 号：	ISBN 978-7-301-24234-6/H·3521
出 版 发 行：	北京大学出版社
地　　　　址：	北京市海淀区成府路 205 号　100871
网　　　　址：	http://www.pup.cn　新浪官方微博:@北京大学出版社
电 子 信 箱：	zpup@pup.cn
电　　　　话：	邮购部 62752015　发行部 62750672　编辑部 62754382 出版部 62754962
印　刷　者：	北京虎彩文化传播有限公司
经　销　者：	新华书店
	650 毫米×980 毫米　16 开本　16 印张　450 千字 1994 年 12 月第 1 版　2001 年 10 月第 2 版 2007 年 1 月第 3 版　2010 年 7 月第 4 版 2014 年 5 月第 5 版　2023 年 4 月第 4 次印刷
定　　　　价：	36.00 元

未经许可,不得以任何方式复制或抄袭本书之部分或全部内容。
版权所有,侵权必究
举报电话:010—62752024　电子信箱:fd@pup.pku.edu.cn

前 言

《美英报刊文章阅读（精选本）学习辅导》（第五版）主要为自修者和初次授课教员而编，因《美英报刊文章选读》（上下册）的部分课文与《精选本》的选文相同，所以，《学习辅导》也可供使用《上下册》的师生参考。

本书助读分四部分：背景知识、语言点、阅读理解和补充阅读。背景知识部分包括 Summary, The Author 和 Background Information。语言点分两部分，I. New Words 和 II. Notes，这是对教材中生词和注释的补充，旨在为自修者和自考者提供帮助。第三部分提供习题参考答案（Reference Answers to Questions）和本课需掌握的重点词语（Words to Know）。习题参考答案旨在帮助学习者加深理解和掌握每课的主要内容。重点词语是学生学习一课后必须掌握的与政治、军事、外交、社会、经济、法律、宗教、文教和科技等相关的词语，与学生在大学一、二年级打基础时要求掌握的有关词语如 byproduct, prolong, steady, prior to, make a comeback 等侧重点有所不同。这些词语和课后注释（Notes）是复习考试的重点，其中有些词语，读者不但要知道意思，还要能用英语释义或译成汉语，如 Foggy Bottom（美国首都华盛顿一地名，喻美国务院及其模糊不清的政策或声明等），Secretary of State（美国国务卿），Speaker（美国众议院或英国议会下院议长），Spokesman/spokeswoman（发言人），Capitol Hill 或 the Hill（美国会山，喻"国"会），the State of the Union message（美国国情咨文），Downing Street（No. 10）（唐宁街10号，喻英"首相府"、"英国首相"、"英国政府或内阁"）和 Buckingham Palace（白金汉宫，喻"英国王室或王宫"）等。

本书有10个附录，其中有外刊课考试的若干说明、标题自我测试和四份考试样题等重要内容。此外，还有一些是读者学习美英报刊的必要参考资料。

本书中出现的缩略词，读者可查缩略词表（Short Forms）。See（cf）Note... of Lesson... 指的是见（参见或比较）课本中课文后的注释；See（cf）Language Point... of Lesson... 指的是见（参见或比较）本书中第二部分的语言点。

  书中的错误或不妥之处望批评指正。如通过电话就与周学艺联系，如通过 email 请与赵林探讨。

周学艺 赵林

E-Mail：Zhou_xueyi@sina.com

Zhao_lin28@aliyun.com

Contents

Lesson One
    China opens doors of state-run companies to world's top talent ……… 1

Lesson Two
    An American in Beijing ……… 9

Lesson Three
    Tiger Mom… Meet Panda Dad ……… 15

Lesson Four
    Is an Ivy League Diploma Worth It? ……… 23

Lesson Five
    Debt Burden Alters Outlook for US Graduates ……… 28

Lesson Six
    The Evolution Wars ……… 36

Lesson Seven
    Obama Wins a Second Term as U.S. President ……… 45

Lesson Eight
    The Economy Sucks. But Is It '92 Redux? ……… 53

Lesson Nine
    Five myths about the American dream ……… 59

Lesson Ten
    Is America's new declinism for real? ……… 66

Lesson Eleven
    Pentegon Digs In on Cyberwar Front ……… 73

Lesson Twelve
    Terrorized by "War on Terror" ……… 78

Lesson Thirteen
    Spies Among Us: Modern-Day Espionage ········· 85

Lesson Fourteen
    Google's Zero-Carbon Quest ········· 91

Lesson Fifteen
    Little Sympathy for Margaret Thatcher Among
    Former Opponents ········· 101

Lesson Sixteen
    Britain's Embattled Newspapers Are Leading the World ······ 107

Lesson Seventeen
    Mrs Windsor, Anyone? ········· 119

Lesson Eighteen
    Rethinking the welfare state: Asia's next revolution ········· 125

Lesson Nineteen
    The hopeful continent: Africa rising ········· 134

Lesson Twenty
    Greece as Victim ········· 141

Lesson Twenty-one
    The Coming Conflict in the Arctic ········· 147

Lesson Twenty-two
    Does Online Dating Make It Harder to Find 'the One'? ······ 155

Lesson Twenty-three
    Yawns: A generation of the young, rich and frugal ········· 160

Lesson Twenty-four
    Ahead-of-the-Curve Careers ········· 166

Lesson Twenty-Five
    Model economies: The beauty business ········· 173

Lesson Twenty-six
    Nanospheres leave cancer no place to hide ········· 180

Lesson Twenty-seven
    Why Bilinguals Are Smarter ················· 185

Lesson Twenty-eight
    Basketball: The incredible story of Jeremy Lin,
    the new superstar of the NBA ················· 191

Lesson Twenty-nine
    He's Back All Right, Now with a Memoir ················· 196

Lesson Thirty
    The reality-television business: Entertainers to the world ······ 203

附　录

I	美国政府 ·················	209
II	英国政府 ·················	214
III	二战以来美国历任总统一览 ·················	217
IV	二战以来英国历任首相一览 ·················	220
V	值得注意的几个词缀 ·················	223
VI	报刊标题常用词汇 ·················	224
VII	标题自我测试 ·················	229
VIII	报刊课考试的若干建议 ·················	234
IX	考试样题 ·················	236

Lesson One

China opens doors of state-run companies to world's top talent

Part One

Summary

　　经历三十多年的改革开放,中国业已发展为第一大外汇储备国(2006年始)、第二大对外贸易国以及全球第二大经济体(2011年始)。这一快速发展离不开廉价劳动力。然而随着我国进入老龄化社会(1999年始),未来中国很难再以同样的经济发展模式来推动经济的可持续发展。有人猜测中国经济将会面临世界经济理论中的"路易斯拐点"(Lewis Turning Point)。我国的经济转型需要大量具备国际竞争力的高端人才。但是,根据麦肯锡全球研究机构和瑞士艺珂人力资源学院等知名机构的报告,中国在基础应用、管理和研究等众多领域面临人才匮乏和人才流失(brain drain),这将严重制约中国各行业的创新和经济发展。如何激活人才培养和人才引进机制,改善人才环境,提高中国的国际竞争力和创新能力等,都是摆在中国面前亟待解决的问题。为此,我国提出科教兴国和人才强国战略。《国家中长期人才发展规划纲要 2010—2020》提出"开发利用国内外人才"、"大力吸引海外高层次人才和急需紧缺专门人才,坚持自主培养开发与引进海外人才并举,积极利用国际教育培训人才。""千人计划"就是其中一个重要举措。目的就是通过提供优厚的薪资和便利的签证条件来吸纳海外专家来华工作,推动技术创新,以提升中国在重点领域的竞争力。

　　本文是一篇专栏评论,作者分析了中国的人才战略,但在呼吁美国重视它可能带来人才竞争的同时,也对通过引进海外人才来解决中国的创新问题提出质疑,认为提高创新能力的最终出路在于创造有利于创新创业的人才环境,而创新需要勇气打破传统,挑战陈规。这在提倡"和谐社会"的中国并不容易。但无论怎样,"千人计划"已经吸引了的经济和其他领域为数众多的优秀海外人才回国创业,他们正在不同的领域发挥作用,必将给中国带来深远的影响。

The Author

Vivek Wadhwa is Vice President of Academics and Innovation at Singularity University; Fellow of Arthur & Toni Rembe Rock Center for Corporate Governance, Stanford University; Director of Research at the Center for Entrepreneurship and Research Commercialization at the Pratt School of Engineering, Duke University; and distinguished visiting scholar, Halle Institute of Global Learning, Emory University.

Wadhwa oversees the academic programs at Singularity University, which educates a select group of leaders about the exponentially growing technologies that are soon going to change our world. In his roles at Stanford, Duke, and Emory universities, Wadhwa lectures in class on subjects such as entrepreneurship and public policy, helps prepare students for the real world, and leads groundbreaking research projects. He is an advisor to several governments; mentors entrepreneurs; and is a regular columnist for *The Washington Post*, *Bloomberg BusinessWeek*, and the American Society of Engineering Education's *Prism* magazine.

Background Information

1. Thousand Foreign Talents Program 千人计划

In 2008, the Chinese government started a plan called the "Overseas High-level Talents Introduction Project" (海外高层次人才引进计划), referred to as the "Thousand Talents Plan". According to national development strategic goals, the Chinese government wanted to introduce about 2,000 scientists and leading talents to China within 5 to 10 years. In order to compete for talents and scientists, the local governments launched the local "Thousand Talents Plan".

According to the project's eligibility criteria(合格标准), employers should be universities, scientific institutions, Chinese-invested enterprises or joint ventures in which Chinese investors have a more than 50 percent stake. The targeted foreign professionals include professors at prestigious universities and scientific research institutions as well as senior technology and management professionals in world-renowned corporations or financial institutions. The Program also seeks those who control intellectual property rights(知识产权) or master core technology and those with overseas experience in starting and running businesses and other skills that China urgently needs.

2. strategic entrepreneurship 战略型企业家素质

Strategic entrepreneurship is a newly recognized field that draws from the fields of strategic management and entrepreneurship. The field emerged officially with the 2001 special issue of the *Strategic Management Journal* on "strategic entrepreneurship"; the *Strategic Entrepreneurship Journal*, appeared in 2007. Strategic entrepreneurship is built around two core ideas. (1) Strategy formulation and execution involves attributes that are fundamentally entrepreneurial, such as alertness, creativity, and judgment, and entrepreneurs try to create and capture value through resource acquisition and competitive positioning. (2) Opportunity-seeking and advantage-seeking—the former is the central subject of the entrepreneurship field, and the latter, the central subject of the strategic management field—are processes that should be considered jointly. This entry explains the specific links between strategy and entrepreneurship, reviews the emergence and development of the strategic entrepreneurship field, and discusses key implications and applications. Its focus has been on how firms systematically discover and exploit opportunities via processes of search, learning, and innovation.

3. Wang Huiyao 王辉耀

Wang Huiyao (1958—) is a well known leading authority on global talent, returnees, overseas Chinese and students, and migration issues and an expert on Chinese firms going global; a founder of a global Chinese think tank(智囊团) and several Chinese well known overseas returnees organizations; a social entrepreneur and a top adviser to the Chinese government at both central and provincial levels as well as to international organizations and Fortune 500 firms. He has a work life span over both Chinese and foreign governments, multinational executive and business entrepreneur and academic circle. He has taught at Peking University, Tsinghua University, University of Western Ontario and was a visiting fellow at Brookings Institution. Currently he is a senior Fellow(高级研究员) at Harvard Kennedy School and he has published over 30 books and over 100 papers. He is also a frequent speaker at various international forums and often interviewed by various well known media.

4. state-owned enterprises 国有企业

A business that is owned and operated for profitby the government is a state-owned enterprise, also referred to as an SOE in initials. The characteristics that define these businesses vary from one country to another.

A state-owned enterprise is usually a legal entity(法人实体). This means that generally it can be held liable(有责任的) and can hold other entities liable. These businesses are often subject to many of the same regulations and procedures private businesses would be subject to.

5. *hexie shehui* or harmonious society 和谐社会

A blueprint for social development featuring decent living standards for the majority of people, a tolerant society and peaceful coexistenceamong humans and between the human society and nature.

The concept was first floated in 2004 and then amplified in October 2006, when the Chinese Communist Party set specific goals for building a harmonious society by 2020. The goals range from fostering the rule of law, substantial protection for private property（私有财产）, developed public services to promoting creativity and more efficient use of resources.

Stemming from ancient Chinese values about harmony, the blueprint underlines the need to fine tune relationship between different social entities. The idea is also evident in the country's foreign policy, particularly in its call for "a harmonious world".

Part Two

Language Points

I. New Words

ambitious /æmˈbɪʃəs/ *adj.* having a desire to achieve a particular and great goal 雄心勃勃的

barrier /ˈbærɪə(r)/ *n.* sth immaterial that impedes or separates;

blocking the way obstacle 障碍

brilliant /'brɪlɪənt/ *adj.* very bright; distinctive; talented 聪明,高智商的

capability /ˌkeɪpə'bɪlətɪ/ *n.* ability; potentiality, capable of doing 能力

commitment /kə'mɪtmənt/ *n.* an agreement, pledge or promise to do sth in the future 承诺

cultivate /'kʌltɪveɪt/ *v.* to raise, to foster the growth of 培养

discrimination /dɪˌskrɪmɪ'neɪʃn/ *n.* prejudiced or biased towards (against sth.) 歧视

evaluate /ɪ'væljʊeɪt/ *v.* to determine or fix the value of 评价

festivity /fe'stɪvətɪ/ *n.* a festive event 庆祝活动,庆典

front-page /'frʌnt'peɪdʒ/ *adj.* printed on the front page of a newspaper; very newsworthy 头版新闻的;很有新闻价值的

innovation /ˌɪnə'veɪʃn/ *n.* the introduction of sth new; being creative 革新,创新

launch /lɑʊntʃ/ *v.* to set up or found and initialize sth. 发起

participate /pɑː'tɪsɪpeɪt/ *v.* to take part in 参与

pose /pəʊz/ *v.* to be the cause of (sth difficult to deal with); present 造成(难题等)

rank /ræŋk/ *n.* relative standing or position among others 排行

secure /sɪ'kjʊə(r)/ *v.* to safeguard; guarantee 确保

setting /'setɪŋ/ *n.* the context or environment in which sth is set 环境,氛围

transform /træns'fɔːm/ *v.* to change in composition or structure 改变,转型

upgrade /ˌʌp'greɪd/ *v.* to raise the quality or level of sth. 提升

victim /'vɪktɪm/ *n.* a person, animal, or thing that suffers pain, death, harm, destruction etc, as a result of other people's actions, or of illness, bad luck etc 牺牲品

II. Notes

1. lay off (Par. 2)—to suspend (workers) from employment with the intention of re-employing them at a later date 解雇、遣散
2. high-tech (Par. 3)—高科技的,"high tech" 的形容词形式,也作 "high-technology"。
3. GDP (Par. 3)—*abrev.* and initials of Gross Domestic Product. It refers to the market value of all officially recognized final goods and services produced within a country in a given period of time. 国内生

产总值

4. China has launched several high-priority programs ... talent demands. (Par. 4)—中国已经启动了几个优先项目以鼓励具有熟练技能的海外华人回国,这一切正是为了满足国内对人才的紧迫需求。
5. state-owned enterprises (Par. 7)—国有企业 (*cf.* state-run company)
6. permanent resident-type visas (Par. 7)—永久居住签证(green card)
7. This announcement was front-page news in China ... were not widely covered. (Par. 8)—这项计划在中国登上了报纸的头条新闻,但是在美国对这类事件却没有广泛的报道,然而,我们不能低估其重要性。

   cover—to report the details of (an event) by a newspaper, TV network etc 包含,覆盖
8. nothing short of(Par. 8)—nothing less than, nothing but(用于加强语气)不少于……的;简直
9. China's future growth ... its population dividend and investment. (Par. 9)—中国未来的发展将更加依赖于这一新人才战略,尽管她过去的成功基本上依靠的是她的人口优势和外国投资 FDI。

   population dividend—advantages obtained from the population—人口优势(指一个国家的年轻劳动人口占总人口比重较大,抚养率比较低,为经济发展创造了有利条件。)
10. The country is determined to win this race if only to ensure it can complete the goal of transforming its economy. (Par. 9)—中国下决心要赢得这场比赛,即使只是为了确保实现其经济转型的目标。
11. research proposal (Par. 11)—a document written by a researcher that provides a detailed description of the proposed program. It is like an outline of the entire research process that gives a reader a summary of the information discussed in a project. (研究计划)
12. research grants (Par. 11)—funding designated for research 研究经费

Part Three

Questions and Answers for Your Reference

1. What is the main reason for China to open its door to talents from other parts of the world?

   China has a severe shortage of skilled talents. The situation will

likely get worse as China's high-tech industries grow and it increases its national R&D spending.
2. What is the "Thousand Foreign Talents Program"?

   The "Thousand Foreign Talents Program" is launched by the Chinese government to bring 2,000 experienced engineers, scientists, and other experts of Chinese origin back from the West.
3. So far, what has China been doing in welcoming the returnees?

   China has recruited more than 1,500 high quality talents, and 300 returnees have been enrolled in management training courses. These individuals, while re-learning how to operate successfully within the Chinese setting, are expected to serve as a critical catalyst in transforming China's innovation environment in ways that will enhance the country's competitive edge across a range of key, strategic industries.
4. What are the favorable conditions offered to attract those overseas talents?

   The Chinese government announced that it would permit foreign nationals to take senior positions in science and technology sectors and state-owned enterprises. They will also pay foreigners salaries equal to what they can earn at top paying jobs in the US. And the government announced that it intended to offer permanent resident-type visas to foreign entrepreneurs.
5. What problems have some of the returnees found after coming back to China?

   Some of the returnees have found themselves victims of discrimination and petty jealousy from those who fell behind. Moreover, they have struggled to re-adapt themselves to China's relationship-oriented culture, which stands in sharp contrast to the performance-oriented culture of the West. For instance, returnees are frequently confounded by the "personalized" ways research proposals are evaluated and research grants are distributed.
6. Why is there hesitation among those overseas Chinese?

   Because they are faced with the challenges of returning. For example, they would prefer their children to complete their education abroad and not have to suffer through China's "examination hell" prior to college.

Words to Know

catalyst, commitment, competitive edge, conducive, cultivate, enroll, entrepreneurship, expatriates, fraud, innovation economy, lay off, high-priority, national priority, plagiarism, rank, recruit, R&D, GDP, re-adapt, re-learning, returnee, state-owned enterprises, state-run companies, strategic entrepreneurs, strategic industries, talent, talent pool, underestimate, upgrade, workforce

Part Four

Supplementary Reading

China approaching the turning point (From The *Economist*, January 31, 2013)

Lesson Two

An American in Beijing

Part One

Summary

对于美国学生来说,出国留学并不是稀罕的事情。随着中国经济的发展和国际地位的提高,中国也成了他们出国深造的新目的地。据统计,在 2005—2006 学年,美国的出国留学生人数是 223,534,其中的 9.3%(20788 人)选择去亚洲国家,而到中国来的人数只有大约 6,000 人。虽然如此,这个数字与过去相比仍显示出逐年上升的趋势。那么,他们为什么选择来中国留学呢?《环球》杂志记者 Lauren Konopacz 在北京的一所大学学习了一个学期之后,根据自己的亲身经历,对为什么出国、为什么选择亚洲、特别是为什么来中国留学这一问题进行了细致的分析。

Lauren Konopacz 认为,许多学生出国留学是为了学习外语,同时还可以增长阅历,扩大视野。另外,由于经济全球化的需要,特别是美国经济与中国经济的密切联系,美国迫切需要懂外语、了解外国文化的人才,因此美国政府出台了鼓励出国留学的政策。出国留学的意义还在于了解不同的文化,从而加深对本民族文化的了解,促进人类文明的发展。

The Author

Lauren Konopacz is an Editorial Intern with *The Globalist*. Lauren Konopacz comes from Sudbury, Massachusetts and is currently a student at the George Washington University, where she is a dual major in Asian Studies and International Affairs. She spent the fall semester of 2007 studying Chinese and politics at Beijing Foreign Languages University, a University in Beijing, China.

Background Information

1. The *Globalist*

The Globalist is a daily online magazine that "focuses on the economics, politics andculture" of globalization. "The Globalist" "aims to provide current and up-to-date news analysis and perspectives on wide-ranging global issues that touch all global citizens." It claims to be a unique international magazine that "accepts articles from authors across the globe and attempts to provide a voice to all in order to better understand the processes and impacts of globalization."

Its offices are based in Washington, DC, United States and it began publishing on January 3, 2000. *The Globalist* was founded by Stephan Richter, who is also its Publisher and Editor-in-Chief. *The Globalist*, in addition to its English-language flagship, also publishes German-and French-language editions.

2. Uncle Sam

Uncle Sam (initials U. S.) is a common national personification of the American government that, according to legend, came into use during the War of 1812 and was supposedly named for Samuel Wilson. The first use of Uncle Sam in literature was in the 1816 allegorical(寓言的)book *The Adventures of Uncle Sam in Search After His Lost Honor* by Frederick Augustus Fidfaddy. An Uncle Sam is mentioned as early as 1775, in the original "Yankee Doodle"(一首在美国广为传唱的歌曲, 康涅狄格州州歌) lyrics of the Revolutionary War. It is not clear whether this reference is to Uncle Sam as a metaphor for the United States. The lyrics as a whole clearly deride the military efforts of the young nation, besieging the British at Boston. The 13th stanza is:

Old Uncle Sam come there to change
Some pancakes and some onions,
For'*lasses* cakes, to carry home
To give his wife and young ones.

Part Two

Language Points

I. New Words

appealing /əˈpiːlɪŋ/ *adj*. attractive pleasing, or interesting 有吸引力的；有趣的

assumption /əˈsʌmpʃn/ *n*. sth that is taken as a fact or believed to be

true without proof; sth taken for granted; a supposition 假定,假设
available /ə'veɪləbl/ adj. (to) able to be had, obtained, used, seen, etc. 可获得的;可用的;可见的
capacity /kə'pæsəti/ n. the amount that something can hold or contain 容量,容积
connection /kə'nekʃn/ n. the state of being connected; relationship 联系;关系
contribute /kən'trɪbjuːt/ v. to join with others in giving (money, help, etc.) 捐献;捐助
emphatically /ɪm'fætɪklɪ/ adv. in a manner that shows emphasis; strongly; forcefully 强调地;强烈地;坚决地
enhance /ɪn'hɑːns/ v. to increase in strength or amount 提高,增加,增强
extensive /ɪk'stensɪv/ adj. large in amount, area, or range; having an effect on or including many parts 大量的;大规模的;广阔的;广泛的;广博的
federal /'fedərəl/ adj. of the central government of the US 美国联邦政府的
grossly /'grəʊslɪ/ adv. very unpleasantly; extremely
institution /ˌɪnstɪ'tjuːʃn/ n. an organization, usually a long-established or well-respected 社会机构
predominance /prɪ'dɒmɪnəns/ n. the state of being powerful, noticeable, or important, or largest in number 占优势,显著,支配地位
refreshing /rɪ'freʃɪŋ/ adj. pleasantly new and interesting 令人欣喜的,使人耳目一新的
senate /'senət/ n. the smaller and more important of the two parts of the central law-making body in such countries as Australia, France, and the US 参议院
steady /'stedɪ/ adj. moving or developing in an even, continuous way; regular 有规则的,平稳的
unequaled /ʌn'iːkwəld/ adj. fml not equaled or surpassed; greater or especially better than any other; matchless (正式)无与伦比的,无双的
Vietnam /ˌvjet'næm/ a country in SE Asia, next to Cambodia and China 越南

II. Notes

1. In the 2005 — 2006 academic year ... to study abroad in Asia. (Par. 2)—根据可获取的最新资料,2005—2006 学年,有 223,534 名美国学生在海外学习。这个数字只相当于全美大学生入学人数的 1%。在这 1% 的学生中,只有 9.3% 的学生选择来亚洲学习。
2. sell out (Par. 3)—sell all of (what was for sale)(货物)(全部)卖完;卖光
3. American Council on Education (Par. 5)—美国教育委员会
4. the U. S. Senate (Par. 8)—美国参议院。(见附录 I"美国政府")
5. Senate Resolution 308 (Par. 8)—(美国)参议院 308 号决议
6. Several of these points address the fact... and foreign skills. (Par. 9)—其中几条谈到,美国联邦政府的各事务处,教育机构以及各大公司都很缺乏具有国际相关知识与技能的专业人才。
    a. address—deal with or discuss
    b. a shortage of—a condition of having less than is needed; an amount lacking (缺乏;短缺,不足)
7. Much of what people consider... and national culture. (Par. 11)—许多人们认为"自我"的东西仅仅是一系列关于生活的信念和设想,并很大程度受到社会环境、经济状况、家庭背景和民族文化等因素的影响。
8. hard though it may be (Par. 21)—though it may be hard
9. Given China's growing economic importance and global predominance (Par. 21)—考虑到中国经济的重要性和在国际的领先地位
    given—if one takes into account; considering 如果考虑到,倘若
10. plus (Par. 21)—in addition; besides
11. bring sth to life (Par. 26)—make sth more exciting or interesting (使某物更生动、有趣)
12. I am confident that... a similar experience. (Par. 28)—I am sure that any student who is willing to expand his worldview and to go to some new places will have a similar experience.

Part Three

Questions and Answers for Your Reference

1. According to the American Council on Education, why is it necessary for students to study abroad?

    According to the American Council on Education, many

students who go abroad have the goal of learning a language. There is no better way to improve language skills than by being immersed in a language other than your own. Studying abroad also offers students an opportunity to travel, to expand their worldview, to enhance the value of a college degree, and to make international connections. Studying abroad can have excellent benefits for future employment opportunities by providing students with international skills and experiences. Connections made while abroad could easily lead to future opportunities.

2. As to the importance of studying abroad, what were listed by Senate Resolution 308?

   An experience of studying abroad is firstly very important for both the students and then for theUnited States as a whole. For the students, learning aboard would enhance their international knowledge and foreign skills, which will prepare them for a good career in the future. At the same time, the expertise and skills would eventually benefit the whole nation when competing in the world. Moreover, by comparing with an alien culture, the students would better understand their own culture, thus expanding their worldview.

3. Why is China the worthy place for U. S. students?

   China is one of America's most important partners in business in Asia, with a large amount of exports and imports. As China keeps booming, it is playing a more and more important role in world economy. Besides, China has a population of 1.3 billion and 5,000 years of uninterrupted history which has long been ignored by most of the westerners. In fact, both its economical presence and cultural presence make it worthwhile for the U. S. students to go.

4. What benefits has the author gained from studying in China?

   By studying in China, the author gained a lot of benefits, especially from the perspective of language, culture and personal experience. Firstly, nothing could be of more help for a language learner than being immersed in the language and talking to the native speakers, which, at the same time, offered a good chance to physically experience the culture there. When the author was in China, he traveled a lot, meeting different people and experiencing new things. Therefore, studying in China really pushed back his horizon and inspired new interests and curiosities.

Words to Know

academic, address, appall, appealing, assumption, ballpark, capacity, contribute, counterpart, cultivate, dugout, dwarf, elective, emphatically, empower, enhance, enroll, extensive, forgo, immerse, institution, intrigue, myriad, predominance, prior to, refreshing, reinforce, render, semester, steady, underrepresented, unequaled, worldview

Part four

Supplementary Reading

Record number of foreign students in U. S. (From *USA Today*, November 12, 2012)

Lesson Three

Tiger Mom...Meet Panda Dad

Part One

Summary

2011年,一位耶鲁大学华裔教授蔡美儿(Amy Chua)出版了 *Battle Hymn of the Tiger Mother*,在中美两国引起了轰动,并引发了一场关于中美教育方式差异的大讨论。现在"虎妈"已经俨然成为了一个"专有名词",比如,一个妈妈比较严厉一些就会被称作"虎妈"。

在书中,蔡美儿介绍了自己如何以中式教育法管教两个女儿:她要求女儿练钢琴和小提琴,从晚饭后开始直到深夜,中间不能喝水,甚至不能去厕所;她不允许孩子有休息日、看电视节目、玩电子游戏,每门功课都至少得A;她还曾因为愤怒而喊自己的小孩"垃圾"。虎妈的严格教育取得了丰硕的成果:大女儿被哈佛大学录取,14岁就在卡内基音乐大厅演奏钢琴;小女儿12岁就成为耶鲁青年管弦乐团首席小提琴手,当她自己选择网球运动作为业余爱好后,在极短的时间内就打败新英格兰地区的种子选手。

"虎妈"式的严厉、传统、不向孩子妥协、培养孩子的竞争意识的教育方式引来不少美国家长的反思,也招来了不少批评。本文《当虎妈遇到熊猫爸爸》即是一篇典型的批评文章。作者艾伦·保罗以一名在北京生活的美国爸爸的亲身经历,提出了在教育中,父亲不应是一个缺席的角色;接着,在描述"中式教育"的成果的同时,指出了其弊端:扼杀孩子们的创造能力和创新精神;随后,作者详细阐释了自己的教育理念:宽松(而非松懈)的教育方式更能够将孩子培养成独立、能干、自信、对社会更有益的人。作者针对虎妈的教育观点进行了一一批驳,比如家里的井然有序是否重要? 美式教育是否落后? 孩子是否应该完全遵从父母的意愿? 是否应该禁止孩子去朋友家过夜? 本文使用了很多口语化的词语(如dad,mom,prep,plus,get over yourself等)和灵活的句式,让全文看上去真实、严肃但又不乏轻松。

本文作者批判了当代美国的一种思潮,即"我们的国家正在被按照类似的方式划分阶层,而且很快就要被中国所赶超。如果你对孩子的教育方法不如他们,就向他们学习好了"。美国近年来对于中国崛起十分警惕,新闻界对于"中美文化差异"、"中国威胁论"的论述层出不穷。经济危机爆发以来,美国民众和媒体的焦虑心理不断累积。2010年12月,美国学生在"学生能力评价国际计划"(PISA)竞赛上大大失利于中国学生后,这种焦虑心理从对中式教育模式中找到发泄口,从对美式教育模式的重新自我肯定中得到了慰藉。这或许就是这种思潮产生的背景和深层原因。

但是,作者一定程度上曲解了《虎妈战歌》中"中国妈妈"的含义,也过于强调对"中式教育"的定义和定性,从而夸大了中美教育方式及教育结果的差别。实际上,正如蔡美儿在书中所说:"我定义的中国妈妈与西方妈妈,都是宽泛的概念。""中国妈妈"在她的定义中并非指身为中国人的母亲,而是指教育方法严格,不遵循西方教育模式的母亲。只要满足这一点,不论国籍种族,都是她眼中的"中国妈妈"。

The Author

Alan Robert Paul, born in 1966, was an online columnist for *The Expat Life*(老外在中国)column of WSJ. com from 2005 to 2008, and was named "Online Columnist of the Year" by The National Society of Newspaper Columnists. In November 2009, Paul signed a deal with Harper Collins for *Big in China: My Unlikely Adventures Raising a Family, Playing the Blues, and Becoming a Star in Beijing*, which was based on *The Expat Life* column. The book was optioned on March 22, 2011 by Montecito Pictures to start development for a cinematic adaptation. Paul is also an author, musician and blogger.

Background Information

1. *Battle Hymn of the Tiger Mother*
《虎妈战歌》/《我在美国做妈妈:耶鲁法学院教授的育儿经》

This is a book by Amy Chua published in 2011. The complete subtitle of the book is: "This is a story about a mother, two daughters, and two dogs. This was supposed to be a story of how Chinese parents are better at raising kids than Western ones. But instead, it's about a bitter clash of cultures, a fleeting taste of glory, and how I was humbled by a thirteen-year-old."

Chua forced her 7-year-old daughter Lulu to practice piano for hours on end, right through dinner into the night, with no breaks for water or even the bathroom, until at last Lulu learned to play the piece. Chua calling her elder daughter Sophia "garbage" after the girl behaved disrespectfully—the same thing Chua had been called as a child by her strict father.

An article published under the headline "Why Chinese Mothers Are Superior" in *The Wall Street Journal* on January 8, 2011, contained excerpts from her book, in which Chua describes her efforts to give her children what she describes as a traditional, strict "Chinese" upbringing. This piece was controversial. Many readers missed the supposed irony and self-deprecating (自贬的) humor in the title and the piece itself and instead believed that Chua was advocating the "superiority" of a particular, very strict, ethnically defined approach to parenting. In any case, Chua defines "Chinese mother" loosely to include parents of other ethnicities who practice traditional, strict child-rearing, while also acknowledging that "Western parents come in all varieties," and not all ethnically Chinese parents practice strict child-rearing.

The *Wall Street Journal* article generated a huge response, both positive and negative. Chua has openly confronted criticism in print and during her book signings. In a follow-up article in the *Wall Street Journal*, Chua explains that "my actual book is not a how-to guide; it's a memoir, the story of our family's journey in two cultures, and my own eventual transformation as a mother. Much of the book is about my decision to retreat from the strict 'Chinese' approach, after my younger daughter rebelled at thirteen."

Part Two

Language Points

I. New Words
annoyance /əˈnɔɪəns/ n. the feeling of being annoyed 烦恼,可厌之事
auditorium /ˌɔːdɪˈtɔːriəm/ n. the space in a theatre, hall, etc., where people sit when listening to or watching a performance 会堂,礼堂
babysitter /ˈbeɪbɪsɪtə(r)/ n. sb who takes care of babies or children while their parents are out 临时受雇代外出的父母照顾小孩的人
bore /bɔː(r)/ n. sth you find it annoying 令人生厌的事;无聊的事
chain /tʃeɪn/ v. to limit the freedom of sb or sth (as if) with a chain 拴住,束缚
chaos /ˈkeɪɒs/ n. a state of complete and thorough disorder and

confusion 大混乱,无序状态

character /ˈkærəktə(r)/ *n*. letter, mark, or sign used in writing or printing 中国字,字体,符号

claw /klɔː/ *n*. a sharp usu. curved nail on the toe of an animal or bird（动物或鸟类的）爪

contemporary /kənˈtemprərɪ/ *adj*. belonging to the same period of time 当代的,同时代的

counterpart /ˈkaʊntəpɑːt/ *n*. a person or thing that has the same purpose or does the same job as another in a different system 两方面地位相当的人（物）

frontline /ˈfrʌntlaɪn/ *n*. the most advanced or important position 第一线,最前线

function /ˈfʌŋkʃn/ *v*. to be in action; work; operate 运行,发挥作用

generalization /dʒenrəlaɪˈzeɪʃn/ *n*. a act or instance of generalizing 归纳,概括

genuine /ˈdʒenjuːɪn/ *adj*. actual, real

hard-driving *adj*. very demanding 要求过高的,严苛的

household /ˈhaʊshəʊld/ *n*. all the people living together in a house 一家人,同住一座房子的人

impulse /ˈɪmpʌls/ *n*. a sudden wish to do sth; sudden urge 突然的欲望,冲动

insane /ɪnˈseɪn/ *adj*. seriously ill in the mind; mad; very foolish

insight /ˈɪnsaɪt/ *n*. a sudden, clear, but not always complete understanding 领悟,顿悟

lonesome /ˈləʊnsəm/ *adj*. lonely

mess /mes/ *n*. untidiness or dirt; dirty material

neurotic /njʊəˈrɒtɪk/ *adj*. unreasonably anxious or sensitive 神经质的,极为焦虑的

New Jersey /njuːˈdʒɜːzi/ *n*. A state of the east-central United States on the Atlantic Ocean（美国）新泽西州

perspective /pəˈspektɪv/ *n*. the way in which a situation or problem is judged 洞察力,视角

pillow /ˈpɪləʊ/ *n*. 枕头,枕垫

ponder /ˈpɒndə(r)/ *v*. to spend time in carefully considering 深思,考虑

portray /pɔːˈtreɪ/ *v*. to describe according to one's opinion 描述,描写

prep /prep/ *v*. *infml* to prepare

prescribe /prɪˈskraɪb/ *v*. *fml* to sate (what must happen or be done in

certain conditions) 规定,指定遵守某事
rear /rɪə(r)/ v. to care for (children or a child) during the early stages of life; bring up
rebellion /rɪ'beljən/ n. an act of opposing or fighting against someone in a position of control 造反,反抗
reign /reɪn/ v. have sovereign power 当政,统治;占主导地位
shallowness /'ʃæləʊnɪs/ n. the state of being shallow 肤浅,浅薄
sideline /'saɪdlaɪn/ n. a line that marks the limit of play at the side of a football field, tennis court, etc. (运动场的)边线
superior /suːˈpɪərɪə(r)/ adj. better in quality or value 上等的,优秀的
thrive /θraɪv/ v. to develop well and be healthy, strong or successful

II. Notes
1. I have watched the uproar over ... Where are the dads? (Par. 1)—I have observed the noisy confusion over the debate of Tiger Mom, and I am getting more and more annoyed because of the fact that a simple question is still not asked: What are the roles and positions of the dads?
2. gold standard(Par. 5)—a paragon of excellence (黄金标准,典范)
3. controlled chaos reigns in our house(Par 7.)—our house is always in a state of disorder but under control
4. sent weak-kneed babysitters scurrying for the door(Par. 7)—frighten feeble babysitters away (使胆小的保姆夺门而逃)
5. It has also been a plus for our children ... (Par. 8)—It has also been favorable for our children.
6. And it introduced them... rather than waiting for things to be perfect. (Par. 8)—And this style of child-rearing made them understand a simple fact at an early age: Life is made by controlled chaos and success is based on planning the path through the chaos, and not on waiting for things to become perfect by themselves.
7. to make a sweeping generalization, moms tend to be more detail oriented and order driven(Par. 9)—to make an overall summary, moms tend to deal mostly in details and keep orders.
8. Her ability to do this... (Par. 9)—"this" here refers to "she cedes to my style of parenting" in the previous sentence.
9. ... the differences are small bore rather than big picture. (Par. 10)—differences of parents on basic values are small, limited, and not vital.
10. have more of an opportunity(Par. 11)—have more opportunities

11. It's not the hyper-orderly household the Amy Chua portrays... (Par. 12)—My home is not as very orderly as her home described by Amy Chua.
12. When they were done, they unwound by picking up video game consoles. (Par. 13)—When they finished their practice, they can only relax by playing video game.
13. It also seems insane to ... that our child-rearing is too laid back. (Par. 14)—It also seems very foolish to take a look at the situation of the upper-middle-class American families that Amy Chua is discussing in her book and quickly come to the conclusion that our way of rearing children is too relaxed.
    a. cast an eye around—look around quickly
    b. laid back—unworried; relaxed
14. ... who has ever stalked a suburban soccer sideline (Par. 14)—who has ever played in a suburban soccer team
15. Forcing a child to constantly bend... constant rebellion and head-butting. (Par. 16)—强迫一个孩子长期屈服于你的意愿要么会使他（她）成为俯首贴耳、凡事没有主见的孩子，要么会导致长期的反叛和顶撞。
16. Aside from being a much cheaper option... with any pillow. (Par. 17)—Sleepover can not only save the money for babysitter, but also help children learn to sleep in any place.
17. Do that and you will have done your job, launching them off with the foundation needed to thrive. (Par. 15)—Do as what I said and you will have accomplished your mission of being parents by preparing children with the basic abilities to grow strong.
    launch off—to start out; to set off

Part Three

Reference Answers to Questions

1. What role should a father play in child-rearing according to the author's experience?
   Based on the author's experience, a father can't just leave child-rearing responsibility to mothers or backseat drive how his children are being raised. He should also shoulder the child-care duties and even fight on the frontline of parenting.
2. What insight is given to the author by his several years in China?

He observed the parenting way claimed by Amy Chua as the best and Chinese way. He pondered the goal and way people are raising kids
3. Why does the author call himself Panda Dad?
   Alan Paul has a strong aversion to the hard-driving "Tiger" parenting, so he uses Panda to cast a contrast which indicates parenting with cuddliness but sometimes show authority.
4. How does the author think about order and chaos at home?
   Alan Paul can tolerate a bit more chaos in his house because he thinks it can give children space to take on responsibilities for their own homework, play time and everything else, make them independent and see their parents pursuing their own interests and careers while also being very involved in one another's lives.
5. According to the article, is the American child-rearing too laid back?
   No, it is too shallow to conclude the American child-rearing too laid back. The Americans have been tried hard enough. The unstructured play in American-children rearing is helpful for children to grow up to be independent, competent and confident.
6. What are the three final goals that everyone should realistically set for raising their kids in the author's view?
   They are getting the children to adulthood without any sleeping, eating or sexual hang-ups.
7. What is the Alan Paul's attitude towards sleepovers?
   Sleepover can not only save the money for babysitters, but also help children learn to sleep at any place which is an ability to make social connections and interactions that they will need through life.

Words to Know

aversion, backseat drive, cast an eye around, cede to, child-rearing, controlled chaos, counterpart, counterproductive, creativity and innovation, freelance, functioning, gold standard, hang-ups, hard-driving, head-butting, hyper-orderly, juggle with, narcissism, parent (*v.*), parenting, perspective, plus, rebellion, stereotype, swap positions, sweeping generalization, talent show, Tiger Mom (debate), unstructured play, unwind

Part Four

Supplementary Reading

Why Chinese Mothers Are Superior (From *The Wall Street Journal*, Jan. 8, 2011)

Lesson Four

Is an Ivy League Diploma Worth It?

Part One

Summary

美国在经济低迷时,曾削减教育拨款,高校学费节节攀升,大学生及其家庭负担日益加重。2011年底,美国学生贷款债务已突破万亿美元大关。截止2012年5月,美国攻读本科学位的人士中,约有94%需要通过借贷支付学费,人均欠债额达到2.7万美元。2012年12月,美国学生贷款拖欠率攀升至20%。由于就业市场不景气,许多美国大学生毕业后难以找到工资足够高的工作来偿付贷款,而学生贷款不能像其他贷款一样能通过破产来注销。因此,有媒体评论说,学生贷款问题有可能引起美国下一次的次贷危机。

有鉴于此,很多美国学生产生了怀疑:投入高额学费就读名校还是对未来最好的投资吗? 作者通过此文讲述了几个美国大学生的真实故事,他们对自己的择校决定心里充满矛盾。作者在文章中还提到,针对美国大学生的现实问题,一些知名大学提高了助学金和奖学金。也有专家指出,就读于哪所学校对于学生未来的影响,并没有他们所学专业、人际关系和实习经历大。但是,这些解释并不能从根本上解决学生的贷款问题和学习需求。

The Author

Melissa Korn is a reporter at *The Wall Street Journal*. Having graduated from the Graduate School of Journalism in Columbia University, she had been a copy editor and reporter at Dow Jones Newswires from 2006 to 2011, and started to work for *The Wall Street Journal* from 2011, covering higher education, with a particular focus on business schools. Her coverage areas include admissions, curriculum, academic research, finances and leadership for undergraduate and MBA programs.

Background Information

Sallie Mae 萨利美（学生贷款市场公司）

Sallie Mae, or SLM Corporation (originally the Student Loan Marketing Association) is a publicly traded U.S. corporation whose operations are originating, servicing, and collecting on student loans. Originally created in 1972, the company now owns offices across the US, and is managing more than $180.4 billion in debt for more than 10 million borrowers. It primarily provides federally guaranteed student loans originated under the Federal Family Education Loan Program (FFELP), but at present, it also provides private student loans.

Part Two

Language Points

I. New Words

commute /kəˈmjuːt/ *vi.* travel back and forth regularly, as between one's place of work and home 通勤；

default /dɪˈfɔːlt/ *n.* act of failing to meet a financial obligation 未履行，拖欠

outcome /ˈaʊtkʌm/ *n.* something that results 结果；成果；出路

overcrowding /ˌəʊvəˈkraʊdɪŋ/ *n.* the state of putting or allowing too many people or things in 过度拥挤

in-state // *adj.* being in the same state 州内的

internship /ˈɪntɜːnʃɪp/ *n.* the period in which a person who gains controlled practical experience 实习

per capita /pəˈkeɪpətə/ *adv.* equally to each individual

pile /paɪl/ to heap (something) in abundance 堆积

plus /plʌs/ *adj.* after a number or quantity to indicate that the actual number or quantity is greater than the one mentioned （用于数字或数量后）多于……的

scholarship /ˈskɒləʃɪp/ *n.* a grant of financial aid awarded to a student, as for the purpose of attending a college 奖学金

II. Notes

1. As student-loan default rates climb ... without having to take on debt. (Par. 4)—Because student-loan default rates go up and college graduates fail to secure jobs, more and more students are stating that

if they go to a less-expensive school rather than an elite school, they can still achieve the same goals. What's more, they do not need to borrow money for their tuition.

  default rates—违约率
  land jobs—to secure jobs 工作有着落;找到工作
  take on debt—to accept debt

2. Top-tier colleges tend to attract recruiting visits from companies that have stopped visiting elsewhere. (Par. 7)—It is easier for elite colleges to attract companies to come to their campuses to recruit graduates while the companies do not go to other colleges any more.

  recruiting visits—校园招聘

3. And overcrowding at state schools means **students could be locked out of required courses and have difficulty completing their degrees in four years.** (Par. 7)—学生可能选不上必修课并且很难在四年内取得学位。

  lock out—关在门外;不准进入……

4. come to terms. (Par. 8)—to accept (sth one does not want to accept)

5. It didn't help that his father attended Princeton University and his uncle, Columbia University. (Par. 10)—His father's and his uncle's diplomas at the two famous Universities did not help him change the school-choosing decision.

6. There is little question that having a college degree gives candidates an edge in the job market. (Par. 12)—It is very probable that having a college degree gives job candidates a competitive advantage in the job market.

  give an edge—占优势

7. Harvard College ... below $60,000. (Par. 16)—Harvard College doesn't require the families which earn an annual income less than $60,000 to pay for their children's tuition fees if their children are enrolled in the college.

8. ... graduate outcomes often have more to do with major and how a student takes advantage of networking and internship opportunities, than with school choice. (Par. 17)—... graduate outcomes often depends more on a student's major and how he/she make use of networking and internship opportunities, and less on their choice about which college to go to.

9. ... had I gone to BC, where that could have taken me... (Par.

20)—假若我去波士顿学院的话，它也会录取我的……　此句是虚拟语气，倒装句 had I gone to BC = if I had gone to BC。
　　　BC—Boston College
10. She says she turned down an offer ... need to pitch in $30,000 annually.
　　　　turn down—to refuse (a request or offer) 拒绝
　　　　pitch in—to invest or spend 投入

Words to Know

Ivy League, scholarship, loan, endowment, take on debt, pile on debt, pay off, land jobs, elite school, top-tier colleges, prestige, income brackets, recruiting visits, come to terms, candidates, in-state students, edge, networking, internship, turn down an offer

Part Three

Reference Answers to Questions

1. Why did not Mr. Schwartz enroll at Cornel University?
　　　Because the University he enrolled at, City University of New York's Macaulay Honors College, is free. What's more, since he wants to be a doctor, going to Cornel University would cost him a large sum of tuition fee, in which he doesn't see the value.
2. What was the general annual cost of top-tier colleges or Ivy League such as Cornell university?
　　　The general annual cost of top-tier colleges is more than $45,000 a year.
3. What is the meaning of the phrase "land jobs" in the seventh paragraph?
　　　It means to secure jobs.
4. What is the reason for those students at state schools who are locked out of required courses and have difficulty completing their degrees in four years?
　　　Because too many students enroll at state schools, and their opportunities to choose required courses are limited. If they cannot finish their required courses on time, they will not complete their degrees in four years.

Part Four

Supplementary Reading

Student loans add stress to young marriages (From *Star Tribune*, April 16, 2013)

Lesson Five

Debt Burden Alters Outlook for US Graduates

Part One

Summary

2008年爆发的金融危机被很多经济学家认为是继20世纪30年代经济大萧条以来最为严重的金融危机。这次危机由美国政府的一系列盲目鼓励购房而发生的次贷危机所触发。在9/11事件和安然、安达信等美国大公司爆出财务丑闻,最后纷纷倒下后,国际资金大规模撤离,美国经济神话破灭。2003年,美国发动的伊拉克战争,更是耗费了8000多亿美元。这使美国财政和贸易都出现了巨额赤字。美国希望藉房地产拉动经济,于是采取宽松的货币政府,鼓励人们购房。这样,即使信用级别低的人也可以轻松拿到购房贷款,次级贷款由此大增。然而从2007年9月开始,出现大量购房者违约现象,导致房贷公司资金链断裂,进而影响金融行业的资金流动性,爆发了金融危机。金融危机爆发以来,已经有100多家规模较大的美国金融机构宣布破产或被兼并,实体经济也遭受重创,导致用人需求下降,社会的整体失业率升高,税收大幅减少。税收的减少使得美国不得不修改预算,包括教育预算也遭到大幅削减,从而使得给大学生提供的奖学金和补贴减少,来自美国中低收入家庭的学生们需要借贷以完成自己的学业。

本文描述的就是在这样的经济背景下,在2012年完成学业,步入社会的美国大学毕业生们的前景问题。他们在2008年金融危机爆发的时候刚刚走入大学校园。四年过去了,他们拿到了自己的学位,可经济依然不见起色,美国整体的失业率高达8%,大学毕业生的失业率也保持在6.8%。更糟糕的是,在经济萧条时期步入职场,使得他们的赚钱能力大打折扣,起薪很低,甚至还影响到自己今后的职业生涯。而在求学时期借下的债务,因就业困难,薪酬不高而难以偿清,这使得很多毕业生后悔自己当初的选择。工作难找,债务难偿,而即使是找到了工作的毕业生也发现,薪酬和职位与自己预期的相去甚远。面对大学生债务过重的情况,美国参议院也在争执如何延长给学生贷款提供补贴。美国总统奥巴马和竞选对手罗姆尼也呼吁采取行动。文章末尾还引用了美国总统奥巴马给纽约巴纳德学院的毕业生发表演讲的部分内容,提到这些毕业生们面临的困难和他自己当年毕业时经历经济危机的情况多么一样。以此结尾,不仅突出了文章的主题:学生债务负担让他们的前途未卜,同时又给读者带来一些宽慰和希望,即这样的经济和就业环境并非此时独有,再大的困难最终也能安然度过,大学毕业生们最终还是能获得成功。

　　本文是一篇评述性新闻报道,介绍了学生债务增加给 2012 年毕业的美国大学生带来的影响。作者对大学生债务的情况、债务增加的原因及影响做了介绍,并将一些研究报告作为引证,文中多次以具体数字来说明问题,凸显报道的客观性,更在文章末尾处引用了奥巴马总统的演讲内容,让读者能够提升到历史角度来看待这一问题,给结尾增添了一抹亮色。文章的立场客观,语言平实,主题突出。但是作者只是提到参议院仍旧在为缓解形势的手段争论不休,而把如何从根本上解决这一问题留给读者自己去思考。不难看出,在某种程度上这一问题解决与否实为政治家和党争的筹码。

The Author

　　Shannon Bond is a reporter and FT. com editor in New York. She joined the FT (*Financial Times*) in 2008 after receiving her MS from Northwestern University's Medill School of Journalism. She has also written for MarketWatch, Politico and UPI. com.

　　Jason Abbruzzese is a web editor at *Financial Times*. After graduating from Boston University with a degree in journalism, he worked for the Sentinel & Enterprise in central Massachusetts before receiving a master's degree in international affairs from the Australian National University. He then wrote for the *Shanghai Business Review*(《上海商评》)as a feature writer before moving to New York City and working for GRITtv with Laura Flanders as a development director.

　　Robin Harding is US Economics Editor for the Financial Times, and covers the US Federal Reserve and the US Treasury(美国财政部). Based in Washington, his beat includes US economics, financial markets and business. He studied economics at Cambridge and also holds a master's degree in economics from Hitotsubashi University(一桥大学) in Tokyo.

Background Information

1. The financial crisis 2008 年金融危机

The 2008 financial crisis is considered to be the worst financial crisis since the Great Depression of the 1930s. It was triggered by a complex interplay of policies, which were adopted by American government to stimulate the economy and encouraged people to buy houses. Banks provided easier access to loans for subprime borrowers (次级贷款人), and over-evaluated the bundled sub-prime mortgages(次级抵押贷款) based on the theory that housing prices would continue to escalate. Unfortunately home prices peaked in the winter of 2005—06 and started to go down, and the house of cards started to crumble(崩溃). People could no longer increase their mortgage debt to pay previous debts. In 2008, approximately 6% of all mortgage loans in United States were in default(违约), and a huge portion of the increased mortgage loan defaults were what are referred to as "sub-prime" loans (次级贷款). The bursting of the U.S. housing bubble, which peaked in 2006, caused the values of securities tied to U.S. real estate pricing to plummet(骤然下降), and resulted in the threat of total collapse of large financial institutions, the bailout(紧急援助) of banks by national governments, and downturns in stock markets around the world. The crisis also played a significant role in the failure of key businesses, declines in consumer wealth estimated in trillions of US dollars, and a downturn in economic activity leading to the 2008 − 2012 global recession and contributing to the European sovereign-debt crisis(欧洲主权债务危机).

2. Scholarships offered by American colleges and universities 美国大学的奖学金

The scholarships provided by colleges and universities in the U.S. may be classified into three categories such as Non-Service Scholarships (非服务性奖学金), Service Assistantships(服务性奖学金) and Loans.

Non-Service Scholarships do not require an individual to perform a past, present or future service in order to receive payment, and include Fellowship(助学金),Scholarship(奖学金), Tuition & Fee Waiver(全免学杂费) and other awards offered by specific institutions, while Service Assistantships require an individual to perform some service in order to receive payment, and include Teaching Assistantship (助教金) and Research Assistantship(助研金).

Generally, a scholarship or fellowship grant is any amount paid orallowed to, or for the benefit of, an individual to aid in the pursuit of study or research. A tuition waiver is a program initiated by states that allows students to attend publicly funded higher education institutions by "waiving" tuition and fees under certain criteria.

Teaching Assistantships are a source of aid provided to graduate students whoassist faculty members in teaching undergraduate classes. A research assistantship is a form of funding in which a student works as an "assistant" in exchange for partial or full tuition and/or a stipend.

Astudent loan is designed to help students pay for university tuition, books, and living expenses. It may differ from other types of loans in that the interest rate may be substantially lower and the repayment schedule may be deferred while the student is still in education. In the United States, there are two types of student loans: federal loans sponsored by the federal government and private student loans, which broadly includes state-affiliated nonprofits and institutional loans provided by schools.

3. The US Senate's wrangle over student loans 参议院关于学生贷款的争斗

With student loans rocketing in recent years, both Democrats(美国民主党) and Republicans(共和党) agreed to freeze student loan rates and keep them from doubling from 3.4 percent to 6.8 percent which would be effective on July 1, 2012. Their chief remaining dispute is how to pay for the $5.9 billion cost of keeping those rates low. When it comes to that, each side has in effect taken a political hostage: House Republicans would cut spending from Obama's prized health care overhaul law(被认为非常重要的奥巴马的医疗保险改革法案), Senate Democrats would boost payroll taxes(工资税) on owners of some private corporations and House Democrats would erase federal subsidies to oil and gas companies. That is why the US Senate was wrangling over how to extend a modest subsidy for student loans.

4. political sensitivity over student debt 关于学生债务的竞选敏感性

2008 financial crisis has casted a great impact on American economy and the world as a whole. With the economic recession, the education budget has been cut greatly and the tuitions and fees have been increased steadily, so much so that many students have to take out loans to pay for their education. According to the New York Fed's(纽约联邦储备银行) quarterly report on household debt, student loan debt hit $904 billion in the first quarter of 2012, up from $241 billion a decade ago. The Consumer Financial Protection Bureau(消费者金融保护局) puts total student loan debt above $1 trillion. According to a *NY Times* report, more than 37 million Americans have some student loans, with an average $23,300 of debt in 2011.

So, instead of young adults graduating with hopes and dreams of a better future, they are graduating with a great burden of loans. With a political sensitivity of getting supports from young voters, the issue of student loans has become a topic focused on by both the Republic and the Democratic, especially in the American general election year of 2012.

Part Two

Language Points

I. New Words

bachelor /ˈbætʃələ(r)/ *n.* bachelor's degree, a first university degree in any of several subjects

burden /ˈbɜːdn/ *n.* sth. that is carried; a heavy duty or responsibility which is hard to bear(负担)　　*v.* to load or trouble 使背负,使苦恼

cite /saɪt/ *v.* to mention, esp. as an example in a statement, argument, etc.

definitely /ˈdefɪnətli/ *adv.* without doubt; clearly

encounter /ɪnˈkaʊntə(r)/ *v.* to meet or have to deal with (sth. bad, esp. a danger or a difficulty); be faced with

finance /ˈfaɪnæns/ *v. rather fml* to provide an esp. large amount of money for (a public activity or organization, business, etc.

initial /ɪˈnɪʃl/ *adj.* which is (at) the beginning

loan /ləʊn/ n. sth. which is lent, esp. money
minimum /'mɪnɪməm/ adj. (being the smallest number, amount, etc.
modest /'mɒdɪst/ adj. not large in quantity, size, value, etc. 不大的，适度的
negative /'negətɪv/ adj. without any active, useful, or helpful qualities; not constructive 消极的；非建设性的
outcome /'aʊtkʌm/ n. an effect; result
percentage /pə'sentɪdʒ/ n. an amount stated as if it is part of a whole which is 100 百分比，百分率
postsecondary adj. of or relating to education taking place following graduation from a high school
pursue /pə'sjuː/ v. to continue steadily with; carry on(继续从事，进行)
statistics /stə'tɪstɪks/ n. a collection of numbers which represent facts or measurements
statistically adv.
survey /'sɜːveɪ/ v. question, examine 调查
transfer /træns'fɜː(r)/ v. to move from place, job, position, etc., to another

II. Notes
1. ... the financial crisis that unfolded ... casting a long shadow over their futures. (Par. 1)—the financial crisis that became spread out when they were freshmen in 2008 is still making their futures uncertain.
      cast a shadow over/on sth. —make sth. dark(给……笼罩上阴影)
2. that (par. 2)—here "that" refers to "the overall unemployment rate."(that 在这个从句里做主语，指代主句里的主语部分，以免重复。)
3. is stuck at (Par. 2)—is fixed at
4. ... the promise of a degree... still burdened by student debt (Par. 3)—the expectation of getting a good job after graduating and getting degrees has turned to disappointment, because they find it difficult to get their first job, and can't earn enough money to pay back the money they had loaned and they are still under the pressure of debts.
5. take into account (Par. 6)—consider
6. pick a school (Par. 6)—choosing a school
7. ... definitely a major factor in that is the more promising outlook for a business major coming out of college (Par. 7)—undoubtedly, the

main reason for me to choose to study business is that a business graduate may have a brighter future. (毫无疑问,我选择读工商专业的主要原因,是工商专业毕业生走出校门后可能会有更好的前途。)
8. take on (Par. 8)—undertaking, handling
9. keep pace with (Par. 15)—go as fast as
10. due to expire (Par. 18)—coming to the end of the expected date
11. strike a sombre note (Par. 19)—to express and communicate a serious and grave opinion

Part Three

Reference Answers to Questions

1. Does on the 2008 financial crisis influences the university graduates?

    The 2008 financial crisis increased the unemployment rate, making university graduates hard to find their first job or even lose part of earning power for the rest of the their career. Students with debt may take on an even heavier burden as they have less ability to repay the loans.

2. What can belearned from the result of Rutgers University's study?

    It can be learned that the graduates who finished college between 2006 and 2011 suffered a lot from the 2008 financial crisis with the high unemployment and reduced wages, and they felt regretful for their previous choices. They thought if they had known that they had to bear such a great burden of the student loans, they would have made different choices as to the majors, universities and jobs.

3. Why does Chelsea Katz want to study business?

    Because she thinks that a business major graduate might have a brighter future, finding a good job and earning more money.

4. What conditions are squeezing American young people's ability to repay the student loans?

    a. Some graduates took the position below their level of education.

    b. Some graduates earned less than what they expected.

    c. Some graduate had to accept job outside their field in order to find work.

    d. The average starting salary dropped compared withyears ago.

    e. The rapidly rising tuition fees surpass the income growth.

5. Why do American students have to borrow more money to finish

their higher education?

Because the public universities have been hit seriously by deep cuts to the state budget, and had to transfer more of the cost burden on to students and their families by increasing tuition and fees and reducing grants.

5. Why do you think the authors cite Mr. Obama's speech in the last paragraph?

President Obamashowed his sympathy for the graduates who are trapped in debts and difficulties in his speech, and shared the same experience and feeling with them. So the authors of the article cite Mr. Obama's speech to reinforce the theme of the article, and at the same time to give a ray of hope to encourage the young people out of plight eventually.

Words to Know

blight, cast a long shadow over, debt burden, disinvest, earning power, expire, financial crisis, graduate degree, harsh reality, initial wages, internship, labour market, median starting salary, mire, outlook, outpace, postsecondary education, professional degree, public institutions, recession, skip, squeeze, state budget, strike a note, subsidy, tuition fee, unemployment rate, unfold, wrangle

Part Four

Supplementary Reading

U. S. colleges punished by financial crisis (From *Reuters*, Oct. 30 2008)

Lesson Six

The Evolution Wars

Part One

Summary

达尔文的进化论从它产生以来就处于争论之中,100多年过去了,科学的发展并没有使分歧统一,相反却使它不断扩大,人们从认识的各个层面对它提出了越来越严厉的批判。在这一背景下,一些人又重新拾起"创世说",认为人类不可能是进化来的,而是上帝创造的。这场科学与宗教之争不可避免地反映到教育领域,就有了本文开头的那一幕:美国一所高中的校监准备在生物课开课时朗读一段文字,意思是说"达尔文的理论只是一种理论,不是事实。智慧设计论是与达尔文的观点不同的另一个关于生命起源的学说,如果学生们感兴趣可以阅读《关于熊猫与人》这本书。学校鼓励学生对任何理论都持有开放的态度。"就连当时的美国总统小布什也说:"两种理论都应该教给学生。"这种把科学与伪科学混为一谈的做法,有如下几方面的原因:(1)自《物种起源》一书发表以来的约150年里,美国人一直不愿接受这一理论。例如,1925年田纳西州的"猴子案审判",以及其他一些州曾出台法律干涉学校传授进化论。(2)达尔文的理论存在许多漏洞。20世纪80年代开始,随着研究的深入,许多科学家、哲学家和神学家撰写了大量论文及著作,指出达尔文理论存在的诸多问题。(3)来自家长的压力。民意测验显示,45%的美国人相信上帝造人说,他们要求校方提供这方面的课程。看来,这场争论仍将是一场持久战。

The Author

ClaudiaWallis is currently a contributor to *Time* magazine. A two-time National Magazine Award finalist, Wallis has worked at *Time* as a staff reporter and editor, and has produced 35 cover stories on education, science, health, psychology, children and family issues. She was the founding editor of *Time for Kids* magazine, and served as editor-at-large from 2003—2007.

Background Information

1. Evolution

Evolution is the change in the inherited characteristics of biological populations over successive generations. Evolutionary processes give rise to diversity at every level of biological organisation, including species, individual organisms and molecules such as DNA and proteins.

All life on Earth is descended from a last universal ancestor that lived approximately 3.8 billion years ago. Repeated speciation and the divergence of life can be inferred from shared sets of biochemical and morphological traits, or by shared DNA sequences. These homologous (同源的) traits and sequences are more similar among species that share a more recent common ancestor, and can be used to reconstruct evolutionary histories, using both existing species and thefossil record. Existing patterns of biodiversity have been shaped both by speciation and by extinction.

Charles Darwin was the first to formulate a scientific argument for the theory of evolution by means of natural selection. Evolution by natural selection is a process that is inferred from three facts about populations: 1) more offspring are produced than can possibly survive, 2) traits vary among individuals, leading to different rates of survival and reproduction, and 3) trait differences areheritable. Thus, when members of a population die they are replaced by the progeny of parents that were better adaptedto survive and reproduce in the environment in which natural selection took place. This process creates and preserves traits that are seemingly fitted for the functional roles they perform. Natural selection is the only known cause of adaptation, but not the only known cause of evolution. Other, nonadaptive causes of evolution include mutation (突变) and genetic drift (遗传漂变).

In the early 20th century, genetics was integrated with Darwin's theory of evolution by natural selection through the discipline of population genetics. The importance of natural selection as a cause of evolution was accepted into other branches of biology. Moreover, previously held notions about evolution, such as orthogenesis and "progress" became obsolete. Scientists continue to study various aspects of evolution by forming and testing hypotheses, constructing scientific theories, using observational data, and performing experiments in both the field and the laboratory. Biologists agree that descent with modification is one of the most reliably established facts in science.

Discoveries in evolutionary biology have made a significant impact not just within the traditional branches of biology, but also in other academic disciplines (e.g. anthropology and psychology) and on society at large.

2. Creation-evolution controversy

The creation-evolution controversy (also termed the creation vs. evolution debate or the origins debate) involves a recurring cultural, political, and theological dispute about the origins of the Earth, of humanity, of life, and of the universe.

This debate rages most publicly in the United States of America, but to a lesser extent also proceeds in Europe and elsewhere, often portrayed as part of a culture war. Christian fundamentalists dispute the evidence of common descent of humans and other animals as demonstrated in modern palaeontology, and those who defend the conclusions of modern evolutionary biology, geology, cosmology, and other related fields. They argue for the Abrahamic religions' accounts of creation, framing it as reputable science ("creation science"). While the controversy has a long history, today it is mainly over what constitutes good science education, with the politics of creationism primarily focusing on the teaching of creation and evolution in public education. The debate also focuses on issues such as the definition of science (and of what constitutes scientific research and evidence), science education, free speech, separation of Church and State, and theology.

Evolution is an undisputed fact within the scientific community and in academia, where the level of support for evolution is essentially universal. The support for Abrahamic accounts or other creationist alternatives is very low among scientists, and virtually nonexistent among scientists in the relevant fields. Unlike the scientific community, a 2012 Gallup survey reports, "Forty-six percent of Americans believe in the creationist view that God created humans in their present form at one time within the last 10,000 years. The prevalence of this creationist view of the origin of humans is essentially unchanged from 30 years ago, when Gallup first asked the question. About a third of Americans believe that humans evolved, but with God's guidance; 15% say humans evolved, but that God had no part in the process."

The debate is sometimes portrayed as being between science and religion, but as the United States National Academy of Sciences states:

Today, many religious denominations accept that biological evolution has produced the diversity of living things over billions of years of Earth's history. Many have issued statements observing that evolution and the tenets of their faiths are compatible. Scientists and theologians have written eloquently about their awe and wonder at the history of the universe and of life on this planet, explaining that they see no conflict between their faith in God and the evidence for evolution. Religious denominations that do not accept the occurrence of evolution tend to be those that believe in strictly literal interpretations of religious texts. (National Academy of Sciences, *Science, Evolution, and Creationism*)

Part Two

Language Points

I. New Words

alongside /əˌlɒŋˈsaɪd/ *adv.* beside or together with

ancestor /ˈænsestə(r)/ *n.* a member of your family who lived a long time ago, esp. if more remote than a grandparent; a forebear (祖先,祖宗)

cautionary /ˈkɔːʃənəri/ *adj.* giving a warning

controversy /ˈkɒntrəvɜːsi/ *n.* a serious argument or disagreement

critique /krɪˈtiːk/ *n.* an article, book, etc., criticizing an idea or a person's system of thought

distract /dɪˈstrækt/ *v.* to make sb stop giving their attention to sth

diversity /daɪˈvɜːsəti/ *n.* the quality of having variety and including a wide range of different people or things

exquisite /ɪkˈskwɪzɪt/ *adj.* extremely beautiful and very delicately made

flaw /flɔː/ *n.* a fault, mistake or weakness, esp. one that happens while sth is being planned or made, or which causes sth not to be perfect

fossil /ˈfɒsl/ *n.* a bone, a shell or the shape of a plant or animal which has been preserved in rock for a very long period (化石)

hard-core /hɑːdkɔː/ *n.* a small group of people within a larger group, who strongly believe in the group's principles and usu. have a lot of power in it (核心部分,中坚分子)

ingenious /ɪnˈdʒiːniəs/ *adj.* cleverly made or planned, involving new ideas, methods, etc.

interfere /ˌɪntəˈfɪə(r)/ v. to come between so as to be a hindrance or an obstacle
invalidate /ɪnˈvælɪdeɪt/ v. to make sth no longer legally or officially acceptable
motto /ˈmɒtəʊ/ n. a short sentence or phrase that expresses a belief or a purpose（格言，座右铭）
nonpartisan /ˌnɒnˈpɑːtɪzæn/ adj. not supporting the ideas of any political party or group
novel /ˈnɒvl/ adj. new and original
probability /ˌprɒbəˈbɪlətɪ/ n. the likelihood of sth happening or being true
proponent /prəˈpəʊnənt/ n. one who argues in support of sth; an advocate
protein /ˈprəʊtiːn/ n. 蛋白质
reconcile /ˈrekənsaɪl/ v. to find a way in which two situations or beliefs that are opposed to each other can agree and exist together
side dish /saɪd dɪʃ/ small amount of food that you eat with a main meal（配菜）
sophisticated /səˈfɪstɪkeɪtɪd/ adj. intellectually appealing; deceptive

II. Notes

1. superintendent of schools (Par. 1)—someone who is in charge of all the schools in a particular area（地方教育官员，教育局长）
2. local school board (Par. 1)—a local board that governs or oversees public schools（地方教育委员会，地方教育董事会）
3. a cautionary preamble (Par. 1)—a preliminary statement giving a warning
4. a question-and-answer session (Par. 3)—a press interview
5. weigh in (Par. 3)—to add a remark to a discussion or an argument
6. an intelligent cause or agent (Par. 3)——一种智慧的起因或力量
    agent—a force or substance that causes a change
7. But to biologists, it smacks of faith-based science. (Par. 4)—但对生物学家来说，智慧设计有着以宗教信仰为基点的科学的意味。
    smack of—seem to have the quality of sth (usu. unpleasant)
8. losing its edge (Par. 4)—losing its advantage over other countries
9. No. 1 topic (Par. 4)—the most important or most noticeable topic
10. executive director (Par. 4)—会长，执行会长
11. Darwin's Theory has been a hard sell to Americans. (Par. 5)—it is very hard to make Americans believe Darwin's theory.

a hard sell—a method of selling in which the seller tries very hard to persuade the customer to buy
12. has as its motto "Teach the controversy" (Par. 6)—has "Teach the controversy" as its motto
13. religious Christians (Par. 7)—people who believe strongly and firmly in Christianity
14. senior fellow (Par. 8)—senior research fellow, a senior member of a group of high ranking teachers at a particular college or university or academic society (高级或资深研究员)
15. mathematics of probability (Par. 9)—概率统计,概率计算
16. sore point (Par. 9)—a subject that sb prefers not to talk about because it is likely to cause offence
17. avoid ... pitfalls of teaching creationism (Par. 9)—avoid likely mistakes or troubles brought by teaching creationism
18. Many scientists have been reluctant ... a meaningful debate about evolution (Par. 10)—Many scientist think that even mentioning intelligent design gives it more credibility than it deserves, so they avoid getting involved in the debate. They don't want to make people believe that intelligent design is a scientific theory equal to evolution.(许多科学家不愿卷入与"智慧设计论"者的辩论,因为这样做会让如下说法披上合理的外衣:关于进化论的争论是有意义的。)
19. peer-reviewed journals (Par. 10)—journals reviewed by similarly qualified scientists or experts in this field
20. To attribute natures' complexity ... to the unseen designer. (Par. 11)—The saying that the nature's complexity is the work of an intelligent designer still can't give a scientific account of the origin of this complexity because the designer is unseen and unknowable.
21. As for gaps in the fossil record ... what they found at the scene. (Par. 12)—至于化石记录中的空白,道金斯说,这就好比侦探抱怨说,根据现场发生的一切,它们无法弄清楚罪行——而且是一桩年代非常久远的罪行——发生过程中的每一分钟的情景。(这里道金斯用了一个比喻来说明证据并不都存在于化石记录中,就像犯罪记录并不都能在现场找到一样,因此我们不能仅以化石记录的缺失来判断物种是被一次性创造的。)
22. there's no reconciling faith with Darwinism (Par. 14)—they can by no means bring themselves to accept Darwinism
23. "The intelligent-design people are trying to ... teach I. D. crap in

the schools" (Par. 15)—In order to teach the worthless idea of intelligent design in schools, advocates for intelligent design refer to their theory as a critical inquiry of science to mislead people. ("智慧设计论者试图误导人们，让人们以为把科学称为不断批判性探索就能为他们在学校教授智慧设计这种无稽之谈大开绿灯。")

Crap—sth which is worthless or useless; nonsense

24. raise the profile (Par. 16)—to add the degree of exposure to public notice（提高知名度）

Part Three

Questions and Answers for Your Reference

1. What will happen in the public high school in rural Dover in the late fall? Why do scientists feel horrible about it?

    Sometime in the late fall, students will be taught intelligent design as the explanation of the origin of life in their biology class. This is a challenge to Darwin's theory which is widely regarded as one of the best-supported ideas in science since it comes from decades of study and objective evidence. Till now Darwin's theory is the only explanation for the rich variety of life forms on Earth, so scientists feel horrible about the teaching of such a pseudoscience.

2. What is President Bush's attitude towards "intelligent design"? What is the effect of his attitude?

    President Bush supports the idea of introducing both evolutionism and "intelligent design" in biology class, although he did not show his support for the "intelligent design" itself. He is very prudent and explains that the idea can "expose people to different schools of thought," but his attitude will further provoke battles on the topic and even bring more political and competitive pressure on science.

3. Has evolutionism been well accepted in America since its birth? What was the "monkey trial"?

    a. Ever since the birth of Darwin's theory, it has been violently attacked. Many people strongly opposed the idea of evolution because it conflicted with their religious convictions. However, Darwin's theory has never been successfully refuted. The notion of evolutionary change is now firmly established as a major pattern of the natural sciences.

    b. The "monkey trial" was a famous case, in which Tennessee school teacher John Scopes was convicted of violating the ban of teaching evolution in 1925. That was a big war between creationism and evolutionism.

4. What are the problems with Darwin's theory, according to the advocates of "intelligent design"?

    The advocates of "intelligent design" put their emphasis on the weaknesses and gaps in evolution. These involve two major ideas:

    1) Living things are too exquisitely complex to have evolved by a combination of chance mutations and natural selection.

    2) Some pieces in the fossil record that may prove the evolution process are missing.

5. Do earlier anti-Darwinists and the proponents of "intelligent design" hold the same point of view? Why?

    Their points are similar in that they all believe in a creator, but they are not exactly the same. The earlier anti-Darwinists, mostly creationists, regarded evolution as a heresy and they openly claimed the role of God. But the proponents of "intelligent design" accept some role of evolution and they avoid bringing God into the discussion.

6. Why do many scientists resist engaging in the new evolution war?

    They think the "intelligent design" is faith-based, so the debate about evolution is not a real scientific argument. They don't want to mislead people into thinking that "intelligent design" is another scientific theory like Darwinism.

7. Why will science teachers choose such expressions as "critical inquiry", "strengths and weaknesses" and "critical analysis" when they teach ideas like "intelligent design"?

    Because it is difficult for people to argue over such benign and earnest language. This can even make people feel the theory a scientific one and avoid violation against the Constitution.

8. What is your opinion of the war between Darwin's theory and "intelligent design"?

    (Open.)

Words to Know

    anti-Darwinism, Baptist Theological Seminary, Cambrian period, chance mutations, Christian fundamentalist, creationism, Darwinism, embolden, evolution wars, evolutionary biology, faith-based science, the First Amendment, flat earthism, fray, Genesis, genetic code, hardcore defenders, I. D. movement, intelligent design, irreducibly complex, legal and political pitfalls, monkey trial, natural selection, *The Origin of Species*, peer-reviewed journals, pseudoscience issue, raise the profile, religious Christians, school board, senior fellow, separation of state and church, sore point, superintendent of schools, think tank, turf battle

Part Four

Supplementary Reading

So Much for Earth Being Special: There Could Be 20 Billion Just Like It (http://science.time.com/2013/11/04/)

Lesson Seven

Obama Wins a Second Term as U. S. President

Part One

Summary

美国大选每四年举行一次,2008年奥巴马在民主党内击败前第一夫人希拉里·克林顿获得党内提名,代表民主党与共和党总统候选人麦凯恩展开竞争,得胜后成为美国历史上第一位黑人总统。当时正值美国深陷次贷危机,奥巴马打着"变革"的大旗,成了无数美国人"无限希望的象征"(a symbol of limitless hope),赢得了众多美国人的支持,轻松击败麦凯恩。四年过去了,2012年的美国仍失业率高,经济增长乏力,社会矛盾突出。奥巴马成了"有限希望的象征"(a symbol of hope's limitations),为了获得连任,奥巴马使出浑身解数,依然难与共和党总统候选人罗姆尼拉开差距,直到选举结果揭晓人们才能确定谁最终胜者,可见四年后的奥巴马已光环不再。但毕竟还是笑到最后,究其原因,本文做了如下分析:第一,他挽救汽车业的举措为他赢得了Ohio州59%的选民支持;第二,决定保留非法移民的在美居留权和工作权,为此他赢得了Florida 60%的选民支持;第三,就在大选投票日前夕,美国遭遇了飓风桑迪(Hurricane Sandy)的袭击,奥巴马应对得当,赢得了New Jersey超过60%选民的支持。综上所述,奥巴马这次小胜罗姆尼的原因在于这三招,这应归功于现任总统执政的优势。

本文是一篇即时性报道,发表于大选日第二天投票结果出炉之时。作者对大选前后的方方面面及共和民主两党候选人输赢做了分析,立场客观。但作者没有分析奥巴马胜选的其他种种原因。如有的是保守州,一般支持共和党;有的是黑人占多数的州,一般支持民主党;有的是传统上支持某党的州;还有的是候选人必须获胜的州,如加州、得州、纽约州,因选民多,选举团(Electoral College)的选举人票也多。总之,胜败原因复杂和众多,非一文所能说清道明的。

The Author

David Alan Fahrenthold, 34, works for *The Washington Post* in the capacity of News Reporter. He covers Congress for the Washington Post.

Background Information

1. Electoral vote 选举人票

US citizens don't vote directly for their President. Instead, they vote for electors who do the actual electing. The United States Electoral College is the institution that officially elects the President and Vice President every four years. Electors are apportioned to each state and the District of Columbia. The number of electors in each state is equal to the number of members of Congress to which the state is entitled. The Twenty-third Amendment has always resulted in the District of Columbia having three electors. There are 538 electors, based on there being 435 representatives and 100 senators, plus the three electors from the District of Columbia.

In all states, except Maine and Nebraska, electors are elected on a "winner-take-all" (赢者全得) basis. That is, all electors pledged to the presidential candidate who wins the most votes in a state. Maine and Nebraska use the "congressional district method", selecting one elector within each congressional district by popular vote and selecting the remaining two electors by a statewide popular vote. No elector is required by federal law to honor a pledge.

This Electoral College has been around for over 200 years. It sometimes gets confusing though. In the past, Al Gore got a half million more votes than George Bush, but he lost the election because George Bush won more electoral votes (or states) than Al Gore. Electoral votes decide who will become President.

2. swing state 摇摆州

In the presidential politics, a swing state (also, battleground state or purple state) is a state in which no single candidate or party has overwhelming support in securing that state's electoral college votes. Such states are targets of both major political parties in the elections, since winning these states is the best opportunity for a party to gain electoral votes. Non-swing states are sometimes called safe states, because one candidate has strong enough support that he or she can safely assume that he or she will win the state's votes.

In 2012, seven states (Colorado, Florida, Iowa, Nevada, New Hampshire, Ohio, Virginia,) emerged as battlegrounds or swing states, or tossup states, which may well determine the 2012 presidential election. President Obama won all seven in 2008, but the Great Recession and the slow and difficult recovery have changed all that. From the start of this campaign, polls showed the president with narrow but persistent leads in the states that would have the final say on Election Day. While the overall vote was close nationally, Mr. Obama defeated challenger Republican Mitt Romney in most of the tossup states.

3. Election Day

Election Day in the United States is the day set by law for the general elections of public officials. It occurs on the Tuesday after the first Monday in November, which is usually also the first Tuesday in November. The earliest possible date is November 2 and the latest possible date is November 8. The recent election was held on November 6, 2012.

For federal offices (President, Vice President, and US Congress), Election Day occurs only in even-numbered years. Presidential elections are held every four years, in years divisible by four. Elections to the House of Representatives and the Senate are held every two years; all Representatives serve two-year terms, while Senators serve six-year terms. General elections in which presidential candidates are not on the ballot are referred to as midterm elections. Terms for those elected begin in January the following year; the President and Vice President are inaugurated on Inauguration Day, usually January 20. Many state and local government offices are also elected on Election Day as a matter of convenience and cost saving.

Election Day is a civic holiday (法定假日) in some states. California Elections Code Section 14,000 provides that employees otherwise unable to vote must be allowed two hours off with pay, at the beginning or end of a shift.

4. the Church of Jesus Christ of Latter-day Saints 耶稣基督后期圣徒教会

It is a Christian church that considers itself to be a restoration of the church founded by Jesus Christ. The church is headquartered in Salt Lake City, Utah, and has established congregations(圣会)called wards or branches and built temples worldwide. Adherents(信徒), referred to as Latter-day Saints or, more informally, Mormons, view faith in Jesus Christ and his atonement(赎罪) as the central tenet(教义) of their religion. LDS theology includes the Christian doctrine of salvation only through Jesus Christ, though LDS doctrines regarding the nature of God and the potential of mankind differ significantly from mainstream Christianity.

In the USA, there has been existing anti-Mormonism, which is discrimination, persecution, hostility or prejudice directed at members of the Latter Day Saint movement. The most strident persecution occurred during the 19th century, particularly during the Utah War of the 1850s, and in the second half of the century. Opponents generally allege that the church's claims to divine origin are false, or that it is non-Christian, or that it is a religion based on fraud or deceit on the part of its past and present leaders.(现在魔门教徒集中在犹他州,该教主张一夫多妻,有教徒曾在加拿大发生过淫乱丑闻。)

Part Two

Language Points

I. New Words

aftermath /'ɑːftəmæθ/ n. the period of time after something such as a war, storm, or accident when people are still dealing with the results

bail /beɪl/ v. also bail out (AE.); bale out (BE.) to escape from a situation that you do not want to be in any more:

boost /buːst/ v. to increase or improve something and make it more successful

bruise /bruːz/ v. to cause injury by a blow to the body or to a fruit, discoloring the skin but not breaking

coalition /ˌkəʊə'lɪʃn/ n. a union of two or more political parties that allows them to form a government or fight an election together 联盟,联合

devout /dɪˈvaʊt/ *a*. sincerely religious, pious

far-reaching /fɑːˈriːtʃɪŋ/ *adj*. having a great influence or effect

governor /ˈgʌvənə(r)/ *n*. the person in charge of governing a state in the U.S.

Latino /ləˈtiːnəʊ/ *n*. sb. of Latin American origin living in the US (*cf*. Hispanic)

perception /pəˈsepʃn/ *n*. the way you think about something and your idea of what it is like 看法,洞察力

reassemble /ˌriːəˈsembl/ *n*. to bring together the different parts of something to make a whole again, after they have been separated

string /strɪŋ/ *v*. to combine things in order to make something that is complete, good, useful etc.

II. Notes

1. narrow victories(险胜)(*cf*. close loss)
2. picked ourselves up (Par. 3)—got up from the ground after we have fallen
3. Romney ... fix it. (Par. 5)—Romney, the former Massachusetts governor, based his campaign on arguing that Obama was not qualified to lead the USA because the U.S. economy was depressed and slow in growth but high in unemployment rate, but he himself was well experienced, and so was qualified.
4. too close to call (Par.7)—势均力敌,难分伯仲
5. He lost among white men by a large margin (Par. 13)—He won much less support of the white men than his rival.
   by a large margin—大幅度地
6. won by double digits (Par. 10)—There are ten percent more women voters who voted for Obama than those who voted for Romney.
7. Mormons had oncebeen persecuted to the desert edge of American civilization. (Par. 17)—Mormons had been treated cruelly and unfairly over a period of time and was almost removed from the American civilization.
8. ... a devout Mormon had fallen just short of the White House. — Romney, a pious Mormon, was only one step away from success.(本句中"a devout Mormon"指的就是与总统一职失之交臂的罗姆尼。)

fall short of sth——to be less than the amount or standard that is needed
9. bail out(Par. 19)——to help (esp. a business) out of difficulties by providing money [cf. bailout n.)紧急注资援助
10. deliver on (Par. 22)——to produce the promised, desired or expected results; come through 兑现(诺言)
11. He did not lay out a broad new agenda in the campaign. (Par. 25)——Obama did not make out his plan more clearly and to a greater extent in this election.

　　lay out——to describe or explain sth clearly
12. campaign trail (Par. 27)——竞选游说的行程
13. lean against (Par. 27)——to be opposed to
14. When one Wisconsin woman picked up … in perspective. (Par. 37)——When one Wisconsin woman picked up the phone to listen to Obama, he had got the chance to make a correct judgment about his running for the second term as the president.

　　put sth in perspective——to judge the importance of sth correctly

Part Three

Reference Answers to Questions

1. What are the main differences between present Obama and the one four years ago in accordance with the text?

　　a. Four years ago he was a hopeful uniter, but now he is a determined fighter for middle-class interests.

　　b. Four years ago, he ran as a symbol of limitless hope, but now he ran as a symbol of hope's limitations.

　　c. Four years ago, he pledged to sweep away Washington's old partisan politics, but now he pledges to plunge into those old politics and fight——battling Republicans.

　　d. Four years ago, his slogan was "Change" which has specific ideas, but now it is "Forward" which is vague in meaning.

2. In what group of people did Obama get the most and least supports?

　　He won strong supports among African Americans, women,

and Latinos and illegal immigrants by a lot but lost among white men by a large margin.
3. What is Obama's campaign slogan for this campaign? And what does it mean?

   In the campaign, Obama has no specific ideas about future terms but a vague slogan "Forward"
4. What were the three actions helping Obama win the reelections?

   One was his decision to bail out theUS auto industry, so most voters in Ohio appreciated it. Another key decision was his choice to give some young illegal immigrants the temporary right to live and work. Most voters in Florida were for him. A third was his properly handling of Sandy. More than 60% of people in New Jersey voted for the president.
5. Make a comment on Mitt Romney's policy in this election?

   a. He lost in the swing states but won supports among the whites.

   b. He attacked Obama's failure in American economy and expressed his business experience uniquely qualified him to fix the economy, but he was not lucky because just weeks before the election day American economy improved, which undermined his attack.

   c. as to his family, this failure in the election means the third unsuccessful attempt to capture the White House.

   d. he was a Mormon, so his close loss was also a milestone for his religion, meaning much to the Church of Jesus Christ of Latter-day Saints

   e. he is strongly against theDodd-Frank financial reforms and the present health-care law, which made him lose a lot.

Words to Know

balance of power, battleground, Capitol Hill, contention, by a large margin, Church of Jesus Christ of Latter-day Saints, deport, Election Day, electoral vote, exit poll, PAC, GOP, governor, Mitt Romney, Mormon, partisan politics, political coalition, second term, swing-state

Part Four

Supplementary Reading

Obama, Romney take on the world in final debate (From the *Washington Post*, Oct. 22, 2012)

Lesson Eight

The Economy Sucks. But Is It '92 Redux?

Part One

Summary

早在 2007 年 4 月,美国第二大次级房贷公司——新世纪金融公司的破产就暴露了次级抵押债券的风险;从 2007 年 8 月开始,美联储作出反应,向金融体系注入流动性以增加市场信心,美国股市也得以在高位维持,形势看来似乎不是很坏。然而,2008 年 8 月,美国房贷两大巨头——房利美和房地美股价暴跌,持有"两房"债券的金融机构大面积亏损。后来,这场始于美国的危机席卷全球,引发了自 20 世纪 30 年代以来最严重的经济危机。

2008 年初,在这样的经济形势下,美国大选的初选也拉开了帷幕。因此,候选人的经济政策对选举结果就起到了关键作用。本文作者把 2008 年与 1992 年进行比较,认为 2008 年的情况更糟,因为 1992 年 Bill Clinton 选举时,经济已经开始复苏,而 2008 年年初的经济刚刚显露出衰退的迹象。作者一方面引用经济学家的观点及美国政府对经济形势的判断,另一方面举出大量的实例,表明了人们对当时经济走势的担忧。

The Author

Daniel Gross (born 1967) is an American journalist and author. Since July 2012 he has been editor of global finance for *Daily Beast/Newsweek*. He was formerly Senior Editor at *Newsweek*, and between 2010 and 2012 was employed at *Yahoo! Finance*.

Background Information

subprime mortgage crisis

The U. S. subprime mortgage crisis was a set of events and conditions that led to a financial crisis and subsequent recession that began in 2008. It was characterized by a rise in subprime mortgage delinquencies and foreclosures, and the resulting decline of securities backed by said mortgages. These mortgage-backed securities (MBS) and collateralized debt obligations (CDO) initially offered attractive rates of return due to the higher interest rates on the mortgages; however, the lower credit quality ultimately caused massive defaults. Several major financial institutions collapsed in September 2008, with significant disruption in the flow of credit to businesses and consumers and the onset of a severe global recession.

There were many causes of the crisis, with commentators assigning different levels of blame to financial institutions, regulators, credit agencies, government housing policies, and consumers, among others. A proximate cause was the rise in subprime lending. The percentage of lower-quality subprime mortgages originated during a given year rose from the historical 8% or lower range to approximately 20% from 2004 to 2006, with much higher ratios in some parts of the U.S. A high percentage of these subprime mortgages, over 90% in 2006 for example, wereadjustable-rate mortgages. These two changes were part of a broader trend of lowered lending standards and higher-risk mortgage products. Further, U.S. households had become increasingly indebted, with the ratio of debt to disposable personal income rising from 77% in 1990 to 127% at the end of 2007, much of this increase mortgage-related.

When U.S. home prices declined steeply after peaking in mid-2006, it became more difficult for borrowers to refinance their loans. As adjustable-rate mortgages began to reset at higher interest rates (causing higher monthly payments), mortgage delinquencies soared. Securities backed with mortgages, including subprime mortgages, widely held by financial firms globally, lost most of their value. Global investors also drastically reduced purchases of mortgage-backed debt and other securities as part of a decline in the capacity and willingness of the private financial system to support lending. Concerns about the soundness of U.S. credit and financial markets led to tightening credit around the world and slowing economic growth in the U.S. and Europe.

The crisis had severe, long-lasting consequences for the U.S. and

European economies. The U. S. entered a deep recession, with nearly 9 million jobs lost during 2008 and 2009, roughly 6% of the workforce. U. S. housing prices fell nearly 30% on average and the U. S. stock market fell approximately 50% by early 2009. As of early 2013, the U. S. stock market had recovered to its pre-crisis peak but housing prices remained near their low point and unemployment remained elevated. Economic growth remained below pre-crisis levels. Europe also continued to struggle with its own economic crisis, elevated unemployment and severe banking impairments (estimated at 940 billion between 2008 and 2012).

Part Two

Language Points

I. New Words

decline /dɪˈklaɪn/ v. to go from a better to a worse position, or from higher to lower; deteriorate 衰落,衰退,下降

designate /ˈdezɪgneɪt/ v. to choose or name for a particular job or purpose 选派;指定;任命

disproportionate /ˌdɪsprəˈpɔːʃənət/ adj. not in proper proportion; not much or too little in relation to someone else 不相称的,不成比例的,不均匀的

notorious /nəʊˈtɔːrɪəs/ adj. famous or widely known for something bad [贬义]臭名昭著的

perilous /ˈperələs/ adj. very dangerous; risky

pro- /prəʊ/ prefix in favor of; supporting

prolonged /prəˈlɒŋd/ adj. continuing for a long time 长期的,持续很久的

recession /rɪˈseʃn/ n. a period of reduce trade and business activity 工商业的衰退期;经济衰退期

squeeze /skwiːz/ n. (esp. in business) a difficult situation caused by short supplies, tight controls, or high costs(尤指商业因供应短缺、管制严、成本高等引起的)拮据;困境

subtle /ˈsʌtl/ adj. clever in arrangement, esp. so as to deceive people 狡猾的,巧妙的

trail /treɪl/ n. a path

well-off /wel'ɔːf/ *adj.* rich

II. Notes

1. "on the campaign trail" (Par. 2)—in the course of the campaign
2. in '92, the economy had already started growing, though a jobless recovery doomed George H. W. Bush's re-election bid anyway. (Par. 2)—1992年，经济已经开始复苏，然而因为没有带来就业机会的增加，老布什的竞选连任注定要失败。
   bid—an attempt to get, win, or attract
3. The lesson? (Par. 2)—What lesson do we learn from George H. W. Bush's re-election?
4. As of this week... (Par. 4)—From this week on...
   as of—starting from (the time stated) 从……时候起
5. But policymakers aren't ready to give up on the business cycle (Par. 5)—Policymakers still have some hope that economy will keep growing.
   give up on—have no further hope for 对……不抱希望，对……表示绝望
6. What gives Paulson hisoptimism? "The president's pro growth policies, the fact that government revenues are coming in ahead of forecasts and that our deficit is now down to 1.2 percent GDP." (Par.5)—是什么让 Paulson 如此乐观呢？总统支持发展的政策，还有政府财政收入超出预算，财政赤字现在降至 GDP 的 1.2%。
7. Recession—defined as a contraction in economic activity... so infrequently. (Par.7)—经济衰退，即经济活动减少，由于不常出现，所以很难预测。
   define... as—show the nature of; characterize（显示……的特征或特性）
8. If theeconomy teeters into ... hit the wall. (Par. 8)—如果今年经济进入衰退期，那是因为消费能力很强的美国消费者已经达到极限。消费占美国经济的百分之七十。
9. At thedank CompUSA store ... the store's going-out-of-business sale. (Par. 10)—Although the prices at CompUSA store are much lower than usual because it is going to close down, there are not many shoppers.
10. housing hot spots—places where housing business is prosperous

11. they account for a disproportionate share of consumer purchase (Par. 17) —The rich make up a large part of consumer purchases.

  account for—make up a particular amount or part of sth （占……比例）

Part Three

Questions and Answers for Your Reference

1. In what ways are the 2008 and 1992 presidential elections similar?

    Both elections took place when economy was in recession and the candidates talked about economy most in their campaign.

2. What is the position of policymakers towards the slowdown of economy?

    Policymakers are reluctant to admit the economic recession and remain optimistic about the economic prospect. Treasury Secretary believes that it is natural that the economy has its ups and downs. The economy is going to continue to grow. President Bush will make proposals to bring the economy back to life. The Federal Reserve has taken action to deal with the financial troubles caused by the subprime mortgage crisis.

3. What is the root of the financial crisis in the Unites States?

    The trouble started with housing. Defaults on subprime mortgage led to a credit squeeze. Home prices fell at an unprecedented percentage in the past year. It led to problems in related industries.

4. How did the U. S. government respond to recessions? Why did it become a hot political issue?

    U. S. Government's responses come in two forms: fiscal policy (stimulus packages) and monetary policy (lowering interest rates). As the primaries roll into economically depressed Michigan, the need for the government to stimulate the economy has become a hot political issue.

5. Why did economists think that the economy could skate by a recession as long as the rich are getting richer and spending?

    Because rich people account for a disproportionate share of

consumer purchases. As long as they keep buying things, the economy can keep growing.

6. Along with the subprime loan problem, what are the other financial problems that banks are faced with?

When the economy slows down, debt of all kinds begins to go bad. Banks have to set aside money for bad loans because of higher write offs of auto and credit-card loans. Even well-off customers are behind in card payments. Take the American Express for example. It took a $440 million charge for bad debt.

7. According to this article, can the government bail out the economy? Why or why not?

Even though the government had taken actions and the Federal Reserve had cut the rate three times, the public still doubted whether it would work or not. Banks recovering from poor lending decisions are less willing to make mortgage loans. And, unlike the argument that the rich will spend anyway, even rich people are struggling and behind in card payment.

Words to Know

bail out, byproduct, cater to, cement shoes, contentious, contract, contractor, crumble, deficit, doom, dour, fret, housing hot spot, lay off, make a comeback, notch, on message, out of business, outlet, pan out, pivot, poll, primary, proactive, prolonged, receipt, recession, redux, remodel, retail, slump, speed bump, squeeze, State of the Union address, suck, tip, write off

Part Four

Supplementary Reading

Government Shutdown? Wall Street Refuses to Panic (From The *Daily Beast*, September 30, 2013)

Lesson Nine

Five myths about the American dream

Part One

Summary

　　"美国梦"是美国这一国家创立伊始就开始或从欧洲大陆移民迁移美洲大陆时的梦想,被视为是美国的灵魂。美国梦曾吸引了世界各地的移民,使它成为了世界上最受欢迎的移民国家,同时也是使其成为最强大国家的源泉。然而随着时代的变化,"美国梦"也在不断拓展。家庭幸福和经济富裕已取代财富成为美国梦的最重要核心定义;拥有不动产不再意味着实现美国梦,反而使部分欲想成为房屋拥有者的美国人陷入资不抵债的泥沼;美国梦式的理想不再是美国人所独有,世界各地的移民都相信美国梦并纷纷涌入美国希望实现其幸福梦想;美国的金融未来走向是美国自身的问题和选择,不应归于中国威胁论。无论美国欠债多少,对其他许多国家而言仍是充满机遇的地方;经济、政治困境不会熄灭美国民众对美国梦的信心和热情,无论有何种困境,梦想终究会实现。

　　本文是一篇典型的摆事实、讲道理的报刊文章,发表于因美国金融海啸、欧债危机使美国和欧洲经济陷入困境,美国梦遭到质疑之际。作者认为,当前人们对美国梦有五种误解:财富是美国梦的核心,美国梦意味着拥有房产,美国梦是美国人的梦想,中国对美国梦产生威胁,经济、政治困境扼杀美国梦。对此他分别进行了点评。本文观点明确,主题突出,论证充分,层次分明。具有典型的报刊社论文体特征,如"现象—分析—结论"的数据论证模式、主题词、情态动词、小句的使用、主谓结构等。不过作者虽然对美国梦的五种误解进行了诠释,但对美国制度本身的问题没有做深层次的分析,另外从文中不难看出,作者对美国梦始终持有一种过分乐观的态度,即无论有多少困难,只要有决心、勤奋努力就一定能实现美国梦。

The Author

Michael F. Ford, is the founding director of the Xavier University's Center for the Study of the American Dream. Ford has a 37-year career in politics, government and business at all levels of American public life. He has held senior staff and senior advisory positions in nine presidential campaigns. Ford also served as executive assistant to the Governor of Ohio and chief of staff for the mayor of Cincinnati. He has a master's degree in government from Georgetown University, was a graduate fellow at the Pennsylvania State University School of Public Administration and received his Bachelor of Arts from Xavier University.

Background Information

1. The American Dream

The American Dream is a national ethos of the US, a set of ideals in which freedom includes the opportunity for prosperity and success, and an upward social mobility achieved through hard work. In the definition of the American Dream by James Truslow Adams in 1931, "life should be better and richer and fuller for everyone, with opportunity for each according to ability or achievement" regardless of social class or circumstances of birth. The idea of the American Dream is rooted in the United States Declaration of Independence which proclaims that "all men are created equal" and that they are "endowed by their Creator with certain inalienable(不能剥夺的) Rights" including "Life, Liberty and the pursuit of Happiness."

The meaning of the "American Dream" has changed over the course of history, and includes both personal components (such as home ownership and upward mobility) and a global vision. Historically the Dream originated in the mystique regarding frontier life(边境生活). The ethos today implies an opportunity for Americans to achieve prosperity through hard work. According to The Dream, this includes the opportunity for one's children to grow up and receive a good education and career without artificial barriers. It is the opportunity to make individual choices without the prior restrictions that limited people according to their class, caste(社会地位), religion, race, or ethnicity

(种族). Immigrants to the United States sponsored ethnic newspapers in their own language; the editors typically promoted the American Dream.

2. The Great Depression 经济大萧条

The Great Depression was a severe worldwideeconomic depression in the decade preceding World War II. The timing of the Great Depression varied across nations, but in most countries it started in 1930 and lasted until the late 1930s or middle 1940s. It was the longest, most widespread, and deepest depression of the 20th century.

The depression originated in the U.S., after the fall in stock prices that began around September 4, 1929, and became worldwide news with the stock market crash of October 29, 1929 (known as Black Tuesday).

Some economies started to recover by the mid-1930s. In many countries, the negative effects of the Great Depression lasted until the end of World War II.

3. The Great Recession 经济大衰退

It is a major global recession characterized by various systemic imbalances and was sparked by the outbreak of the U.S. subprime mortgage(次级房贷)crisis and financial crisis of 2007−2008.

The global recession has affected the entire world economy, with greater detriment to some countries than others. The economic side effects of the European sovereign debt crisis(欧洲主权债务危机), austerity(紧缩), high levels of household debt, trade imbalances, high unemployment and limited prospects for global growth in 2013 and 2014 continue to provide obstacles to full recovery from the Great Recession.

The initial phase of the ongoing crisis, which manifested as a liquidity crisis(清偿危机), can be dated from August 7, 2007, when BNP Paribas(法国巴黎银行)terminated withdrawals from three hedge funds(对冲基金)citing "a complete evaporation of liquidity". The bursting of the U.S. housing bubble, which peaked in 2006, caused the values of securities tied to U.S. real estate pricing to drop sharply, damaging financial institutions globally.

Part Two

Language Points

I. New Words

attain /əˈteɪn/ v. to succeed in achieving sth. after trying for a long time（最终）获得

boost /buːst/ v. to increase or improve sth. and make it more successful 增加, 促进

coin /kɔɪn/ v. to invent a new word or expression, esp. one that many people start to use 创造（新词）

creditor /ˈkredɪtə(r)/ n. a person, bank, or company that you owe money to 债权人, 贷方

deduction /dɪˈdʌkʃn/ n. the process of taking away an amount from a total, or the amount that is taken away 扣除, 减除

epic /ˈepɪk/ n. a book, poem, or film that tells a long story about brave actions and exciting events 史诗

guarantee /ˌɡærənˈtiː/ n. a formal written or oral promise to materialize sth. 担保, 保证

institution /ˌɪnstɪˈtjuːʃn/ n. an established organization or foundation, esp. one dedicated to education, public service, or culture 机构, 公共机构

odds /ɒdz/ n. difficulties which make a good result seem very unlikely 阻碍, 困难

perception /pəˈsepʃn/ n. the way you think about sth. and your idea of what it is like 看法, 理解

pre-date v. to be built or formed, or to happen, at an earlier date than sth. else in the past 位于……之前

recession /rɪˈseʃn/ n. a difficult and hard time in economy when there is less trade, business activity etc. in a country than usual（经济）衰退; 不景气

renter /ˈrentə(r)/ n. one that receives payment in exchange for the use of one's property by another. 出租人, 房东

security /sɪˈkjʊərəti/ n. (usu. pl.) an official piece of writing, esp. a bond or piece of stock, giving owner the right to certain property 证券

trillion /ˈtrɪljən/ n. the number of 13 digits 1,000,000,000,000 万亿

II. Notes

1. ... material comfort that is not necessarily synonymous with Bill Gates-like riches (Par 1)... ——being rich enough but may not so wealthy as the richest figures in the world like Bill Gates and etc. 物质享受并不等同像比尔·盖茨那样的人一样富有
2. A fat bank account can be a means to these ends(Par 2)... ——With a large amount of money in the bank account, it is possible for people to achieve these aims.

    fat——thick and heavily-loaded, here referring to containing a large amount of money 银行里有大笔存款可以实现一些目标
3. special interests (Par 7)... ——special interest groups in general, or a group of people who have particular demands and who try to influence political decision making process by lobbing and contributing.(特殊利益集团)
4. In the midst of (Par 8)... ——在……期间
5. out of one's hands (Par 12)... ——out of one's control 某人对某事失控
6. While they may be worried about future generations, their dream today stands defiantly against the odds (Par 15)——Although they may be worried about the future of their offspring, they can still challenge all the difficulties and make their dream come true. 虽为后人担忧,仍力克困难实现美梦。

    against the odds——in spite of all the barriers

Part Three

Reference Answers to Questions

1. What is the core of American dream?

    The core of American dream is no longer getting rich only. More and more Americans choose "a good life for family" and "financial security" as their utmost American dream. Freedom, opportunity and the pursuit of happiness are still core part of their American dream, while wealth has become only a means to realize their dream rather than their ultimate goal.

2. Is the American dream American?

American Dream had already existed before 1931 and sustained today with more and more immigrants who came to America seeking to realize their American dream. American dream nowadays is not only for American, but a symbol of approach to success and the pursuit of happiness to everyone who has a dream.

3. American Dream fits perfectly into human nature, e. g. humans all want food and shelter, better ones too. This is why so many immigrants go to the U. S. to have their dreams fulfilled?

4. Why isn't homeownership ranked first or second by most people in the American dream?

Although owning real estate is important, but to some Americans, it is not as important as people are led to believe. To some Americans, the mortgage loan they take is far beyond their real value of the property, making them much pressured with bank account deficit, to whom "a good job," "the pursuit of happiness" and "freedom" are much closer. Those who benefit a lot from housing boost are those special interest groups rather than most Americans.

5. Do you think China is a threat to the American Dream?

No, I don't think so. Although many Americans chose China as the country to represent future as US economy has suffered severely, China won't be a threat to the American dream with the following reasons:

a. China is not the only country who holds large part of US debts, Japan, Britain and other country also hold US debts. Neither of these countries should be blamed for America's financial recession, instead, American itself should take the blame for the current financial situation.

b. Although China is rising both economically and politically, the United States owns unparalleled advantage in low-carbon energy research and education system due to its profound accumulation of talents as the world's land of opportunity.

c. The real reason for Western countries to propagate the "China conspiracy" is that they are afraid that China will challenge the existing international status when it becomes strong. They hope

to restrict the rise of China by means of the "China conspiracy" as political trick.
6. How do economic decline and political gridlock influence the American Dream?

   The economic decline and political gridlock made many Americans lose their confidence and trust in American system and government, but they still hold a belief that they can attain their American dream no matter how the government behaves.

Words to Know

against the odds, American dream, attain, boost, chart(v.), coin, counterintuitive, defiant, discrepancy, dub, Federal Reserve, Great Depression, Great Recession, gridlock, homeownership, mortgage, myth, odd, real estate, respondent, security, special interest, spree, subsidy, synonymous, tax break, underwater

Part Four

Supplementary Reading

Civic Illiteracy: A Threat to the American Dream (From *Huffington Post*, 2012—4—30)

Lesson Ten

Is America's new declinism for real?

Part One

Summary

本文发表于 2008 年 11 月,当时的美国经济由于次贷危机的影响处于非常困难的时期。因此,有些人又提出了美国即将衰退的观点。美国国家情报委员会在 2008 年 11 月 20 日公布的一份报告中说:"美国将继续在全球事务中扮演突出的角色,但它只是许多重要角色当中的一个。"这与其四年前报告中的说法大相径庭。这种观点是美国国内普遍蔓延的"新衰落主义"的一部分,完全失去了小布什执政时期和美国一统天下的单极时代的自信。

"新衰落论"的提出有三方面的原因:第一,伊拉克和阿富汗战争表明,军事上的强大并不能转化为政治上的胜利。第二,中国和印度的崛起预示着美国作为世界最大经济体的日子已经屈指可数了。第三,金融危机是人们意识到美国经济处于入不敷出的境地,美国模式出了问题。

一些新出版的著作和文章也表达了人们对"新衰落论"的认识。最有代表性的是 Fareed Zakaria 著的《美国后的世界》(*The Post-American World*)和 Andrew Bacevich 的《权利的局限》(*The Limits of Power*)。这又使人想起 1988 年发表的 Paul Kennedy 教授的书《大国的兴衰》(*The Rise and Fall of the Great Powers*)。

论最后,作者指出,美国历史上的衰落论都被事实证明是错误的,言外之意是这次也会如此。全文表现了美国人目前的心理状态:对衰落的恐惧,同时还保留着不愿承认即将衰落的美国人的傲慢。

The Author

Gideon Rachman became chief foreign affairs columnist for the Financial Times in July 2006. He joined the FT after a 15-year career at The Economist, which included spells as a foreign correspondent in

Brussels, Washington and Bangkok.

He also edited The Economist's business and Asia sections. His particular interests include American foreign policy, the European Union and globalisation.

Background Information

1. National Intelligence Council (NIC)

The National Intelligence Council is the center for midterm and long-term strategic thinking within the United States Intelligence Community (IC). It was formed in 1979. According to its official website:

- It leads the IC's effort to produce National Intelligence Estimates and other documents;
- It supports (and reports to) the Director of National Intelligence;
- It serves as a focal point for policymakers' questions;
- It contributes to the effort to allocate IC resources in response to policy changes; and
- It communicates with experts inacademia and the private sector to broaden the IC's perspective.

The NIC's goal is to provide policymakers with the best information: unvarnished, unbiased and without regard to whether the analytic judgments conform to current U.S. policy.

One of the NICs most important analytical projects is a Global Trends report produced for the incoming US president. The report is delivered to the incoming president between Election Day andInauguration Day, and it assesses critical drivers and scenarios for global trends with an approximate time horizon of fifteen years. The Global Trends analysis provides a basis for long-range strategic policy assessment for the White House and the intelligence community. The NIC's most recent Global Trends report, "Global Trends 2030: Alternative Worlds" was released in December 2012.

On February 2, 2007, the Office of the Director of National Intelligence, and the National Intelligence Council released the National Intelligence Estimate (NIE)—"'Prospects for Iraq's Stability: A

Challenging Road Ahead' Unclassified Key Judgments".

2. *The Post-American World*

The Post-American World is a non-fiction book by Indian American journalist Fareed Zakaria. It was published in hardcover and audiobook formats in early May 2008 and became available in paperback in early May 2009; the Updated and Expanded Release 2.0 followed in 2011. In the book, Zakaria argues that, thanks to the actions of the United States in spreading liberal democracy across the world, other countries are now competing with the US in terms of economic, industrial, and cultural power. While the US continues to dominate in terms of political-military power, other countries such as China and India are becoming global players in many fields.

The book peaked at #2 on *The New York Times* non-fiction hardcover best-seller list and at #47 on the *USA Today* Top 150 Best-Selling Books list. Reviewers commented that Zakaria's writing was intelligent and sharp, yet accessible to general audiences. A few reviewers also wrote that the book was similar to an extended essay with journalistic style writing.

3. *The Rise and Fall of the Great Powers*

The Rise and Fall of the Great Powers: Economic Change and Military Conflict from 1500 to 2000, by Paul Kennedy, first published in 1987, explores the politics and economics of the Great Powers from 1500 to 1980 and the reason for their decline. It then continues by forecasting the positions of China, Japan, the European Economic Community (EEC), the Soviet Union and the United States through the end of the 20th century.

Kennedy argues that the strength of a Great Power can be properly measured only relative to other powers, and he provides a straightforward and persuasively argued thesis: Great Power ascendancy (over the long term or in specific conflicts) correlates strongly to available resources and economic durability; military overstretch and a concomitant relative decline are the consistent threat facing powers whose ambitions and security requirements are greater than what their resource base can provide for.

Part Two

Language Points

I. New Words

address /əˈdres/ n. a formal speech
aggressive /əˈgresɪv/ adj. assertive, bold, and energetic; fast growing
agonised /ˈægənaɪzd/ adj. distressed with extreme pain; tortured
assumption /əˈsʌmpʃn/ n. sth that is taken as a fact or believed to be true without proof 假定
brisk /brɪsk/ adj. quick and active; lively
broadly /ˈbrɔːdlɪ/ adv. mainly; generally
budget /ˈbʌdʒɪt/ n. an estimate of expected income and expense for a given period in the future 预算
capture /ˈkæptʃə(r)/ v. to represent or record in lasting form 表现；记录
civilian /səˈvɪlɪən/ adj. of, pertaining to, formed by, or administered by people who are not on active duty with a military, naval, police, or fire fighting organization 平民的；非军事的
corps /kɔː(r)/ n. a military organization consisting of officers and enlisted personnel or of officers alone 军团
deficit /ˈdefɪsɪt/ n. the amount by which a sum of money falls short of the required or expected amount; a shortage 赤字, 亏空
dominance /ˈdɒmɪnəns/ n. the fact or position of dominating; importance, power, or controlling influence 优势；支配地位
issue /ˈɪʃuː/ v. to publish
markedly /ˈmɑːkɪdlɪ/ adv. strikingly; conspicuously; obviously
presidency /ˈprezɪdənsɪ/ n. the office, function, or term of office of a president 总统的职位；总统任期
prominent /ˈprɒmɪnənt/ adj. noticeable; easily seen; of great importance, fame etc
strive /straɪv/ v. to exert oneself vigorously; make strenuous efforts; try hard
Texan /ˈteksən/ adj. of Texas or its people
trait /treɪt/ n. a distinguishing characteristic or quality, esp. of one's personal nature 个性；特征
translate /trænsˈleɪt/ v. to be changed or transformed in effect 转化

underlie /ˌʌndəˈlaɪ/ v. to be a hidden cause or meaning of 构成……的潜在原因,成为……的基础

underline /ˌʌndəˈlaɪn/ v. to indicate the importance of; emphasize, as by stressing or italicizing 强调

II. Notes

1. for real—real; serious; actual
2. The latest report... has made headlines around the world. (Par. 3)—The latest report has become the headlines in newspapers and of radio and TV broadcasts around the world.
3. sit up (Par. 4)—become interested or astonished
4. a broader intellectual trend (Par. 4)—a more general idea held by many scholars, academics etc
5. the financial crisis has fed the notion that the US is living beyond its means (Par. 5)—the financial crisis has provided reasons for people to think that the US is using up more resources or money than it can afford.
6. we exercised that power for a while only to realise that it was ephemeral (Par. 6)—we used that power for a short period of time and in the end we came to understand that it could not last long.
7. Professor Kennedy's argument that previous great powers had succumbed to "imperial over-stretch" resonated in the US at a time when many were worried by Reagan-era budget deficits and Japan's growing economic power. (Par. 9)—肯尼迪教授认为,以前的大国都败于"帝国过度扩张",这一看法当时在美国引起极大反响,当时许多人对里根时代的预算赤字以及日本日益壮大的经济实力表示担心。
8. Odd as it is to recall... (Par. 11)—Although it is strange to recall...

Part Three

Questions and Answers for Your Reference

1. What is the difference between the latest global trends report and the one issued four years ago?

   The latest report foresees "a world in which the US plays a prominent role in global events, but the US is seen as one among many global actors". The report issued four years ago had projected "continuing US dominance".

2. What does "new declinism" mean?

It means that Americans, especially the intellectuals, think that America is in decline. They have lost the aggressive confidence of the Bush years and the "unipolar moment". It is new because there were times in US history when people had similar thoughts.

3. What are the reasons of the new declinism?

There are three reasons: First, the wars in Iraq and Afghanistan have made it clear that US military supremacy does not automatically translate into political victory. Second, the rise of China and India suggests that America's days as the world's largest economy are numbered. Third, the financial crisis has fed the notion that the US is living beyond its means and that something is badly wrong with the American model.

4. What does William Wohlforth of Dartmouth College think of the new declinism?

He pointed out that America may recover from the new declinism just like before and there may be a resurgence of American confidence.

5. Why does the writer think that the new declinism may be more soundly based than the previous ones?

Because he thinks thatChina may pose more challenge to the US than the Soviet Union and Japan since it has a large size and a record of sustained and dynamic economic growth.

6. What do you think of America's decline? And China's rise?

(Open.)

Words to Know

aggressive, American model, assumption, constraint, decline, declinism, deficit, dissipate, dominance, dynamic, high-tech, inadequate, intelligence agencies, intelligence establishment, introspection, outperform, predecessor, Reagan-era; reminiscent, resonate, resurgence, security establishment, succumb, supremacy, sustained, unipolar, unleash, world view

Part Four

Supplementary Reading

Declinism's Fifth Wave (From *The American Interest*, the January/February issue)

Lesson Eleven

Pentegon Digs In on Cyberwar Front

Part One

Summary

网络给我们带来无比的方便和想象空间。然而,凡事都有两面,它是个无规范的新生事物。强国每天都发生网络攻击事件,尤其是美国,叫得最凶,宣称国土安全部的网站多次被黑客成功入侵,被迫切断与有关部门的联系;因经济数据被窃,美国企业每年仅在知识产权方面的损失就高达数十亿美元;国防部计算机每天都遭到数十万次攻击,连部长的电子邮箱也被破解过,等等。

其实,美国在网络安全竞赛中走在世界各国的前面。小布什政府就将网络安全纳入其国土安全计划,并于2002年11月成立了国土安全部,下设国家网络空间安全中心。

2009年6月,美国防部长盖茨宣布,美国正式组建了"网络战司令部",隶属美军战略司令部。在同年初出台的《四年任务与使命评估报告》中,美国防部列举了美军需要发展的八种"核心能力",其中包括网战能力。美国防部提出,鉴于美军在正规作战方面享有优势,今后将重点发展非正规战能力,特别是网战等新型作战能力。

本文对五角大楼实施网络战的现状和实战培训都做了报道。网战吸引了媒体的报道,2013年6月11日斯诺登就是通过英国《卫报》(*The Guardian*)将美国的NSA丑闻公布于众,然后全球各新闻媒体无不加以刊载。

The Author

Julian E. Barnes, Pentagon reporter at the *Wall Street Journal* (WSJ), covers the military and national security for the WSJ since 2010.

Background Information

Cyberwarfare 网络战

Cyberwarfare is a form of information warfare sometimes seen as analogous to (类似于) conventional warfare, and in 2013 was, for the first time, considered a larger threat than Al Qaeda or terrorism, by many U.S. intelligence officials.

U.S. government security expert Richard A. Clarke, in his book *Cyber War* (May 2010), defines "cyberwarfare" as "actions by a nation-state to penetrate another nation's computers or networks for the purposes of causing damage or disruption." The *Economist* describes cyberspace as "the fifth domain of warfare," and William J. Lynn, U.S. Deputy Secretary of Defense, states that "as a doctrinal matter, the Pentagon has formally recognized cyberspace as a new domain in warfare... [which] has become just as critical to military operations as land, sea, air, and space."

Part Two

Language Points

I. New Words

accelerate /əkˈseləreɪt/ v. to cause to move faster, or to happen faster

acknowledge /əkˈnɒlɪdʒ/ v. to admit or accept that sth. is true or that a situation exists 承认(事实、局面等)

airman /ˈeəmən/ n. a member of their country's air force

airstrike /ˈeəˌstraɪk/ n. an attack in which military aircraft drop bombs 空袭, 空中打击

amid /əˈmɪd/ prep. while noisy, busy, or confused events are happening 在……过程中;在……中

curriculum /kəˈrɪkjələm/ n. the subjects that are taught by a school, college, etc., or the things that are studied in a particular subject 课程 *plural* curricula, *or* curriculums

dominance /ˈdɒmɪnəns/ n. the fact of being more powerful, more important, or more noticeable than other people or things 支配; 控制

elite /eɪˈliːt/ *adj.* an elite group contains the best, most skilled or most experienced people or members of a larger group 精英的；精锐的；王牌的

expertise /ˌekspɜːˈtiːz/ *n.* special skills or knowledge in a particular subject, that you learn by experience or training 专门知识或技能

exploit /ɪkˈsplɒɪt/ *v.* To use or develop sth fully so as to get profit

famed /feɪmd/ *adj.* well-known

initiative /ɪˈnɪʃətɪv/ *n.* an important new plan or process to achieve a particular aim or to solve a particular problem 积极的行动

navy /ˈneɪvi/ *n.* the branch of a country's military forces that is concerned with attack and defense at sea

Marine /məˈriːn/ *n.* the Marine Corps, a part of the U.S. Armed forces consisting of soldiers who are based on ships. They are often considered to be the bravest and most skilled soldiers in the U.S. forces, and are often sent into battle first. They are also know for having a very tough training program. 美国海军陆战队

publicize /ˈpʌblɪsaɪz/ *v.* to give information about sth. to the public, so that they know about it 宣传；宣扬

suppress /səˈpres/ *v.* to prevent sth. from growing or developing, or from working effectively 镇压，压制

terminal /ˈtɜːmɪnl/ *n.* a piece of computer equipment consisting of at least akeyboard and a screen, that you use for putting in or taking out information from a large computer 终端；终端机

II. Notes

1. hunt down(the subtitle)—to search for a person or animal until you catch them, esp. in order to punish or kill them(搜索直至找到)
2. emerging battlefield(Par. 1)—Here refers to a new battlefield—cyber battlefield.
    emerging—coming into existence; developing
3. build up (Par. 2)—to cause to increase, develop, or become gradually larger
4. Whilecyber may not look or smell ... is the same. (Para. 5)—Although war on the Internet are not fought with any real weapons like fighter aircrafts and bomber aircrafts (as in a traditional war), it plays an important role in any potential conflict in 2012.
5. the Obama administration(Para. 5)—(奥巴马政府)the executive branch headed by President Obama. In US, the US or federal

government is different from a specific leader administration.
6. "Our curriculum is based on attack, exploit and defense of the cyber domain," (Para. 14)—Our training courses are mainly about the skills of attacking, using and developing, and defending the cyberspace.
7. a Syrian nuclear facility(Para. 15)—叙利亚的一处核设施

   facility—a place or building used for a particular purpose or activity
8. inaugural students(Para. 17)—the first group of students
9. measure up (Para. 18)—to be good enough to do a particular job or to reach a particular standard(符合标准;达到期望)

Part Three

Reference Answers to Questions

1. Why does the Pentagon show much interest in cyberwarfare?

   Because cyberwarfarehas the newer, more high-tech and often more secretive capabilities; and cyberweapons could help suppress enemy air and sea defenses.
2. What is the Air Force version of the Navy's "Top Gun" program mainly about?

   Its new course trains airmen working at computer terminals how to hunt down electronic intruders, defend networks and launch cyberattacks.
3. How does the U.S. Cyber Command deal with the cyber world?

   It marshals cyberwarfare capabilities from across the military and integrates them with expertise at the National Security Agency. Some of the defenses could someday be extended to the private sector.
4. Why does the Air Force set up the "aggressor" team?

   Because the aggressor acts as a hacker testing the Air Force's cyberdefenses.
5. Why is it important to add the cyberwarfare course to the most elite school?

   Because it is important to change the mindset of the military, where many still regard radios, telephones and computers as communications tools—not targets and weapons.

Words to Know

adversary, aerial combat, Cap., Col., cyber, cyberattack, cyber capabilities, cyber domain, cyber power, cyberspace, cyberwar, cyberweapon, deploy, dig in, drone, elite school, Gen., incapacitate, Lt Col., Marine, measure up, NSA, Pentagon, reconnaissance, terminal, US Cyber Command

Part Four

Supplementary Reading

Pentagon Expanding Cybersecurity Force to Protect Networks Against Attacks (From *The New York Times*, January 27, 2013)

Lesson Twelve

Terrorized by "War on Terror"

Part One

Summary

自 2001 年发生"9·11"事件以来,美国及其盟友便展开了这场以"消灭国际恐怖主义"为目标的全球性战争,即反恐战争(War on Terror)。然而,这场反恐战争在打击恐怖主义的同时,却对整个社会的心理、文化、价值观等各方面产生了消极影响。本文作者认为,布什政府过于强化"反恐战争",制造了人们的恐惧心理,结果是损坏了美国民主和美国在全世界的声誉。恐怖主义并不是敌人,而是通过屠杀手无寸铁的平民而达到政治目的的工具。

本文作者一针见血地指出,这种状况是美国当局有意制造的,因为恐惧可以压倒理性,强化人们的各种情感,而政客们就可以利用公众的情感达到自己的目的。例如,若不是布什政府把伊拉克拥有大规模杀伤性武器与9·11恐怖袭击联系起来,对伊开战就不可能得到国会的支持。另外,2004年小布什竞选连任成功的部分原因也是这种战争心理。总之,作者对反恐战争的负面影响做了全面深刻的剖析,尖锐批评了在"9·11"之后的一系列错误做法。

The Author

Zbigniew Kazimierz Brzezinski (/ˈzbɪgnjuː bɜrˈzɪnski/; Polish born March 28, 1928) is a Polish American political scientist, geostrategist, and statesman who served as United States National Security Advisor to President Jimmy Carter from 1977 to 1981. Brzezinski is currently Robert E. Osgood Professor of American Foreign Policy at Johns Hopkins University's School of Advanced International Studies, a scholar at the Center for Strategic and International Studies, and a member of various boards and councils. He appears frequently as an expert on the PBS program *The News Hour with Jim Lehrer*, ABC

News' *This Week with Christiane Amanpour*, and on MSNBC's *Morning Joe*, where his daughter, Mika Brzezinski, is co-anchor. His son, Mark Brzezinski, is an American diplomat and the current United States Ambassador to Sweden since 2011. (兹比格涅夫·布热津斯基生于波兰华沙,美国著名的国际关系学者、地缘战略家、国务活动家。曾任卡特政府的国家安全顾问,目前美国重量级智囊之一。)

Background Information

1. war on terror

The war on terror (also known as the Global War on Terrorism) is a term commonly applied to an international military campaign which started as a result of the 11 September 2001 terrorist attacks on the United States. This resulted in an international military campaign to eliminate al-Qaeda and other militant organizations. The United Kingdom and many other NATO and non-NATO nations such as Pakistan participate in the conflict.

The phrase "War on Terror" was first used by U. S. President George W. Bush on 20 September 2001. The Bush administration and the Western media have since used the term to signify a global military, political, lawful, and conceptual struggle—targeting both organizations designated as terrorist and regimes accused of supporting them. It was typically used with a particular focus on countries supporting militant Islamists, al-Qaeda, and other jihadi groups.

Although the term is no longer officially used by the administration of U. S. President Barack Obama (which instead uses the term Overseas Contingency Operation), it is still commonly used by politicians, in the media and by some aspects of government officially, such as the United States' Global War on Terrorism Service Medal.

Civilian as well as military personnel that are held as prisoners or detainees by the U. S. in the War on Terrorism are neither considered suspected criminals, nor prisoner of war, but unlawful combatants, denied protection by the Geneva Conventions.

2. Al-Qaeda

Al-Qaeda (/æl'kaɪdə/ Arabic, translation: "The Base" and alternatively spelled al-Qaida and sometimes al-Qa'ida) is a global militant Islamist organization founded by Osama bin Laden in Peshawar, Pakistan, at some point between August 1988 and late 1989, with its originsbeing traceable to the Soviet War in Afghanistan. It operates as a network comprising both a multinational, stateless army and a radical Sunni Muslim movement calling for global Jihad and a strict interpretation ofsharia law. It has been designated as a terrorist organization by the United Nations Security Council, NATO, the European Union, the United Kingdom, the United States, India and various other countries (see below). Al-Qaeda has carried out many attacks on non-Sunni Muslims, non-Muslims, and other targets it considers *kafir*(异教徒).

Al-Qaeda has attacked civilian and military targets in various countries, including the September 11 attacks, 1998 U.S. embassy bombings and the 2002 Bali bombings. The U.S. government responded to the September 11 attacks by launching the War on Terror. With the loss of key leaders, culminating in the death of Osama bin Laden, Al-Qaeda's operations have devolved from actions that were controlled from the top-down, to actions by franchise associated groups, to actions of lone wolf operators.

Characteristic techniques employed by Al-Qaeda include suicide attacks and simultaneous bombings of different targets. Activities ascribed to it may involve members of the movement, who have taken a pledge of loyalty to Osama bin Laden, or the much more numerous "al-Qaeda-linked" individuals who have undergone training in one of its camps in Afghanistan, Pakistan, Iraq or Sudan, but who have not taken any pledge. Al-Qaeda ideologues envision a complete break from all foreign influences in Muslim countries, and the creation of a new worldwide Islamiccaliphate. Among the beliefs ascribed to Al-Qaeda members is the conviction that a Christian-Jewish alliance is conspiring to destroy Islam. As Salafist jihadists, they believe that the killing of civilians is religiously sanctioned, and they ignore any aspect of religious scripture which might be interpreted as forbidding the murder of civilians and internecine fighting. Al-Qaeda also opposes man-made laws, and wants to replace them with a strict form of sharia law.

Al-Qaeda is also responsible for instigating sectarian violence among Muslims. Al-Qaeda is intolerant of non-Sunni branches of Islam and denounces them by means of excommunications called "takfir". Al-Qaeda leaders regard liberal Muslims, Shias, Sufis and other sects as heretics and have attacked their mosques and gatherings. Examples of sectarian attacks include the Yazidi community bombings, the Sadr City bombings, the Ashoura Massacre and the April 2007 Baghdad bombings.

Part Two

Language Points

I. New Words

apologist /əˈpɒlədʒɪst/ *n.* a person who strongly supports a particular belief and can give arguments in defence of it 辩护者

assessment /əˈsesmənt/ *n.* (an example of) the act of calculating or deciding the value or amount of sth 评价，估计

billboard /ˈbɪlbɔːd/ *n. AmE* a high fence or board on which large advertisements are stuck 广告牌

conviction /kənˈvɪkʃn/ *n.* the act of convicting or being convicted of a crime 定罪；宣判有罪

divided /dɪˈvaɪdɪd/ *adj.* separated into opposing groups; being an important cause of disagreement 有分歧的，(意见)不一致的

entertain /ˌentəˈteɪn/ *v.* to hold in the mind; harbor; cherish

foster /ˈfɒstə(r)/ *v.* to help (feelings or ideas) to grow or develop 培养，助长

generate /ˈdʒenəreɪt/ *v.* to cause (esp. feelings or ideas) to exist; produce

initiate /ɪˈnɪʃieɪt/ *v.* to be responsible for starting 创始；发起

intensify /ɪnˈtensɪfaɪ/ *v.* to (cause to) become stronger or greater

Nazi /ˈnɑːtsi/ *n. & adj.* 纳粹分子(的) Nazism *n.* 纳粹主义

oblivious /əˈblɪviəs/ *adj.* not noticing; unaware

panel /ˈpænl/ *n.* a group of usually well-known speakers or entertainers who answer questions to inform or amuse the public, usually on a radio or television show 专门小组；专题讨论小组

prompt /prɒmpt/ *v.* to cause or urge

propagation /ˌprɒpəˈgeɪʃn/ *n.* the act of spreading to a great number of people 传播；普及

prophecy /ˈprɒfəsi/ *n.* a statement telling sth that will happen in the

future, esp. one based on one's personal feelings rather than on any proof 预言
reference /'refrəns/ *n.* (an example of) mentioning
Semitic /sə'mɪtɪk/ *adj.* belonging to a race of people which includes the Jews and Arabs; Jewish 闪米特人的; 犹太人的
spanning /'spænɪŋ/ *prep.* including
undermine /ʌndə'maɪn/ *v.* to weaken or destroy gradually
vagueness /'veɪgnəs/ *n.* the quality or state of being not clearly described, expressed, known, or established

II. Notes

1. The "war on terror" has created a culture of fear in America. (Par. 1)—The "war on terror" has frighten the Americans, and this fear is shown in everything they do, in their attitude, belief and behavior.
   culture—collective attitudes and behavior
2. The damage these three words have done ... when they were plotting against us in distant Afghan caves. (Para. 2)—这几个词给我们造成的损失比那些"9·11"事件的狂热份子当初在阿富汗山洞里密谋策划时所梦想的要大得多, 这是我们自己造成的损失。
3. Terrorism is not an enemy but a technique of warfare-political intimidation through the killing of unarmed non-combatants. (Para. 2)—恐怖主义不是敌人, 它是一种通过杀害手无寸铁的平民而进行的、用战争威胁以实现政治目的的手段。
4. the war of choice (Para. 3)—the war that is generally preferred or supported
   of choice—that is generally preferred
5. in the event of (Para. 5)—if there should be
6. Such fear-mongering, reinforced by security entrepreneurs, the mass media and the entertainment industry, generates its own momentum. (Par. 7)—这种兜售恐惧的做法愈演愈烈, 保安公司老板、媒体和娱乐业使其势头更猛。
7. siege mentality (Par. 9)—a state of mind whereby one believes that one is being constantly attacked, oppressed, or isolated 被围心态
8. a case in point (Par. 12)—an example that proves the subject under consideration
9. Someday Americans will be as ashamed ... prompting intolerance against the few. (Par. 14)—总有一天, 美国人会为目前这种做法感

到惭愧,就像他们现在为从前的事情感到惭愧一样。在美国历史上,曾经发生过由于多数人的恐慌而引发对少数人的过激行为的先例。

Part Three

Questions and Answers for Your Reference

1. What is the "three-word mantra" in the author's opinion? What is his attitude to this mantra? Can you explain it in your own words?

    The "three-word mantra" is "war on terror". The author's attitude toward it is basically negative. He says that the mantra has had a very bad impact on America, causing a mentality of fear in the US civilians, spoiling US's standing in the world, and greatly undermining US's strength against terrorism actually.

2. What's the Bush Administration's main objective of referring to "war on terror" constantly?

    The major objective for the Bush Administration to refer to "war on terror" constantly, according to the author, is to create a "culture of fear", so that the public could be misled to follow the policies the politicians want to pursue, esp. to vote for them.

3. What phenomena can show that "America has become insecure and more paranoid"?

    One thing showing "America has become insecure and more paranoid" is the endless increase of the sites as potentially important national targets for would-be terrorists, from 160 sites in 2003 to 300,00 at the time the author wrote the article. Another phenomenon is the "security check" in office buildings and so on.

4. Why does the author say that "the 'war on terror' has encouraged legal and political harassment of Arab Americans"?

    The discrimination against Arabs, such as drivers in turbans taken as suspicious terrorists, films produced with evil characters with recognizable Arab features, and animus towards Muslim travelers, has stimulated a strong Islamophobia. This atmosphere has encouraged legal and political harassment of Arab Americans.

5. What is the reason for the author's view that "the 'war on terror' has gravely damaged the United States internationally"?

The rough treatment of Iraqi civilians by the U. S. military has prompted a widespread sense of hostility toward the United States in general. The victimization of Arab civilians angers Muslims watching the news on television. And the resentment is not limited to Muslims. A BBC poll in 27 countries resulted in the United States being rated as a country with "the most negative influence on the world."

Words to Know

Al-Qaeda, brainwashing, demoralizing, fanatic, harassment, Holocaust, Islamophobia, legal procedures, mobilize, momentum, paranoia, paranoid, Pearl Harbor, pernicious, pervasive, premium, proliferate, prophecy, psyche, scenario, security checks, siege mentality, solidarity, stereotype, suicide bomber, susceptible, terrorism, terrorist attack, undermine, weapons of mass destruction (WMD).

Part Four

Supplementary Reading

Edward Snowden: US surveillance 'not something I'm willing to live under' (From The *Guardian*, July 8, 2013)

Lesson Thirteen

Spies Among Us: Modern-Day Espionage

Part One

Summary

　　此桩俄罗斯间谍案始于 2010 年 6 月 27 日,美国司法部和 FBI 对已布控十年的 10 名俄间谍实施抓捕,经审判和美俄双方交涉后,他们被判驱逐出境,并于 2010 年 7 月 10 日在奥地利维也纳机场与被俄收押的美谍交换。至此,两国落网特工案和平落幕。

　　事实上,跨国情报工作由来已久,派遣情报工作人员在他国活动一直是各国政府心照不宣的潜规则,尽管冷战已经结束 20 多年,但情报工作仍然是很多国家政治、军事、外交等工作的重要辅助。不仅如此,在网络、新科技和各级部门对情报需求激增的推动下,所有形式的间谍活动实际上都在增多。公司、恐怖分子和私人侦探也参其中:恐怖组织利用网络收集情报实施阴谋;企业间相互刺探比比皆是;私人侦探业也因网络技术的发展而趋向多元化,他们则由调查人员升级为监控人员,承接的业务也由帮助客户从间扩展至反间。现当代情报活动不再是专注于战争或国际政治,而是全方位领域进行。

　　本文是一篇综述报道,发表于俄罗斯谍案尘埃落定之时。作者从政府、恐怖组织、商业以及民间侦探等方面对当前各国间谍活动的现状做了分析,脉络清楚,观点明确,事例丰富,语言精辟。从中我们可看出,从间和反间的盛行都源于各国、各组织、各企业间各种各样的利益关系,高科技的发展使谍战更加多样化。

The Author

　　McKay Coppins is a reporter for *Newsweek* and *The Daily Beast* covering politics and national affairs. His writing has also appeared in *The Daily Caller* and Salt Lake City's *Deseret News*.

Background Information

1. The Cold War 冷战

The Cold War, often dated from 1947 to 1991, was a sustained state of political and military tension between powers in the Western Bloc(西方集团), dominated by the U.S-led NATO among its allies, and powers in the Eastern Bloc(东欧集团), dominated by the Soviet led Warsaw Pact (华沙公约). This began after the success of their temporary wartime alliance against Nazi Germany, leaving the USSR(苏联) and the US as two superpowers with profound economic and political differences. A neutral faction arose with the Non-Aligned Movement(不结盟运动国家组织) founded by Egypt, India, and Yugoslavia(南斯拉夫); this faction rejected association with either the US-led West or the Soviet-led East.

2. 9/11 "9·11"恐怖袭击事件

The September 11 attacks refers to a series of four coordinated terrorist attacks launched by the Islamic terrorist group al-Qaeda(伊斯兰恐怖主义基地组织) upon the United States in New York City and the Washington, D.C. area on September 11, 2001.

Four passengerairliners were hijacked(劫持) by 19 al-Qaeda terrorists so they could crash into buildings in suicide attacks(自杀性袭击). Two of those planes, American Airlines Flight 11 and U.S. targets Flight 175, were crashed into the North and South towers, respectively, of the World Trade Center(世贸中心) complex in New York City. Within two hours, both towers collapsed with debris and the resulting fires causing partial or complete collapse of all other buildings in the WTC complex, as well as major damage to ten other large surrounding structures. A third plane, American Airlines Flight 77, was crashed into the Pentagon(五角大楼), the headquarters of the United States Department of Defense(美国国防部), leading to a partial collapse in its western side. The fourth plane, United Airlines Flight 93, was targeted at the United States Capitol(美国国会大厦) in Washington, D.C., but crashed into a field near Shanksville(尚克斯维尔), Pennsylvania, after its passengers tried to overcome the hijackers. In total, almost 3,000 people died in the attacks, including the 227 civilians and 19 hijackers aboard the four planes.

The destruction of the Twin Towers(美国纽约双子星大厦) and other properties caused serious damage to the economy of Lower Manhattan and had a significant negative impact on global markets. Cleanup of the World Trade Center site was completed in May 2002, and the Pentagon was repaired within a year. Numerous memorials have been constructed, including the National September 11 Memorial & Museum in New York, the Pentagon Memorial, and the Flight 93 National Memorial in Pennsylvania.

Part Two

Language Points

I. New Words

bound /baʊnd/ *adj.* be forced to do what a law or agreement says you must do 受约束的

bug /bʌg/ *n.* a small piece of electronic equipment for listening secretly to other people's conversations 窃听器

chatter /'tʃætə(r)/ *n.* informal talk, esp. about things that are not serious or important 闲聊,琐碎的谈话

cheat /tʃiːt/ *v.* to be unfaithful to your husband, wife, or sexual partner by secretly having sex with someone else. to lie to sb.(在男女关系上)表现不忠,欺骗

conviction /kən'vɪkʃn/ *n.* a decision in a court of law that someone is guilty of a crime, or the process of proving that someone is guilty 定罪

corporate /'kɔːpərət/ *adj.* belonging to or relating to a corporation 公司的

derive /dɪ'raɪv/ *v.* to get or obtain sth from sth else 源自,得自

dispatch /dɪ'spætʃ/ *v. fml* to send someone or sth somewhere for a particular purpose 派遣

incidentally /ˌɪnsɪ'dentli/ *adv.* used to add sth to what was said before, either on the same or another subject 顺便地,附带地

jet /dʒet/ *n.* a fast plane with a jet engine 喷气式飞机

merger /'mɜːdʒə(r)/ *n.* a joining together of two or more companies or organizations to form larger one 合并,兼并

nation-state /'neɪʃnstˈeɪt/ *n.* a nation that is a politically independent country 民族国家,单一民族为主的独立国家

private-eye *n. infml.* a private detective(个人或单位雇用的)私人侦探
recipient /rɪˈsɪpɪənt/ *n.* someone who receives something 接受者
shade /ʃeɪd/ *n.* slight difference in sth. 差别,不同
soar /sɔː(r)/ *v.* to increase quickly to a high level 猛增,高涨
transmitter /trænsˈmɪtə(r)/ *n.* equipment that sends out radio or television signals 发射机,发射台
vibration /vaɪˈbreɪʃn/ *n.* a continuous slight shaking movement 振动,颤动

II. Notes

1. But intelligence experts weren't the least surprise. (Par. 1)—But intelligence experts were not surprised at all. 情报专家们丝毫不感到惊讶

    no the least—not at all

2. espionage of all shades (Par. 3)—spying in all kinds of forms

3. ...are returning the favor. (Par. 5)—As U.S. has focused much of its recent spying on Iran, North Korea, and China, these countries' spying is also targeted on U.S. in return. 有"投桃报李"之意,这里指双方各自以对方为刺探重点。

4. are under the false impression that (Par. 9)—to believe that something is true when it is not 误解

5. "cave-dwelling terrorists" (Par. 9)—terrorists who live in the cave in remote mountainous areas to escape from surveillance. 藏匿于山洞的恐怖分子

6. suicide bombing (Par. 10)—instance in which a person straps explosives onto his body and detonates them in a crowded public area (usually as an act of terrorism) 自杀式炸弹袭击

7. give them an edge(Par. 11)—give them an advantage (over sth.) 提供有力条件

8. that billion-dollar merger-and-acquisition deals... spies getting involved. (Par. 11)—almost all the large merger-and-acquisition deals with billion-dollar worth have much do to with the contribution of commercial espionages who have aggressively pursued confidential information for the corporations. 现在任何一笔价值数十亿美元的并购协议都一定会有技艺高超的间谍参与其中。

9. "moonlight" for major corporations (Par. 12)—to have a second job for big corporations 在大公司兼职

10. track corporate jets (Par. 12)—to monitor the flight records of corporate jets to keep the board of directors under surveillance. 监视公司的喷气公务机出行情况
11. he's going to fool around... (Par. 15)—he's going to have a sexual relationship with someone else's wife 他要去干男盗女娼之事
12. get the goods (Par. 15)—to have or find proof that someone is guilty of a crime 取证
13. much of his business is derived from spouses who suspect infidelity (Par. 15)—much of his business is from the married couples who distrust the spouse' faithfulness and ask detective agency to investigate whether their spouse has sex with another person or not. 很多生意是从调查夫妻丑闻得来
14. grow in sophistication (Par. 17)—become more advanced and complex in technology 产品的精细化

Part Three

Reference Answers to Questions

1. Is espionage mostly a product of the Cold War? Why or why not?

    No, espionage has been conducted for centuries. It never stopped but continues, and espionage of all shades has actually increased since the Cold War.

2. What is the focus of modern professional spying?

    Today's professional spying is largely about tracking terrorists' activities and monitoring public communications for suspicious chatter by hacking others websites.

3. How many "secret agents" are there currently undercover in the U.S.?

    It's unknown. Because spying in itself must be kept a secret.

4. According to experts, who are the most dangerous spies?

    The most dangerous spies are often the ones not working for recognized government. Among them, independent terrorists had even destroyed the government intelligence operations.

5. What is the focus of modern corporation espionage?

    Not only competitors snoop around corporations, foreign

governments may also regularly spy on those major companies with the following focuses:
  a. Detect deception in negotiators
  b. Surveil competing investors
  c. Glean intelligence that could give them an edge in their dealmaking.
6. According to the passage, what contributes most to modern espionage?

Words to Know

adept, agent, bug sweep, CIA, conviction, counterintelligence, counterterrorism, cripple, cyberattack, deception, double agent, deport, emanate, espionage, firewall, fool around, get the goods, glean, keep tabs on, KGB, infidelity, infiltrate, intelligence, looking over one's shoulders, merger, MI5, moonlight, paparazzi, private investigator, ring, secret agent, snoop, suicide bombing, surveillance, ubiquitous, undercover

Part Four

Supplementary Reading

The Art of Industrial Espionage (FROM *The Independent*, May 24, 2012)

Lesson Fourteen

Google's Zero-Carbon Quest

Part One

Summary

　　搜索引擎巨头谷歌曾制定了一项雄心勃勃的计划来实现公司的目标：成为全球最节能的企业。为实现这一"零碳"(zero-carbon)大计，它采取了三方面的措施：(1)向从垃圾堆放场和养猪场收集沼气的组织机构购买碳信用，以抵消谷歌排放的温室气体；(2)减少服务器机群和办公等的能源消耗，并更多地使用零碳排放的风能和太阳能；(3)对绿色电力、风能和太阳能等清洁能源行业投资。

　　但要达此目标并非易事，谷歌在探索中已经尝到了一些苦头。2007年谷歌创始人之一的拉里·佩奇推出 RE＜C（renewable energy is cheaper than coal，指"可再生能源比煤炭便宜"）项目，之后不久，他又启动了一系列绿色臭鼬工厂项目（green skunkworks projects），并向太阳能和地热能等绿色能源行业进行风险投资。然而能源是一个资本更为密集型的领域，且盈利周期也比硅谷 IT 企业长，对于硅谷这家在发电方面根本没有经营经验的公司而言，要实现推动可再生能源比化石燃料更便宜这一目标可谓是难上加难。2011 年，一群不明白谷歌为何要投资于清洁能源技术的股东对公司发起责难，批评谷歌在绿色科技方面的投资缺乏透明度。谷歌于 2011 年底终于悄悄地放弃了它努力 4 年的 RE＜C 项目，放弃了成为清洁能源创新者的努力，但它并未停止对绿色电力的投资。

　　尽管谷歌在不断净化公司的行为，但它仍是一个污染制造者。它购买碳补偿，并认为创设碳补偿的最佳方式是付款购买来自于垃圾堆放场及养猪场的沼气排放。迄今为止，谷歌通过投资于清洁能源行业或购买碳信用使其公司达到了约 500 万吨的碳补偿额度，使谷歌至少在帐面上实现了碳中和。当被问到何时能真正实现碳中和时，谷歌高管说他们不知道。不过，从事绿色项目让谷歌摆脱了只顾挣钱的形象。

　　本文是一篇软新闻，结构比较自由。作者采用了第一人称，通过自己乘坐谷歌公司为员工提供的免费班车的亲身经历,自然导入谷歌计划成为全球最节能的企业这一"零碳"(zero-carbon)大计,增强了新闻的趣味性和可读性。作者对谷歌为实现零碳排放所采取的三方面措施进行了详细的介绍,分析其利弊得失,对谷歌公司所作的努力给予了肯定,但是也指出这是一条艰难的绿色长征之路。

The Author

Brian Dumaine is the senior editor-at-large for *Fortune*, and has worked at Fortune for 28 years in various writing and editing positions including assistant managing editor. He directs Fortune's green technology and environmental policy stories. Dumaine is the author of *The Plot To Save The Planet: How Visionary Entrepreneurs and Corporate Titans Are Creating Real Solutions to Global Warming*, which explores partnerships between entrepreneurs and environmentalists. He has won numerous journalism awards and written more than 100 feature stories for the magazine, including covers such as "America's Toughest Bosses," "The Innovation Gap," and "America's Smartest Young Entrepreneurs."

Background Information

1. zero carbon 零碳排放

Zero carbon refers to zero carbon dioxide emissions. It is a scientific term and a scientific reality for climate change mitigation. It means that all industrial sources of CO_2 have to be converted to run on zero carbon emitting energies. It also means no more carbon emissions being added to the atmosphere, from any additional source to the natural carbon balance of the planet that existed before industrialization.

2. Carbon Footprint 碳排放量

A Carbon Footprint is the measure given to the amount of greenhouse gases produced by burning fossil fuels, measured in units of carbon dioxide (i. e. Kg). Carbon offsets enable people and organizations to reduce their carbon footprint.

3. server farms 服务器机群

A server farm or server cluster is a collection of computer servers usually maintained by an enterprise to accomplish server needs far beyond the capability of one machine. Server farms often consist of thousands of computers which require a large amount of power to run and keep cool. At the optimum(最佳的)performance level, a server farm has enormous costs associated with it, both financially and environmentally. Server farms often have backup servers(备份服务器), which can take over the function of primary servers(主服务器)in case of a primary server failure. Server farms are typically co-located with the network switches and/or routers(路由器)which enable communication between the different parts of the cluster and the users of the cluster. The computers, routers, power supplies, and related electronics are typically mounted on 19-inch racks in a server room or data center.

4. carbon offsets 碳补偿

A carbon offset is a reduction in emissions of carbon dioxide or greenhouse gases made in order to compensate for or to offset(补偿)an emission made elsewhere. Carbon offsets are measured in metric tons (公吨) of carbon dioxide-equivalent (CO_2e). One carbon offset represents the reduction of one metric ton of carbon dioxide or its equivalent in other greenhouse gases. Offsets are typically achieved through financial support of projects that reduce the emission of greenhouse gases in the short-or long-term. The most common project type is renewable energy, such as wind farms, biomass(生物燃料) energy, or hydroelectric dams. Others include energy efficiency projects, the destruction of industrial pollutants or agricultural byproducts, destruction of landfill methane, and forestry projects.

5. carbon neutral 碳中和

Carbon neutral refers to achieving net zero carbon emissions by balancing a measured amount of carbon released with an equivalent amountof offset, or buying enough carbon credits to make up the difference. Buying enough carbon credits(碳信用)to make up the difference is even treated as a way to carbon neutral.（碳中和与碳补偿从本质来说意义相同,是现代人为减缓全球变暖所作的努力之一。利用这种环保方式,人们计算自己日常活动直接或间接制造的二氧化碳排放量,并计算抵消这些二氧化碳所需的经济成本,然后个人付款给专门企业或机构,由他们通过植树或其他环保项目抵消大气中相应的二氧化

碳量。)

6. carbon credits 碳信用

Carbon credits are a highly regulated medium of exchange used to offset(补偿), or neutralize(中和) carbon dioxide emissions. A single carbon credit generally represents the right to emit one metric ton of carbon dioxide or the equivalent mass of another greenhouse gas. Carbon credits and carbon markets are a component of national and international attempts to mitigate the growth in concentrations of greenhouse gases. There are many companies that sell carbon credits to commercial and individual customers who are interested in lowering their carbon footprint or the total amount of carbon emissions that result from their activities on a voluntary basis. Larger companies, governments and other entities may be required by law to purchase carbon credits in order to emit greenhouse gases. (碳信用, 即一些公司或个人把碳排放权当做商品交易, 每一个碳信用代表一吨二氧化碳或与其相当的其他温室气体的排放权, 购买者可通过向某些处理二氧化碳或甲烷气体的公司购买碳信用来抵消自己超过额度排放的温室气体)

7. skunkworks projects 臭鼬工厂项目

A skunkworks project isa project typically developed by a small and loosely structured group of people who research and develop a project primarily for the sake of radical innovation. The expression "skunk works", or "skunkworks", is widely used in business, engineering, and technical fields to describe a group within an organization given a high degree of autonomy and unhampered by bureaucracy, tasked with working on advanced or secret projects. These projects are often undertaken in secret with the understanding that if the development is successful then the product will be designed later according to the usual process. (臭鼬工厂, 指用非常规的方式进行某些秘密项目研究的一小群人, 宗旨是用极少的管理限制来迅速发展某物。)

8. renewable energy/renewables 可再生能源

Renewable energy is energy that comes from resources which are continually replenished such as sunlight, wind, rain, tides, waves and geothermal heat. The share of renewables in global electricity generation is around 19%, with 16% of electricity coming from hydroelectricity and 3% from new renewables (small hydro, modern biomass, wind, solar, geothermal, and biofuels).

9. the National Center for Public Policy Research 美国全国公共政策研究

The National Center for Public Policy Research, founded in 1982, is a self-described conservative think tank in the US. Amy Ridenour is its president, and her husband is the vice president. NCPPR's work is in the areas of environmental, regulatory, economic, and foreign affairs. NCPPR is a member of the Cooler Heads Coalition, whose object is described as "dispelling the myths of global warming by exposing flawed economic, scientific, and risk analysis".

Part Two

Language Points

I. New Words

brainpower /ˈbreɪnpaʊər/ *n.* intelligence, or the ability to think 脑力,智力(IQ 智商)

capital-intensive /ˌkæpɪtlɪnˈtensɪv/ *adj.* a capital-intensive business, industry etc needs a lot of money in order to operate properly (企业、工业等)资本密集的

charger /ˈtʃɑːdʒər/ *n.* a piece of equipment used to put electricity into a battery 充电器

commute /kəˈmjuːt/ *v.* to regularly travel a long distance to get to work 长途上下班,通勤

customize /ˈkʌstəmaɪz/ *v.* to change sth to make it more suitable for you, or to make it look special or different from things of a similar type 定做,定制

disband /dɪsˈbænd/ *v.* to stop existing as an organization, or to make sth do this (使组织等)解散;解体

double-decker /ˈdʌblˈdekə/ *n.* a bus with two stories

emit /ɪˈmɪt/ *v.* to send out gas, heat, light, sound etc 散发,发出(气、热、光、声音等) **emission** *n. usu. pl.* a gas or other substance that is sent into the air 排放

equity /ˈekwəti/ *n. tech* shares in a company from which the owner of the shares receives some of the company's profits rather than a fixed regular payment (分享红利而非固定股息的)分红股票

errand /ˈerənd/ *n.* a short journey in order to do sth. for sb., for example delivering or collecting sth. for them(短程)差事；跑腿

formula /ˈfɔːmjələ/ n. a series of numbers or letters that represent a mathematical or scientific rule 公式；方式

geek /giːk/ n. someone who is not popular because they wear unfashionable clothes, do not know how to behave in social situations, or do strange things 怪人

generation /ˌdʒenəˈreɪʃn/ n. the process of producing sth. or making sth. happen 生产，产生

gigawatt /ˈdʒaɪɡəwɒt/ n. 千兆瓦，十亿瓦 giga- prefix（用于构成名词）a billion (used with units of measurement) 十亿，千兆（与度量单位连用）

green-tech adj. 绿色科技的　　tech=technology

hop /hɒp/ v. infml to move somewhere quickly or suddenly 跳跃

indulge /ɪnˈdʌldʒ/ v. to let yourself do or have sth. that you enjoy, esp. sth. that is considered bad for you(使自己)沉溺于，沉湎于

innovative /ˈɪnəveɪtɪv/ adj. using clever new ideas and methods 运用新观念和新方法的

issue /ˈɪʃuː/ v. to officially make a statement, give an order, warning etc 发出(声明)；颁布，发出(命令、警告等)

landfill /ˈlændfɪl/ n. a place where waste is buried under the ground 垃圾填埋场

productivity /ˌprɒdʌkˈtɪvəti/ n. the rate at which goods are produced, and the amount produced, esp. In relation to the work, time and money needed to produce them 生产效率，生产力

priority /praɪˈɒrəti/ n. the thing that you think is most important and that needs attention before anything else 优先处理的事，当务之急

thermal /ˈθɜːməl/ adj. relating to or caused by heat 热的，热量的

transparency /trænsˈpærənsi/ n. the quality of glass, plastic etc that makes it possible for you to see through it (玻璃、塑料、事务的)透明(性)

ultimately /ˈʌltɪmətli/ adv. finally, after everything else has been done or considered 最终

II. Notes

1. Google (GOOG) (Par. 2)—GOOG 是谷歌公司在纳斯达克的股票代码
2. price tag(Par. 2)—the amount that sth. costs 标价，价签
3. energy efficient (Par. 4)—节能，高效能

4. a very tall order (Par. 4)—a request or piece of work that is almost impossible, a mission impossible 很难实现的要求；很难完成的工作
5. To reach its audacious zero-carbon goal, Google is taking a three-pronged approach. (Par. 5)—In order to achieve its great but difficult-to-reach goal of becoming a zero-carbon company, Google is taking measures from three aspects. 为实现大胆的碳零排放的目标，谷歌采用三种措施
6. issue a staff memo (Par. 7)—发布一则给员工的内部文件

    memo—a short official note to another person in the same company or organization; (internal) paper, document(致公司或组织内部另一人的)公务便条
7. The catch? The existing power infrastructure... buying carbon credits. (Par. 7)—要点何在？现有能源基础设施高度依赖化石燃料，迄今为止全球尚没有一家公司能不借助购买碳信用而实现这一目标。

    fossil fuel—fuel such as coal or oil that is produced by the gradual decaying of animals or plants over millions of years 化石燃料，如煤、石油等
8. press release(Par. 8)—an official statement giving information to the newspapers, radio, or television 新闻发布
9. This goal, however, turned out to be more devilish than anyone thought. (Par. 8)—But Google eventually found that it was extremely difficult to achieve this goal. 谷歌终于发现这一目标的实现比想象的难

    put that in perspective(Par. 10)—
10. put sth. in perspective—to judge the importance of sth correctly—正确看待，正视
11. The good news:... would have been much worse. (Par. 10)—What is comforting is that if Google hadn't started trying to become carbon neutral by buying carbon credits and investing in clean-energy businesses, the amount of its carbon emission in 2011 would have been more than 1.5 million tons. 值得庆幸的是……
12. Server farms also account for Google's biggest use of energy. (Par. 12)—Server farms are also the biggest user of energy in the company. 大量的服务器群是谷歌公司耗电大户
13. Now the economic incentive exists to cut energy use. (Par. 13)—

Now that the person paying the utility bills and the one buying the computers is the same, he/she would think more about how to spend less on energy. 为节能存有经济方面的考虑

　　incentive—sth. that encourages you to work harder, start a new activity etc

14. cites as an example the search giant's new server farm in Finland (Par. 13)—cites the search giant's new server farm in Finland as an example 以谷歌——搜索引擎巨人在芬兰新建的一个服务器机群作为例子。

　　cite...as an example—take sth for example 引用…作为例子

15. It couldn't have helped that... was spending money on clean tech. (Par. 16)—Though Google execs explain that not much money was invested in clean tech, Google has been severely criticized by some shareholders, who could not understand why Google invested in clean tech, for spending too much on that. 谷歌在清洁能源技术上的大量投资在他们的一些股东看来无济于事。

16. wind and solar farms(Par. 17)—风力和太阳能发电厂

17. to the tune of (Par. 18)—*infml* (used to emphasize how large an amount or number is) 高达…

18. This type of deal... by federal tax credits. (Par. 18)—The federal tax credits make Google's investment in wind and solar projects, which is a form of tax equity investment, more pleasant and rewarding. 这类交易在形式上是税收公平投资的一种,联邦税收减免待遇令其更具吸引力。

　　a. tax equity—税收公平

　　b. tax equity investment—指具有应纳税收入,但希望避税的投资者以购买项目开发企业的税额减免权为条件参与的投资。

　　c. tax credits—an amount of money on which you do not have to pay tax 税额减免指可从应纳税额中直接减去某些费用和支出,给予税额优惠的制度。

　　d. sweeten—if you sweeten sth. such as an offer or a business deal, you try to make someone want it more by improving it or by increasing the amount you are willing to pay 通过改善条件或提高价格等使报价或交易等更有诱惑力

Part Three

Reference Answers to Questions

1. Why does Google offer the free ride of luxury double-decker buses to its employees on Mountain View campus?

    a. Google's bus service actually save the company money in that it will cost much more for Google to build the parking lotsfor all of its employees since real estate in Mountain View is expensive. And the land saved from building the parking lotscan be used for new buildings.

    b. Google's bus service can be taken as an employee perk, and at the same time, it offers the employees some extra working hours on their way to and from work—such added productivity also benefits the company.

    c. It is more environment-friendly to have all Google's employees commute by buses than by their own cars. That's what Google is striving for—to reduce the emission of carbon dioxide.

2. What makes Larry Page determined to build the nation's first zero-carbon company?

    For the reasons of a growing population, increasingly scarce resources, and climate change, Page believes that the corporate world needs to operate more sustainably, and that it's essential for Google to find creative solutions to energy issues.

3. How is Google going to reach its audacious zero-carbon goal?

    According to the news story, Google is taking a three-pronged approach.

    a. First, it's making its server farms, office buildings, and commuting habits more energy efficient.

    b. Then the company is investing heavilyin solar and wind producers to make clean energy more available.

    c. Finally, it is buying enough carbon offsets to make the company carbon neutral until it can meet its overall goal.

4. What green powers are mentioned in the passage? And what is the conventional power?

The green powers mentioned in the passage are: solar power, geothermal energy, and wind power. The conventional power refers to the electricity generated from coal, oil, and other fossil fuels.

5. What has Google done to make it a carbon-neutral company? Do those measures really work?

Googlecontinues to buy carbon credits and invests in some methane-capture projects to make its carbon offset real.

Yes. Google has spent upwards of $15 million investing in or purchasing carbon credits for dozens of such projects. That will offset about 5 million tons of CO_2—more than enough to make Google a carbon-neutral company on paper.

Words to Know

audacious, charger, carbon offsets, carbon neutral, carbon credits, cutting-edge, electrics, embark, emit, equivalent, facility, formula, geothermal, green-tech, grid, hybrid, infrastructure, initiative, innovative, methane, opportunity cost, priority, renewable, sustainable, utility

Part Four

Supplementary Reading

THE CLOUD FACTORLES:

Power, Pollution and the Internet (From *The New York Times*, Sept. 22, 2012)

Lesson Fifteen

Little Sympathy for Margaret Thatcher Among Former Opponents

Part One

Summary

英国前首相玛格丽特·撒切尔因中风于2013年4月8日走完了她生命的旅程,这个曾经叱咤英国政坛11载、毁誉参半的英伦女首相给英国社会留下了太多的争议。

1979年5月3日保守党大选获胜,撒切尔夫人出任首相,成为英国历史上第一位女首相。当时"铁娘子"面对一个经济陷入衰退、严重通胀、失业率高居不下的英国,她开出的药方是:私有化、减税、放松管制以鼓励竞争、削弱工会力量。她认为,国企必定是没有效率的,将之私有化有助于提高公司治理和效率。之后英国经济果然有了起色,但英国社会为此付出了很大的代价,犯罪率上升,社区破裂和分化。因为她在经济好转后并非给工人等底层阶级经济上平等对待。

"撒切尔主义"(Thatcherism)带来的不仅是英国社会的分裂,还有思想的分裂。20世纪80年代,撒切尔夫人采取强硬措施,压制矿工工会罢工,警察与矿工发生流血冲突。撒切尔夫人在压制工会方面取得胜利,但从此成为英国北部矿工社区憎恨的政治人物。因此,撒切尔夫人去世后的几个小时,一些憎恶她的矿工欢呼为"伟大一天"。

公众对撒切尔推行的人头税(Community Charge)政策十分不满,她还坚持欧洲政策,引起党内分裂。她的心腹、外交大臣Geoffrey Howe因对欧共体的政见不同而辞职,引发危机。接着保守党的其他议员也开始倒戈,最终迫使她辞职。她离开唐宁街10号(10 Downing Street)时的眼泪在英国民众中掀起一场轩然大波:支持者认为她带领英国走出了经济困境,提高了英国的国际地位,实现了国家现代化;反对者认为她就是一个不折不扣的独裁者、自大狂,几乎毁掉了英国的福利制度。

本文对撒切尔死后英国社会的反应作了生动细致的描述,尤其是那些对撒切尔不满的群体。本文大量使用引语,一方面使文字新闻变得直观、生动,另一方面也提高了新闻的真实性,让说话者的形象跃然纸上。

The Author

Michael White (1945—) is an assistant editor and has been writing for the *Guardian* for more than 30 years, as a reporter, foreign correspondent and columnist. He was political editor from 1990—2006, having previously been the paper's Washington correspondent (1984—1988) and parliamentary sketchwriter (1977—1984).

Background Information

1. Margaret Thatcher

Margaret Hilda Thatcher, Baroness Thatcher (1925—2013) was a British politician who was the Prime Minister of the United Kingdom from 1979 to 1990 and the Leader of the Conservative Party from 1975 to 1990. She was the longest-serving British Prime Minister of the 20th century and is the only woman to have held the office. A Soviet journalist called her the "Iron Lady", a nickname that became associated with her uncompromising politics and leadership style. As Prime Minister, she implemented policies that have come to be known as Thatcherism.

Originally a research chemist before becoming a barrister (律师), Thatcher was elected Member of Parliament (MP) for Finchley in 1959. Edward Heath appointed her Secretary of State for Education and Science in his 1970 government. In 1975, Thatcher defeated Heath in the Conservative Party leadership election to become Leader of the Opposition (反对党) and became the first woman to lead a major political party in UK and Prime Minister after winning the 1979 general election. Then she introduced a series of political and economic initiatives intended to reverse high unemployment and Britain's struggles in the wake of the Winter of Discontent and an ongoing recession. Her political philosophy and economic policies emphasized deregulation (反常规), flexible labour markets, the privatisation of state-owned companies, and reducing the power and influence of trade unions. Thatcher's popularity during her first years in office waned amid recession and high unemployment until the 1982 Falklands War (马岛战争) brought a resurgence of support, resulting in her re-election in 1983.

Thatcher was re-elected for a third term in 1987. During this period her support for a Community Charge (popularly referred to as "poll tax" was widely unpopular and her views on the European Community were not shared by others in her Cabinet (内阁). She resigned as Prime Minister and party leader in November 1990, after Michael Heseltine launched a challenge to her leadership. After retiring from the Commons in 1992, she was given a life peerage (贵族爵位) as Baroness (女男爵) Thatcher, of Kesteven in the County of Lincolnshire, which entitled her to sit in the House of Lords. After a series of small strokes (中风)in 2002 she was advised to withdraw from public speaking, and in 2013 she died of another stroke in London at the age of 87.

2. UK miners' strike (1984—1985)

The UK miners' strike of 1984—1985 was a major industrial action affecting the British coal industry. It was a defining moment(大事) in British industrial relations, and its defeat significantly weakened the British trade union movement. It was also seen as a major political victory for Margaret Thatcher and the Conservative Party. The strike became a symbolic struggle, as the National Union of Mineworkers (NUM) was one of the strongest unions in the country, viewed by many, including Conservatives in power, as having brought down the Heath government in the union's 1974 strike. The later strike ended with the miners' defeat and the Thatcher government able to consolidate its fiscally conservative program. The political power of the NUM was weakened permanently.

Part Two

Language Points

1. New Words

assessment /əˈsesmən/ *n.* appraisal; evaluation

brutality /buːˈtæləti/ *n.* cruel and violent behavior, or an event involving cruel and violent treatment 野蛮行径;残暴行为

clerical /ˈklerɪkl/ adj. relating to office work, esp. work such as keeping records or accounts 职员的

counter-demonstration /ˈkaʊntəˌdemənˈstreɪʃən/ n. a demonstration held in opposition to another demonstration

cripple /ˈkrɪpl/ v. to damage sth badly so that it no longer works or is no longer effective

faithful /ˈfeɪθfl/ n. the people who are very loyal to a leader, political party, etc. 信徒

inhibit /ɪnˈhɪbɪt/ v. to restrain, hinder, arrest, or check (an action, impulse, etc.) 抑制；禁止

legacy /ˈleɡəsɪ/ n. sth that happens or exists as a result of things that happened at an earlier time 遗产

livelihood /ˈlaɪvlihʊd/ n. a means of supporting one's existence, esp. financially or vocationally; living

mourn /mɔːn/ v. to feel very sad and to miss sb after they have died 哀悼，悼念

opponent /əˈpəʊnənt/ n. sb who disagrees with a plan, idea, or system and wants to try to stop or change it

prolong /prəˈlɒŋ/ v. to deliberately make sth such as a feeling or activity last longer

prompt /prɒmpt/ v. to make people say or do sth as a reaction 激起，唤起（思想、感情等）

sectional /ˈsekʃən/ adj. of a particular group within a community or country（社会或国家中）某群体的

sentiment /ˈsentɪmənt/ n. fml an opinion or feeling you have about sth

synthetic /sɪnˈθetɪk/ adj. not real or genuine; artificial

tramp /træmp/ v. to walk somewhere slowly and with heavy steps

workaholic /ˌwɜːkəˈhɒlɪk/ n. infml sb who cannot stop working, and does not have time for anything else 工作迷

wreck /rek/ v. to completely spoil sth so that it cannot continue in a successful way 破坏；摧毁

II. Notes

1. Here in Ireland... and caused great suffering. (Para. 3)—在爱尔兰，她（撒切尔）实行古老的严酷军国主义政策，导致长期战争和苦难。（20世纪，爱尔兰共和军为北爱尔兰与爱尔兰统一对英国发动了一系列袭击事件。为此英国政府专门设立了关押该军的梅兹监狱。1981年，该狱发生集体"绝食抗议"事件。因为撒切尔夫人不妥协，7个月饿

死 16 人。)
2. Any satisfaction thatBritain's first female prime minister... and wrecked their communities. (Para. 5)—人们对英国第一位女首相，同时也是他们的敌人的死去感到满足，这种满足在一些人心中还掺杂了强烈的愤怒和悔恨，因为他们觉得是撒切尔主义毁掉了他们的生活，也破坏了他们的社会。
3. a shadow of its once mighty self (Para. 6)—the influence of the Durham Miners Association is much smaller than before
    shadow—a remnant or vestige(遗迹，残余)
4. In 1979 it could take several months to obtain a phone—a landline installed by a state monopoly, the Post Office. (Para. 8)—因"皇家邮政"一直垄断经营，(效率低下，)1979 年安装一部固定电话要等上数个月的时间。(英国"皇家邮政"在国内邮递行业长达 350 年的垄断于 2006 年 1 月 1 日走到终点。)
5. But such talk will not sway the likes of Hopper. (Para. 9)—The remarks of Thatcher supporters will not change the minds of people like Hopper.
    the likes of—someone or sth similar to; the equal of

Part Three

Reference Answers to Questions

1. After hearingof Mrs Thatcher's death, how did the media react?
    News of her death prompted expressions of satisfaction and even delight on social media.
2. How did Gerry Adams comment on Mrs Thatcher's political legacy?
    He thought that Thatcher hurt the Irish and British people, prolonged the war and caused great suffering.
3. What did David Hopper think of Mrs Thatcher's policies?
    He thought that herpolicies absolutely destroyed the working people. It was coup de grace to the miners union.
4. How do the party faithful feel about Mrs Thatcher?
    She wasmore admired than loved.
5. How didKen Livingstone think of Mrs Thatcher?
    He blamed Mrs Thatcher for causing unemployment and leaving

people dependent on welfare.
6. What do you think about MrsThatcher?
    (Open.)

Words to Know

assessment, counter-demonstration, cripple, demonise, divisive, extraordinary, Fleet Street, inhibit, legacy, militaristic, miners union, mingle, monopoly, mourn, opponent, party faithful, prime minister, prolong, scapegoat, synthetic, Thatcherism, Tory, tweet, workaholic

Part Four

Supplementary Reading

Margaret Thatcher dead: The vile outpouring of hate shows there is no respect any more (from *the Mirror*, April 14, 2013)

Lesson Sixteen

Britain's Embattled Newspapers Are Leading the World

Part One

Summary

传统报纸由于年轻人纷纷投入网络和电视的怀抱而发行量锐减,英国报纸如同其他纸质媒介一样,命运同样堪忧,但也有乐观派如俄裔英国富商列别捷夫逆风而行,控股《独立报》、《伦敦晚报》,相信报业革新会带来新的生机。众所周知,英国报纸市场的竞争一向异乎寻常的残酷,报纸众多,又无政府资助,更有国家支持的强劲对手 BBC(原 BBC 个别王牌主持人的性丑闻,给 BBC 带来的影响不容忽视)。然而,步履维艰的英国报业却能推陈出新,不断尝试新的版式和定价,虽然尝试的方向截然不同,但主要有三个潮流:其一,以新闻集团为代表所尝试的收费方式。尽管其对手幸灾乐祸地笑话其网站流量的骤降,但拥有四家英国明星报业《泰晤士报》、《星期天泰晤士报》、《太阳报》和《世界新闻报》的新闻集团并不忧心,希望通过捆绑服务寻求出路;其二,以《每日邮报》为代表的观点,认为足够大的在线广告量是挣钱的主要途径,他们通过其网站清新的文字,明星新闻,尤其是吸引眼球的泳装美女报道取得了巨大的成功,直追门户网站雅虎和微软产品网站(MSN.com);第三个创新代表是俄罗斯大亨列别捷夫旗下的《独立报》和《伦敦晚报》。他们是采取免费赠送(《伦敦晚报》)和低价(如 The i)策略。免费的《伦敦晚报》发行量比之前翻了一倍多。谁将赢得这场战争?这有待时间的检验。毋庸置疑,他们的勇气可嘉。

本文是一篇针对热点问题的分析性深度报道。文章对英国报业的困境、革新作了条理清晰的分析和评论。本文具有论点明确,结构清楚,语言生动,新闻文体特征典型,如使用新词和俚语,句式富有变化等特点。但本文对革新三大趋势的归类颇为牵强,如第二大革新手段是保证网站文字的质量、利用名人效应和女性暴露的图片吸引读者,实际这是报纸经营的常见手段;免费赠送、低价更是商界竞争中常用的途径,且地铁的免费报纸派送、自由取之早已有之。是否革新？人们难免质疑。尝试虽大胆，结果并不一定能成功，是否可以称之为革新也值得商榷，或许用"重整旗鼓"（renew or stage a comeback）更为妥切。

Background Information

1. *Daily Express*《每日快报》

A daily national middle market tabloid newspaper in the United Kingdom. *Express* Newspapers currently also publishes the *Sunday Express* (launched in 1918), the *Daily Star* and the *Daily Star Sunday*. It is the flagship title of Express Newspapers. In July 2011 it had an average daily circulation of 625,952. Founded in 1900 by Sir Arthur Pearson, it was one of the first papers to carry gossip, sports, and women's features, and the first newspaper in Britain to have a crossword. Its success was partly due to an aggressive marketing campaign and a vigorous circulation war with other populist newspapers. The arrival of television and the public's changing interests took their toll on circulation. With the exception of the 2001 general election, when it backed the Labour Party（英国工党）, the newspaper has declared its support for the Conservative Party（英国保守党）at every general election since World War II.

2. *Daily Mirror*《每日镜报》

A British national daily tabloid newspaper which was founded in 1903. Its Sunday sister paper is the *Sunday Mirror*. It had an average daily circulation of 1,083,938 in March 2012. It was launched on 2 November 1903 by Alfred Harmsworth (later Lord Northcliffe) as a newspaper for women, run by women. He said, "I intend it to be really a mirror of feminine life as well on its grave as on its lighter sides.... to be entertaining without being frivolous, and serious without being dull". It cost one penny. In 1919, some issues sold more than 1 million copies a day, making it the largest daily picture paper. In 1963 a restructuring of the media interests of the Harmsworth family led to the Mirror becoming a part of International Publishing Corporation. The *Daily Mirror* has traditionally backed the Labour Party at general elections. It won "Newspaper of the Year" in 2002 at the British Press Awards（英国新闻奖）.

3. *Independent*《独立报》

A British national morning newspaper published in London by Independent Print Limited. The *Independent* became known for its unorthodox and campaigning front pages, which frequently relied on images, graphics or lists rather than traditional headlines and written news content. Nicknamed the *Indy*, it was launched in 1986 and is one of the youngest UK national daily newspapers. The daily edition was named National Newspaper of the Year at the 2004 British Press Awards. In July 2012, it had an average daily circulation of 83,619, and the Sunday edition had a circulation at 118,759. When the paper was established in 1986, the founders intended its political stance to reflect the centre of the British political spectrum and thought that it would take readers primarily from *The Times* and *The Daily Telegraph*. It is now seen as leaning to the left, making it more a competitor to *The Guardian*, though like its rival, it also features conservative columnists. The *Independent* tends to take a classical liberal, pro-market, stance on economic issues. On 23 January 2008, The *Independent* relaunched its online edition, www. independent. co. uk.

4. *Evening Standard*《伦敦晚报》

A local, free daily newspaper (since May 2009 styled the *London Evening Standard*), published Monday to Friday in tabloid format in London, United Kingdom. It is the dominant regional evening paper for London and the surrounding area, with coverage of national and international news and City of London finance. In October 2009, the paper ended a 180-year history of paid circulation and became a free newspaper, doubling its circulation as part of a change in its business plan. It was founded by barrister Stanley Lees Giffard on May 21, 1827, as the *Standard*, which gained eminence for its detailed foreign news. The newspaper has sponsored the annual Evening Standard Theatre Awards(伦敦晚报戏剧奖) since the 1950s. The newspaper has also awarded the annual Evening Standard Pub of the Year (年度晚报酒吧) and the Evening Standard British Film Awards (伦敦晚报电影奖) since the 1970s. The paper also supplies occasional CDs and DVDs for promotions. It also gives Londoners a chance to win exclusive tickets to film premieres and sports tournament tickets, such as the Wimbledon

Ladies Singles Final. In February 2010, a paid-for circulation version became available in suburban areas of London for 20p. The newspaper won the Media Brand of the Year and the Grand Prix Gold awards（大奖赛金奖）at the Media Week awards in October 2010. The Standard also won the daily newspaper of the year award at the London Press Club Press Awards（伦敦新闻俱乐部新闻奖）in May 2011.

5. *News of the World*《世界新闻报》

A national red top newspaper（彩印的小报）published in the United Kingdom from 1843 to 2011. It was at one time the biggest selling English language newspaper in the world, and at closure still had one of the highest English language circulations. Originally established as a broadsheet by John Browne Bell, later by Rupert Murdoch's media firm News Limited (reorganized as News International), it was transformed into a tabloid in 1984 and became the Sunday sister paper of *The Sun*. The newspaper concentrated on celebrity-based scoops and populist news. It had a reputation for exposing national or local celebrities as drug users, sexual peccadilloes（轻罪）, or criminals. Sales averaged 2,812,005 copies per week in October 2010. From 2006, allegations of phone hacking began to engulf the newspaper. News International announced the closure of the newspaper on July 7, 2011. The scandal deepened when the paper was alleged to have hacked into the phones of families of British service personnel killed in action. Senior figures on the newspaper have been held for questioning by police investigating the phone hacking and corruption allegations. Arrested on July 8, 2011 were former editor Andy Coulson and former *News of the World* royal editor Clive Goodman, the latter jailed for phone hacking in 2007. The former executive editor Neil Wallis was arrested on July 15, 2011 and former editor Rebekah Brooks, the tenth person held in custody, on July 17, 2011.

6. *The Times*《泰晤士报》

A British daily national newspaper published by Times Newspapers, since 1981 a subsidiary of News International, itself wholly owned by the News Corporation group headed by Rupert Murdoch. *The Times* has had an online presence since March 1999, originally at *the-times.co.uk* and later at *timesonline.co.uk*, aiming at daily readers. There are also iPad and Android editions of both newspapers. It was printed in broadsheet format for 219 years, but switched to compact size in 2004 in an attempt to appeal more to younger readers and commuters using public transport. Though traditionally a moderate newspaper and sometimes a supporter of the Conservatives, it supported the Labour Party in the 2001 and 2005 general elections. *The Times* had an average daily circulation of 393,814 in February 2013. In April 2009, the *timesonline* site had a readership of 750,000 readers per day. As of October 2011, there were around 111,000 subscribers to the *Times'* digital products.

7. The Sunday Times《星期日泰晤士报》

The largest-selling British national "quality" Sunday newspaper. It is published by Times Newspapers Ltd, a subsidiary of News International, which is in turn owned by News Corporation. *Times* Newspapers and *The Sunday Times* were founded independently and have been under common ownership only since 1966. They were bought by News International in 1981. While some other national newspapers moved to a tabloid format in the early 2000s, *The Sunday Times* has retained the larger broadsheet format. It sells more than twice as many copies as its sister paper, *The Times*, which is published Monday to Saturday. It was Britain's first multi-section newspaper and remains substantially larger than its rivals. Besides the main news section, it has News Review, Business, Sport, Money and Appointments sections-all broadsheet.

8. wine club

It is designed to provide customers with a series of wine bottles on a monthly or quarterly basis that they would otherwise have to find and purchase on their own. It often behaves in a themed manner, providing recipients with red wines, white wines, or a mixture of the two. Most frequently offered by vineyards or specialty wine shops, it can also be found as independent bodies. Paul Kalemkiarian claims to have invented the idea of wine in the mail in 1972, while managing a small liquor store in Palos Verdes Estates, California. When a customer needed advice on a wine purchase, he would direct him or her toward a bottle of red wine and a bottle of white wine that he had designated as the "monthly selections." Soon customers began to request that these selections be delivered to their homes, and Kalemkiarian's teenage son, would load up the truck and make his rounds. Common wine clubs are created by wineries themselves, wine stores, internet retailers or large media companies such as the *New York Times* and the *Wall Street Journal*, among others. The *Times* follows this way to attract its readers.

9. The Sun《太阳报》

A daily national tabloid newspaper published in the United Kingdom and Ireland. It is published by the News Group Newspapers division of News International, itself a wholly owned subsidiary of Rupert Murdoch's News Corporation. It had an average daily circulation of 2,409,811 copies in January 2013. On February 26, 2012, *The Sun on Sunday* was launched to replace the defunct *News of the World*, employing a number of its former journalists.

10. The Wall Street Journal《华尔街报》

An American English-language international daily newspaper with a special emphasis on business and economic news. It is published in New York City by Dow Jones & Company, a division of News Corporation, along with the Asian and European editions of the *Journal*. It is the largest newspaper in the United States, by circulation. According to the Audit Bureau of Circulations, it has a circulation of 2.1 million copies (including 400,000 online paid subscriptions), as of March 2010, compared to *USA Today*'s 1.8 million. Its main rival, in the business newspaper sector is the London-based *Financial Times*. The *Journal* primarily covers American economic and international business topics, and financial news and issues. Its name derives from Wall Street, located in New York City, which is the heart of the financial district.

11. The Daily Mail《每日邮报》

A British daily middle-market tabloid newspaper, the first British paper to sell a million copies a day. First published in 1896, it is the United Kingdom's second biggest-selling daily newspaper after *The Sun*. Its sister paper *The Mail on Sunday* was launched in 1982. It was, from the outset, a newspaper for women, being the first to provide features especially for them, and is the only British newspaper whose readership is more than 50 percent female, at 53 percent. It had an average daily circulation of 1,991,275 copies in April 2012. It has over 100 million unique visitors per month to its website.

12. Yahoo《雅虎》

An American multinational internet corporation (Yahoo! Inc.). Headquartered in Sunnyvale, California, it is widely known for its web portal, search engine, and related services. It is one of the most popular sites in the United States. According to news sources, roughly 700 million people visit Yahoo! websites every month. Yahoo! itself claims it attracts "more than half a billion consumers every month in more than 30 languages." Yahoo! Inc. was founded by Jerry Yang and David Filo in January 1994 and was incorporated on March 1, 1995. On July 16, 2012, former Google executive Marissa Mayer was named as Yahoo! CEO and President.

13. MSN.com《微软门户网站》

A collection of Internet sites and services provided by Microsoft (the Microsoft Network or MSN). The Microsoft Network debuted as an online service and Internet service provider on August 24, 1995, to coincide with the release of the Windows 95 operating system. Once a simple online service for Windows 95, an early experiment at interactive multimedia content on the Internet, and one of the most popular dial-up Internet service providers, MSN is now officially closed down. Microsoft used the MSN brand name to promote numerous popular web-based services in the late 1990s, most notably Hotmail and Microsoft Messenger service, before reorganizing many of them in 2005 under another brand name, Windows Live. *MSN.com* was the 17th most visited domain name on the Internet.

14. *The i*《独立报的姊妹报》

A British newspaper published by Independent Print, owned by Alexander Lebedev, which also publishes *The Independent*. The newspaper, which is aimed at "readers and lapsed readers" of all ages and commuters with limited time, costs 20 pence, and was launched on 26 October 2010. In October 2012 it had an average daily circulation of 304,691, significantly more than *The Independent* and a 44% increase over the past year. The paper is now running Monday to Saturday.

15. *The Guardian*《卫报》

A British national daily newspaper. The newspaper's online offering is the second most popular British newspaper website, after the *Daily Mail*'s *Mail Online*. Its sister papers include *The Observer* and *The Guardian Weekly*. It has grown from a 19th-century local paper to a national paper associated with a complex organisational structure and international multimedia and web presence. *The Guardian* in paper form had a certified average daily circulation of 204,222, behind *The Daily Telegraph* and *The Times*, but ahead of *The Independent*. In the last UK general election in 2010, the paper supported the Liberal Democrats, who went on to form a coalition government with the Conservatives. *The Guardian Weekly*, which circulates worldwide, contains articles from *The Guardian* and its sister Sunday paper *The Observer*, as well as reports, features, and book reviews from *The Washington Post*(美国的《华盛顿邮报》) and articles translated from *Le Monde*(法国的《世界报》).

16. *The Racing Post*《赛马邮报》

A British daily horse racing, greyhound racing and sports betting newspaper, appearing in print form and online. From May 30, 2011 to July 3, 2011 it had a circulation of 56,507.

Part Two

Language Points

I. NewWords

assemble /əˈsembl/ v. to bring together, to put together 组装

assumption /əˈsʌmpʃən/ n. sth. that you think is true although you have no definite proof, to imagine, to anticipate 认为, 想象, 预期

boldness /ˈbəuldnəs/ n. the state or quality of being impudent or arrogantly self-confident, daring 大胆, 冒失, 趾高气扬

commentator /ˈkɔmənteɪtə/ n. sb. who knows a lot about a particular subject, and who writes about it or discusses it on the television or radio, in newspapers 评论员

commuter /kəˈmjuːtə/ n. sb. who travels a long distance to work every day 每日通勤人员

compelling /kəm'pelɪŋ/ *adj.* very interesting or exciting, so that you have to pay attention 引人入胜的,扣人心弦的

counter-intuitive /ˈkaʊntə-ɪn'tjuːɪtɪv/ *adj.* used to describe sth that does not happen in the way you would expect it to, unexpected 出乎意料的

crush /krʌʃ/ *v.* to defeat sb completely, to fall all of sudden 击溃,倒塌

cut-down /kʌt-daʊn/ *adj.* reduced 消减

distribution /ˌdɪstrɪ'bjuːʃən/ *n.* when goods are supplied to shops and companies for sale 分配,分销

drastic /'dræstɪk/ *adj.* extreme and sudden and violent 急剧的,突发的

expertise /ˌekspəː'tiːz/ *n.* special skills or knowledge in a particular subject, that you learn by experience or training 专业技能

extract /ɪk'strækt/ *v.* to get sth. which you want from sb. such as information, money, help etc, esp. when they do not want to give it to you 引用,摄取,获得

fearsome /'fɪəsəm/ *adj.* very frightening, afraid 害怕的,恐惧的

hail /heɪl/ *v.* to acclaim enthusiastically, to cheer 欢呼

hook /hʊk/ *n. infml* to succeed in making sb. interested in or attracted to sth. 勾引,使感兴趣

intriguing /ɪn'triːgɪŋ/ *adj.* interesting, attractive for being strange, mysterious, or unexpected 引起好奇心,有迷惑力的

marketer /'mɑːkɪtə/ *n.* one that sells goods or services in or to a market, esp. one that markets a specified commodity 营销商

migrate /maɪ'greɪt/ *v.* to move from one place to another 移居,流动

newsagent /'njuːzˌeɪdʒənt/ *n. BrE* sb. who owns or works in a shop that sells newspapers, magazines, sweets and cigarettes 报刊经销商 (*AmE* newsdealer)

read /riːd/ *n.* sth. that you spend time reading 所读之物

savage /'sævɪdʒ/ *adj.* ferocious; fierce

shelve /ʃelv/ *v.* to put sth on a shelf, esp. books

staff /stɑːf/ *v.* to be or provide the workers for an organization 招聘,成为雇员

steer /stɪə/ *v.* to take sb. or sth. or cause them to go, in the direction in which you want them to go 驱使,转向

II. Notes

1. look doomed (Par. 1)—seem to be dying out unavoidably 看上去奄

奄一息的人
2. shed about two-thirds of their circulation (Par. 1)—their circulation dropped by about two-thirds 报纸发行量剧减三分之二
3. hail the death of newspapers (Par. 1)—to welcoming the decline of newspapers
4. a tabloid that has been caught up in a celebrity phone-hacking scandal (Par. 3)——一家陷入名人电话窃听丑闻的小报

　　be caught up—to become involved or entangled with 被抓住，卷入

　　phone-hacking—stealing information about sb's phone calls 这是一个新合成的词，其结构是"宾语（phone）＋动词（hack）＋ing"。"hack"意为"to break into a server, Website, etc. from a remote location to steal or damage data"，即"黑客攻击"。
5. a drastic drop in traffic(Par. 5)—a sudden and serious fall in the flow of data on the Internet 网站流量骤降
6. dedicated readers(Par. 5)—people who continue to read the paper (here the *Times*) and stick to it no matter what happens 忠实的读者
7. iPad applications (Par. 216)—苹果平板电脑的应用程序
8. get to the point (Par. 6)—to reach the goal; be so successful that
9. make the top spot(Par. 7)—to be No.1
10. a breezy read (Par. 8)—web pages which are fresh and pleasant to read 爽读，轻松阅读
11. a cut-down *Independent* (Par. 9)—a reduced edition of *Independent* 缩减版的《独立报》
12. face a harder road (Par. 11)—have more difficulties ahead 前途坎坷
13. prop up (Par. 11)—to prevent (*The Independent*) from falling/death by putting *The i* under it; support/ fuel (*The Independent*) 崛起，支撑
14. a halfway house between free and premium papers (Par. 11)—a compromising solution which is a combination of free and high-quality newspapers 介于自由化和高标准之间的报纸
15. It may well be that none of them does. (Par. 12)—It is very likely that none of the three innovations will be successful. 很有可能三项革新无一成功
16. But none can be faulted for lack of boldness. (Par. 12)—However, all three innovations are bold enough. 但三项革新均不乏勇气
17. closest to the cutting edge(Par. 13)—the most advanced; playing

the leading role in the field 最先进,领先

Part Three

Reference Answers to Questions

1. Why is Britain's newspaper market the world's most savage one?

    a. There are nine national daily papers with a circulation of more than 200,000.

    b. advertising has migrated online more quickly than elsewhere. Since 2009 more advertising money has been spent on the internet than on newspapers, according to ZenithOptimedia, a marketer.

    c. British papers receive no government funding (as is the case in France, for example). Most of them are privately owned, they enjoy free competition.

2. Do online paywalls do good to Britain's embattled newspapers? Why or why not?

    No. News Corporation is experimenting with an exceptionally tough online paywalls on its four British titles—the *Times*, the *Sunday Times*, the *Sun and* the *News of the World*, but unfortunately, they have resulted in a drastic drop in traffic. It's estimated that only 14% of regular *Times* readers and just 1% of non-regular ones subscribe to the website. The other former *Times* readers head for the BBC's free website instead.

3. Why is News Corporation's main goal to hook readers on a bundle of services?

    News Corporation succeeds in in-house ads offering entertainments to readers, from iPad applications to theatre tickets and Italian holidays. The firm wants to make its newspaper subscription a must. If so, some forms of bundling service will be unavoidable.

4. How could the Daily Mail's website be successful?

    The Daily Mail has become the world's second-biggest newspaper website and is even likely to become the top spot whenthe *New York Times* goes behind a paywall. Its impressive achievement is made by its breezy writings, by the reports of celebrity news, particularly reports involving attractive women in swimsuits, by lots of news aggregators' link, etc.

5. What are the three main trends of innovation in Britain's newspapers?

    a. Online paywall. It starts from News Corporation, who owns the *Times*, the *Sunday Times*, the *Sun and* the *News of the World*. *The Times* does not allow people to read any articles for free. As a result, only a very small percentage of regular readers subscribe to the website, which does not worry News Corporation, because the firm attaches importance to dedicated readers and make money by offering various services.

    b. Attractive content. For example, the *Daily Mail* becomes the world's second-biggest newspaper website by providing breezy writings, celebrity news, particularly reports involving attractive women in swimsuits, and online news aggregators as well.

    c. Going free or very cheap. The representative of this trend is Lebedevs' British papers. *The Evening Standard*'s circulation has more than doubled since going free, to 700,000. Distribution costs have plunged. The *i*, which is quite cheap, now runs the same ads as in the *Independent*, which has little attraction to marketers, to keep alive both.

Words to Know

ad slots, aggregator, bottom-feeding, breezy read, celebrity, scandal, circulation, the cutting edge, dedicated readers, distribution, format, halfway house, iPad applications, News Corporation, online paywall, phone-hacking, premium papers, state-sanctioned, subscription, subscribe, tabloid, top spot, online traffic

Part Four

Supplementary Reading

    New Mail on Sunday Mag. Is a Happy Event for Print (From The *Observer*, April 13, 2013)

Lesson Seventeen

Mrs Windsor, Anyone?

Part One

Summary

　　这是一篇评论君主制和共和制的文章,作者从历史角度加以论述,先说现在,再说以往君主制的变迁。英国 17 世纪曾实行过共和制,不过只有 11 年光景便又恢复了君主制。经过这一场血腥的 civil war 和共和国及光荣革命后,英国的 monarch 便成了 constitutional one。君主不再享有至高无上的权力,而由 Parliament 取而代之。作者还用民意测验的数据说话,阐明当今的君主制是受绝大多数英国人欢迎的,主张共和的不过是一小批自由派和中左人士。王室经历了戴安娜事件后,绯闻不再发生,已经恢复了元气,女王的威望比以往更高。作者说她能使英国国泰民安,这样的君主制能被共和制取而代之吗? 况且有评论说,英国整体本质上就是个"disguised republic"。

The Author

　　Matthew Lewis Engel(1951—), is a British writer and editor who began his career in 1972. He worked on *The Guardian* newspaper for nearly 25 years, reporting on a wide range of political and sporting events including a stint as Washington correspondent beginning on 9/11. He now writes a column in the *Financial Times*. Engel edited the 1993—2000 and 2004—2007 editions of *Wisden Cricketers' Almanack*, with a short break when he worked in the US. He has been a strong critic of the International Cricket Council, international cricket's ruling body. He remains associated with the almanack, and now edits a new publishing imprint Wisden Sports Writing, which aims to publish top-class books on all sports.

Background Information

1. Prince William's Wedding

Prince William Arthur Philip Louis of Wales (born 1982), is the elder son of Charles, Prince of Wales, and Diana, Princess of Wales, and grandson of Queen Elizabeth II and Prince Philip, Duke of Edinburgh. His wedding to Kate Middleton took place on April 29, 2011. London became the focus of the world that day and huge crowds turned out to watch the Royal procession of horse drawn carriages that made their way from Westminster Abbey back to Buckingham Palace, where the wedding reception took place.

2. The English Civil War (1642—1651)

The English Civil War (1642—1651) was a series of armed conflicts and political machinations between Parliamentarians(议会党人) and Royalists(保皇党人). The first(1642—46) and second(1648—49) civil wars pitted the supporters of King Charles I against the supporters of the Long Parliament(长期议会), while the third war(1649—51) saw fighting between supporters of King Charles II and supporters of the Rump Parliament(残阙议会). The Civil War ended with the Parliamentary victory at the Battle of Worcesteron 3 September 1651.

The War led to the trial and execution of Charles I, the exile of his son, Charles II, and replacement of English monarchywith, first, the Commonwealth of England(1649—53), and then with a Protectorate(护国公政体)(1653—59), under Oliver Cromwell's personal rule. The monopoly of the Church of England on Christian worship in England ended with the victors consolidating the established Protestant Ascendancy(新教优势) in Ireland. Constitutionally, the wars established the precedent that an English monarch cannot govern without Parliament's consent, although this concept was legally established only with the Glorious Revolution(光荣革命) later in the century. (英王成为立宪君主[constitutional monarch], 其实就是有名无实, 一切权力受到宪法限制而归议会, 君主不过是个摆饰[figurehead]。见《导读》五章二节英国"国王")

3. Charles I (1600—1649)

He was monarch of the three kingdoms of England, Scotland, and

Ireland from 27 March 1625 until his execution in 1649. Charles engaged in a struggle for power with the Parliament of England. Many of his subjects opposed his attempts to overrule and negate parliamentary authority. Charles's last years were marked by the Civil War, in which he fought the forces of the English and Scottish parliaments. He was defeated in the First Civil War (1642 — 45), after which Parliament expected him to accept its demands for a constitutional monarchy (君主立宪制). He instead remained defiant by attempting to forge an alliance with Scotland and escaping to the Isle of Wight. This provoked the Second Civil War(1648—49) and a second defeat for Charles, who was subsequently executed for high treason. The monarchywas abolished and a republic called the Commonwealth of England, also referred to as the Cromwellian Interregnum, was declared. Charles's son, Charles II, who dated his accession from the death of his father, did not take up the reins of government until the restoration of the monarchyin 1660.

Part Two

Language Points

I. New Words

bonnet /ˈbɒnɪt/ n. (宽边的)包头软帽
bore /bɔː(r)/ n. a dull uninteresting person, esp. one who talks continually or repeatedly in an uninteresting way
contract /ˈkɒntrækt/ v. fml to get ot begin to have (sth bad, esp. an illness)感染(疾病);染上(恶习)
coverage /ˈkʌvərɪdʒ/ n. the news as presented by reporters for newspapers or radio or television
deprivation /ˌdeprɪˈveɪʃn/ n. act of depriving someone of food or money or rights 剥夺,免职
emit /ɪˈmɪt/ v. to send out (heat, light, smell, sound, etc.)
enthusiast /ɪnˈθjuːzɪæst/ n. a person who is habitually full of enthusiasm, esp. for the stated thing 热心者,热衷于……的人
execution /ˌeksɪˈkjuːʃn/ n. (a case of) lawful killing as a punishment 依法处决
gent /dʒent/ n. infml a gentleman
inconclusive /ˌɪnkənˈkluːsɪv/ adj. not leading to a clear decision or

result 非决定性的,无结果的

landau /'lændɔː/ n. a four-wheeled horsedrawn carriage with two seats and a top that folds back in two parts 活顶四轮马车

laughing-stock /'lɑːfɪŋstɒk/ n. someone or sth that is regarded as foolish and causes unkind laughter 笑柄

leftish /'leftɪʃ/ adj. of a political view that favours greater political changes 左派的,激进的

legacy /'legəsɪ/ n. money or other property passed on or left behind by sb or sth 遗产

legitimate /lɪ'dʒɪtɪmət/ adj. correct or allowable according to the law; reasonable

neutral /'njuːtrəl/ n. one who does not side with any party in a war or dispute 中间派,中立者

prevail /prɪ'veɪl/ v. to gain control or victory

II. Notes

1. a pretty decent attendance (Par. 2)—the number of people who attended was not small
2. street party (Par. 2)—an outdoor party for all the residents of a street or neighbourhood(街头派对,街道聚会)
3. put finishing touches to sth (Par. 2)—to make final adjustments of completing sth(做最后的润饰)
4. culminate in (Par. 5)—to reach the highest point, degree, or stage of development in; end in(达到……高峰;终于)
5. a number in line with similar polls throughout the past 60 years (Par. 6)—the result of the poll was consistent with similar polls in the past 60 years
6. At the behest of the FT's photographer... (Par. 7)—In answer to the request of the *Financial Times* photographer...
   at the behest of—at the requeet of 在……要求下
7. There was a bad run for the monarchy... (Par. 10)—There was a bad time for the monarchy
8. run—a continuous or sustained period; tendency or trend
   retreated into seclusion (Par. 11)—moved back from (here government or state affairs) and lived a life away from other people (隐退). In 1861, her husband, Albert, died. Victoria's grief was so great that she did not appear in public for three years and did not

open Parliament until 1866; her prolonged seclusion damaged her popularity.
9. began to exhibit signs of George IV-ishness (Par. 11)—began to show characters the same as or similar to those of George IV
10. The Queen is there by consent (Par. 13)—The Queen is head of state when people agree.
11. Between the flag-wavers and the placard-wavers (Par. 14)—between the supporters and abolitionists of the monarchy
12. But I suspect that single questioner spoke for apathetic England. (Par. 19)—But I think the person who asked that question expressed the views of all those English people who are indifferent to this issue.

Part Three

Reference Answers to Questions

1. Are there many Britons against monarchy according to the author?
   No. Only a handful of people have expressed their dislike for the monarchy.
2. What does the slogan "Don't jubilee've it!" on the placard mean?
   It means: don't take part in any celebration for the Queens's diamond jubilee.
3. How do you understand the slogan "9,500 nurses or 1 Queen?"
   The slogan means that the expenses of the Queen are equal to those of 9,500 nurses. It suggests that the royal family's life is extravagant and so people choose to have more nurses instead of a queen.
4. Why do you think the majority of Britons give their support to the royal family?
   They think that their country can benefit a lot economically from it, and their state is safer and more stable with it.
5. In your view, which is better for Britain, monarchy or Republicanism?
   (Open.)

Words to Know

accession, ambivalent, anti-royalist, apathetic, Oliver Cromwell, Charles I/II, civil war, David Cameron, the Conservative Party, constitutional, contradiction, diamond jubilee, Edward VII/VIII, Elizabeth II, French Revolution, George III/IV, golden jubilee, indoctrination, institution, Labour, Labour Party, legitimate, log-cabin-to-president tradition, Long Parliament, monarch, monarchy, MP, nuisance, Plaid Cymru, reign, republicanism, royal family, Rump Parliament, Tory, Victoria, Westminster Abbey, William IV, Windsor.

Part Four

Supplementary Reading

"In this special year, I dedicate myself anew to your service": Queen's vow as Diamond Jubilee celebrations begin with 62-gun Royal Salute on Accession Day (From *Daily Mail*, Feb 6, 2012)

Lesson Eighteen

Rethinking the welfare state:
Asia's next revolution

Part One

Summary

近年来亚洲国家经济发展形势大好,脱贫后,民众对国家福利制度的诉求越来越高。大多数亚洲国家已开始从只发展经济向建设福利国家的道路转轨。例如,2012年印度尼西亚政府承诺到2014年将为全民提供医疗保险;中国仅用两年时间便将2.4亿农村人口也纳入了社保覆盖范围,这一数字超过美国享受公共退休金的总人数。作为对比,欧洲福利制度的成型则花费了半个多世纪,同时这些福利国家还不得不面对人口老龄化和财政赤字等问题,欧债危机就是实例。西方国家的福利发展史为亚洲国家福利制度的制定与实施提供了借鉴,以免后继者重蹈覆辙。福利制度首先应关注两个问题:一是人口,二是规模。针对这两题,文章给出了应对挑战的灵丹妙药:第一,由于人们寿命预期的提升,建议延长从业者的退休年龄;第二,亚洲政府需要确定福利制度的目标群体;第三,亚洲国家政府的改革者应保持制度的灵活性和创新性;最后,全体国民都应认识到,福利制度的实施不完全是经济问题,也是政治问题。亚洲公民应未雨绸缪,努力长期工作,避免让子孙后代跌入背负债务包袱的深渊。

  这是一篇评论性政论文章,立场客观,语言平实,分析理性,见解深刻,对各国福利制度发展中的问题分析到位,对亚洲国家的发展潜力持乐观态度。作者运用大量的数据和具体事例来支持其观点,还通过大量的对比来说明问题。针对亚洲民众对福利国家制度表现出的越来越高的诉求,结合西方在该制度发展中的教训,作者指出了亚洲国家福利制度高歌猛进地实施中出现的问题,对其进行了分析,并给出了建设性意见。同时我们也应看到在某些城乡二元对立的国家,福利制度覆盖至农民,不仅是个经济问题,也是关乎全民公平与正义的社会问题。另外,从就业的角度看,延长退休年龄对青年人就业机会的冲击也是政策制定者需要慎重考虑的。

Background Information

1. Welfare state 福利体制;福利国家

It is the concept and obligation of government in which the state plays a key role in the protection and promotion of the economic and social well-being of its citizens. It is based on the principles of equal opportunity, equitable distribution of wealth, and public responsibility for those unable to avail themselves of the minimal provisions for a good life. The general term may cover a variety of forms of economic and social organization. The sociologist T. H. Marshall identified the welfare state as a distinctive combination of democracy, welfare and capitalism.

Modern welfare states include the Nordic (北欧的) countries, such as Iceland, Sweden, Norway, Denmark, and Finland which employ a system known as the Nordic model. The welfare state involves a transfer of funds from the state, to the services provided (i. e. healthcare, education) as well as directly to individuals.

The welfare state is funded through redistributionist taxation (税收的再分配) and is often referred to as a type of "mixed economy". Such taxation usually includes a larger income tax for people with higher incomes, which is called a progressive tax (累进税,即对收入相对较高的群体收更多的税). This helps to reduce the income gap(贫富差距) between the rich and poor. (normally indicated by Gini coefficient) When income inequality is low, aggregate demand (总需求) will be relatively high, because more people who want ordinary consumer goods and services will be able to afford them, while the labor force will not be as relatively monopolized (垄断) by the wealthy.

2. China's welfare system and the health insurance

Social welfare in China, for which the Ministry of Human Resources and Social Security(人力资源和社会保障部) is responsible, has undergone various changes throughout history.

In pre-1980s, China as a socialist state attempted to meet the needs of society from cradle to grave(从生到死). Child care, education, job placement, housing, subsistence (维持生活), health care, and care for the elderly were largely the responsibility of the work unit as administered through state-owned enterprises and agricultural communes and collectives. As those systems disappeared or were reformed, the "iron rice bowl" approach to welfare changed. Article 14 of the constitution stipulates that the state "builds and improves a welfare system that corresponds with the level of economic development."

In 2004, China experienced the greatest decrease in its poorest population since 1999. People with a per capita income (人均收入) of less than 668 in RMB; (US＄80.71) decreased 2.9 million or 10 %; those with a per capita income of no more than 924 RMB (US＄111.64) decreased by 6.4 million or 11.4%, according to statistics from the State Council's Poverty Reduction Office (国务院扶贫办公室).

Welfare reforms since the late 1990s have included unemployment insurance, medical insurance, workers' compensation insurance, maternity benefits, communal pension funds (公积金), individual pension accounts, universal health care, and a carbon tax.

China is also undertaking reform of its health-care system. The New Rural Co-operative Medical Care System (NRCMCS,农村合作医疗体系) is a 2005 initiative to overhaul the healthcare system, particularly intended to make it more affordable for the rural poor. Under the NRCMCS, the annual cost of medical coverage is 50 yuan (US＄7) per person. Of that, 20 yuan is paid in by the central government, 20 yuan by the provincial government and a remaining 10 yuan is made by the patient. As of September 2007, around 80% of the rural population of China had signed up (about 685 million people). The system is tiered (分层的), depending on the location. If patients go to a small hospital or clinic in their local town, the system will cover roughly 70－80% of their bill. If the patient visits a county clinic, the percentage of the cost being covered falls to about 60%. If the patient requires a specialist in a modern city hospital, the policies would cover about 30% of the bill.

The Ministry of Health of the State Council (国务院卫生部) oversees the health services system and nearly all the major medical facilities are run by the government.

3. Social Security in the United States 美国社会保障制度

In theUnited States, Social Security refers to the Old-Age, Survivors, and Disability Insurance (OASDI) federal program(养老,幸存者和残疾保险). The original Social Security Act (1935) and the current version of the Act, as amended, encompass several social welfare and social insurance programs.

Social Security is primarily funded through dedicated payroll taxes called Federal Insurance Contributions Act tax (FICA:联邦保险贡献法案税). Tax deposits are formally entrusted to the Federal Old-Age and Survivors Insurance Trust Fund(联邦养老和遗属保险信托基金), the Federal Disability Insurance Trust Fund(联邦养残疾保险信托基金), the Federal Hospital Insurance Trust Fund(联邦医院保险信托基金), or the Federal Supplementary Medical Insurance Trust Fund(联邦补充医疗保险信托基金) which comprise the Social Security Trust Fund. Upward redistribution of income is responsible for about 43% of the projected Social Security shortfall over the next 75 years.

According to economist Martin Feldstein, the combined spending for all social insurance programs in 2003 constituted 37% of government expenditure and 7% of the gross domestic product. Social Security is currently estimated to keep roughly 40 percent of all Americans age 65 or older out of poverty.

Part Two

Language Points

I. New Words

acute /ə'kjuːt/ *adj*. quick to notice and understand things 反应敏捷
ageing /'eɪdʒɪŋ/ *adj*. becoming old
budget /'bʌdʒɪt/ *n*. the money that is available to an organization or person, or a plan of how it will be spent 预算
deficit /'defɪsɪt/ *n*. the difference between the amount of sth that you have and the higher amount that you need 赤字
dynamic /daɪ'næmɪk/ *adj*. full of energy and new ideas, and determined to succeed 有力,有信心的
emerging /i'mɜːdʒɪŋ/ *adj*. in an early state of development 正在显现的

equate /ɪˈkweɪt/ v. to consider or make equal 使平等
extend /ɪkˈstend/ v. to affect or include people, things, or places 表达, 包含
fraction /ˈfrækʃn/ a very small amount of sth
gape /geɪp/ v. to come apart or open widely 开放, 分开
gaping /ˈgæpɪŋ/ adj. a gaping hole, wound, or mouth is very wide and open 开放的
handout /ˈhændaʊt/ n. an amount of money or goods given to people who need them 分发之物
innovative /ˈɪnəveɪtɪv/ adj. an innovative idea or way of doing sth is new, different, and better than those that existed before 创新的
oblige /əˈblaɪdʒ/ vt. to make it necessary for (someone) to do sth 有责任去做
recipient /rɪˈsɪpɪənt/ n. someone who receives sth 收授者
redistribution /ˌriːdɪstrɪˈbjuːʃn/ n. economics the theory, policy, or practice of lessening or reducing inequalities in income through such measures as progressive income taxation and antipoverty programs 再分配
revenue /ˈrevənjuː/ n. money that a business or organization receives over a period of time, esp. from selling goods or services 收益
thrift /θrɪft/ n. wise and careful use of money, so that none is wasted 节俭, 节约
tricky /ˈtrɪkɪ/ adj. difficult to handle or deal with; full of hidden or unexpected difficulties
withdraw /wɪðˈdrɔː/ v. to take money out of a bank account 取款

II. Notes

1. abject poverty (Para. 2)—赤贫
2. public pensions, national health insurance, unemployment benefits and other hallmarks of social protection (Para. 2)—公共养老金, 国家医疗保险, 失业救济金及其他社会保障制度
3. shifting gear (Para. 2)—换挡, 喻转变
4. role model (Para. 4)—楷模; 榜样; 典范
5. interest groups (Para. 5)—a group of people who work together to achieve a particular goal, especially by putting pressure on the government (利益集团)
6. The eventual result, all too often... an ever-bigger state. (Para. 5)—Eventually, it turns out that these countries have been suffering

from an economic stagnation because of the growing financial burden to pay for the spending on social welfare. 最终的结果通常是更大程度上的经济呆滞

  all too often—通常，往往

7. a first-world rate of government spending but third-world public services (Para. 6)—相当于第一世界国家的政府支出，提供的却是第三世界国家的公共服务。

8. They have little desire to replace traditions of hard work and thrift with a flabby welfare dependency. (Para. 7)—They will encourage people to stick to the traditional virtues of hard work and thrift instead of encouraging them to rely on the welfare system. 他们几乎没有愿望去取代传统上努力工作，勤俭节约式的对少量福利的依赖。

9. The region's giants... tiny Singapore (Para. 7)—The big Asian countries should learn from Singapore rather than Greece. Small as it is, Singapore provides its people the best schools, while the government spending is only a fifth of GDP. 亚洲地区的大国不是从希腊而是从很小的新加坡得到鼓舞。

10. Even now... except sub-Saharan Africa. (Para. 7)—即使在今天，相对该地区经济体的规模来说，社会开支也只有富裕国家平均水平的30%左右，在新兴世界中仅仅高于撒哈拉沙漠以南的非洲国家。

11. Today China... the ratio will have fallen to two. (Para. 8)—Today China has five persons working to support every old person to get the public welfare. But by 2035 there will be only two persons who can work to support an old person. 今天的中国，每5个工作的人养活一位老人，但到了2035年，只有2个工作的人养活一位老人了。

12. The size of most Asian pensions... at an early age. (Para. 11)—The money people of Asian countries can get from their public pension is not much, but they can withdraw and use this money at an early age because people retire early in these countries. 多少亚洲国家的退休金不多，但人们年岁不大时就可支取了。

13. In fast-ageing societies... the young. (Para. 12)—The governments should not reduce the public spending on the old because they need the money to support the increased number of the young. 在迅速老龄化的社会，给老人的待遇不应再挤压出对年轻人的投入。

14. From making electronic health records... modern technology.

(Para. 13)—亚洲国家可以用现代技术来创立新型高效的福利给付系统,比如广泛采用电子档案、通过手机来管理转移性支付等等。

15. The continent's citizens...rich-world counterparts. (Para. 14)—这块大陆上的公民也必须对未雨绸缪心甘情愿,加长工作时间,并且避免让子孙后代背负沉重债务包袱:与之相对的富国公民至今缺少这些美德。("Virtues" here refers to "a willingness to plan ahead, work longer and eschew handouts based on piling up debt for future generations".)

Part Three

Reference Answers to Questions

1. What was the most important mission of the major Asian countries in the past decades? And what do their people concentrate on most in recent years?

    Their most important mission used to be building a wealthy state simply, now it shifts to build a welfare state.

2. Building their welfare states, what achievements have the big giants of Asia accomplished and what problems have they got?

    Achievements are outstanding:

    a. Indonesia's government promised to provide all its citizens with health insurance by 2014.

    b. In just two years China has extended pension coverage to an additional 240 million rural folks.

    c. In India some 40 million households benefit from a government scheme to provide up to 100 days' work a year at the minimum wage.

    d. India has extended health insurance to some 110 million poor people.

    However, various problems have also risen, such as insufficient social spending, ageing populations, regional income disparities and informal economy, gaping budget deficits, and social inequalities.

3. What lessons should the Asian countries learn from the western countries and what suggestions does the author offer?

    While building their welfare system, the Asian countries should follow the following lessons:

  a. learn to cope with ageing population and gaping budget deficits.

  b. make sure therecipients of welfare spending are the needed and try to avoid inequalities.

  c. be more careful about the entitlement system and notto make unaffordable promises.

  d. try to avoid economic sclerosis.

The author offers 4 suggestions:

  a. They should pay even more attention to the affordability over time of any promises.

  b. Asian governments need to target their social spending more carefully.

  c. Asia's reformers should concentrate on being both flexible and innovative.

  d. The Asian citizens will have to show a willingness to plan ahead, work longer and eschew handouts based on piling up debt for future generations: virtues that have so far eluded their rich-world counterparts.

4. Why does the author say that social protection often aggravated inequalities?

    Because he thinks that pension and health care would flow toaffluent urban workers but not to the real poor.

5. Do you agree with the author's opinion that different countries will and should experiment with various welfare models?

    I agree with the author more or less. Then deliver one of the four basic principles discussed in the passage. (Refer to Question 3 listed above)

Words to Know

abject poverty, budget deficit, entitlements system, health insurance, healthcare, income disparity, minimum wage, pension, public spending, safety net, social security, subside, the emerging world, vibrant/dynamic economy, welfare state

Part Four

Supplementary Reading

China's Golden Decade Brings Some Relief to Rural Poor (From the *Guardian*, Nov-5, 2012)

Lesson Nineteen

The hopeful continent: Africa rising

Part One

Summary

  非洲尼日利亚南部，有一个名为奥内特沙市场，场内各家商品货物堆积如山，购买人群摩肩接踵，一片繁忙景象。这个据称是世界上最大的市场是整个新兴非洲经济的缩影。过去的十年中，世界上发展最快的十个国家中就有六个是非洲的。其中八年非洲的发展超过了东亚国家，国际货币基金组织希望其发展速度在后面的两年中与亚洲持平。商品繁荣是非洲崛起的部分原因，人口同样是重要因素。文章提醒对非洲发展过于乐观的人能看到非洲依然存在很多问题，比如大多数非洲人仍然生活在极度贫困中，食品生产下滑，人均寿命低下，干旱和饥饿依然在非洲肆虐，气候还在恶化，森林减少、沙漠化加重。除了自然环境与生产的问题外，盗贼猖獗、道德败坏、无政府现象、腐败等同样制约着非洲的进一步发展。非洲崛起是不争的事实，一些基本数据显然在往正确的方向攀升。非洲拥有成长最快的中产阶级；外资在过去的十年中增加了十倍；中国改善了非洲的基础设施，提高了其制造业水准；其他非西方国家正效仿中国，紧随其后。另外，非洲人对技术的热情也大大促进了它的发展，手机用户拥有量超过了美洲、欧洲，手机银行和电话农业信息服务因为其道路条件太差反而得到了长足的发展，移动网络的覆盖面比例已经高于印度。全民的健康状况也得到了改善。越来越多的非洲国家公民享有更多的民主。整个社会人群中受过良好教育的工作适龄年轻人进入了就业市场，出生率也渐渐减缓。非洲正享受着亚洲国家三十年前享受过的"人口红利"——拥有大量的年轻成人对于经济蒸蒸日上的任何国家都是有益的。当然，崛起的非洲仍然需要深入改革，政府要改善经济增长的基本条件，如税收、土地所有权问题；政要们要认清形势，适时放权。西方政府也应对非洲开放贸易，而不仅仅是随意分发些救济物资。

本文是一篇经济时文。文章对非洲经济的飞速增长和依然面临的问题作了细致、全面而带有政治偏见的分析。观点明晰,结构合理,语言易懂,具备新闻文体特征,如使用合成词、俚语等。

Background Information

1. the Onitsha market 奥尼沙市场

Onitsha is a city of southeast Nigeria on the Niger River (尼日尔河). Its market is so well-known that it is called a market town. The Onitsha market is one of the largest markets in West Africa.

2. IMF 国际货币基金组织

IMF (The International Monetary Fund) is an international organization that was initiated in 1944 at the Bretton Woods Conference (布雷顿森林会议) and formally created in 1945 by 29 member countries. The IMF's stated goal was to stabilize exchange rates and assist the reconstruction of the world's international payment system post-World War II. Countries contribute money to a pool through a quota system (配额制) from which countries with payment imbalances can borrow funds temporarily. Through this activity and others such as surveillance (监管) of its members' economies and policies, the IMF works to improve the economies of its member countries. The IMF describes itself as "an organization of 188 countries, working to foster global monetary cooperation, secure financial stability, facilitate international trade, promote high employment and sustainable economic growth, and reduce poverty around the world."

3. southern Africa 南部非洲

Southern Africa is the southernmost region of the African continent, variably defined by geography or geopolitics. In the UN scheme of geographic regions, Southern Africa is composed of five countries: Botswana (博茨瓦纳), Lesotho (莱索托), Namibia (纳米比亚), South Africa (南非) and Swaziland (斯威士兰). The region is sometimes reckoned to include other territories, such as Angola, Mauritius, Zambia (赞比亚), Zimbabwe (津巴布韦), etc. Another geographic delineation for the region is the portion of Africa south of the Cunene (库内纳河) and Zambezi Rivers (赞比西河)—that is, South

Africa, Lesotho, Swaziland, Namibia, Botswana, Zimbabwe and the part of Mozambique (莫桑比克) which lies south of the Zambezi River. This definition is most often used in South Africa for natural sciences and particularly in guide books such as Roberts' Birds of Southern Africa. The terrain of Southern Africa is varied, ranging from forest and grasslands to deserts. The region has both low-lying coastal areas, and mountains. In terms of natural resources, the region has the world's largest resources of platinum (铂金) and the platinum group elements, chromium (铬), vanadium (钒), and cobalt (钴), as well as uranium (铀), gold, titanium (钛), iron and diamonds. The region is distinct from the rest of Africa, with some of its main exports including platinum, diamonds, gold, and uranium, but it is similar in that it shares some of the problems of the rest of the continent. While colonialism has left its mark on the development over the course of history, today poverty, corruption, and HIV/AIDS are some of the biggest factors impeding economic growth. The pursuit of economic and political stability is an important part of the region's goals. South Africa is the dominant economic "superpower" of the region. South Africa's GDP alone is many times greater than the GDPs of all other countries in the region.

Part Two

Language Points

I. New Words

backdrop /'bækdrɒp/ *n.* the conditions or situation in which sth happens 背景

boost /buːst/ *v.* to increase or improve sth and make it more successful 促进，推动

Brazil /brəˈzɪl/ *n.* the largest country in South America 巴西

breakneck /'breɪknek/ *adj.* very fast and dangerous 高速而危险的

corruption /kəˈrʌpʃən/ *n.* dishonest, illegal, or immoral behaviour, esp. of someone with power 腐败

decent /'diːsənt/ *adj.* of a good enough standard or quality 不错的，体面的

hemisphere /'hemɪsfɪə/ *n.* one half of the earth's surface (地球的) 半球

hub /hʌb/ *n.* the central and most important part of an area, system, activity etc, which all the other parts are connected to 中心

knock-on /'nɒkɒn/ *adj.* When an event or situation has a knock-on effect, it causes other events or situations, but not directly 连锁反应的

lifespan /'laɪfspæn/ *n.* the average length of life of a sort of animal or plant 生命周期

Malaysia /mə'leɪʒə/ *n.* a country in southeast Asia. It is a member of the British Commonwealth (英联邦) 马来西亚

noxious /'nɒkʃəs/ *adj.* harmful and unpleasant 有害的,不吉祥的

revenue /'revənju/ *n.* money that the government receives from tax 税收收入

rivalry /'raɪvəlrɪ/ *n.* competition; a case of being rivals 竞争,对抗

slowdown /'sləʊdaʊn/ *n.* a reduction in activity or speed

soar /sɔː/ *v.* to rise rapidly or to a very high level

tenfold /'tenfəʊld/ *adv.* ten times as much or as many of sth 成十倍的

title /'taɪtl/ *n. law* the legal right to have or own sth 所有权

transformative /træns'fɔːmətɪv/ *adj.* able to produce a big change or improvement in a situation 变换,转型的

Turkey /'tɜːkɪ/ *n.* a country which is mainly in west Asia but partly in southeast Europe, between the Mediterranean (地中海) and Black Seas. 土耳其

II. Notes

1. Even allowing for the knock-on effect of... (Par. 2)—In fact, taking into account its indirect influence on... 允许连锁反应的发生
     allow for—to consider the possible facts, problems, costs etc. involved in sth. when making a plan, calculation, or judgment 考虑到

2. the commodities boom (Par. 3)—the prosperity of the commodities 商品繁荣

3. Optimism about Africa needs to be taken in fairly small doses (Par. 4)—It's too hasty to think optimistically about Africa 对非洲前程的乐观要谨慎
     in small doses—for a short period of time

4. on the march (Par. 4)—becoming stronger and more popular quickly

5. tainted with corruption (Par. 5)—influenced by corruption 受腐败影响

6. there is talk of... (Par. 5)—there is information or news that people talk about and hear about a lot, but that is not official. 传闻
7. ... are following its lead (Par. 7)—are imitating (China) 效仿追随
8. call centres (Par. 7)—offices where people answer customers' questions, make sales etc by using the telephone rather than by meeting people 电话咨询中心
9. a huge boon (Par. 8)—a great help and benefit to improve the quality of life 极大的帮助
10. a taste of (Par. 9)—a short experience of sth. that shows you what it is like 尝试
11. get a boost (Par. 10)—get helps for sth. to increase, improve, or become successful 启动,发动,推动
12. tail off (Par. 10)—become gradually less, smaller etc, and often stop or disappear completely 消失,完结
13. keep their noses out of the trough (Par. 12)—*spoken* to avoid becoming involved in sth. that is not your concern 不卷入,不参与
14. dish out aid (Par. 13)—to distribute assistance; give help to various countries in a careless way 随便,不用心的帮助
15. total openness (Par. 13)—being willing to accept new ideas and new people completely 敞开心扉的
16. the transformative promise of growth (Par. 14)—a sign that sth. good may happen and will produce a big change or improvement 带来增长的转变迹象

Part Three

Reference Answers to Questions

1. How is today's economic development in Africa compared with East Asia and the whole world?

   In eight of the past ten years, Africa has grown faster than East Asia, including Japan. Even allowing for the knock-on effect of the northern hemisphere's slowdown, the IMF expects Africa to grow by 6% in 2011 and nearly 6% in 2012, about the same as Asia. Over the past decade six of the world's ten fastest-growing countries were African.

2. When optimism is shown about Africa, what other obstacles is Africa facing now?

   Most Africans live on less than two dollars a day; food production per person has slumped; the average lifespan in some countries is under 50; drought and famine persist; the climate is worsening, with deforestation and desertification still on the march. In addition, kleptocracies, noxious politics, shoddy election, corruption, etc. are obstacles that Africa is facing, too.

3. What are favorable to Africa's economic growth?

   Africa is now having a fast-growing middle class; foreign countries are increasing their investments; Non-western countries are helping improve its infrastructure and manufacture; its light manufacturing and services are growing fast. Its enthusiasm for technology, for example, high proportion of mobile-internet services, the improvement of African's health, growing productivity, boosts the growth as well. Peace and Freedom play an important role. Meanwhile, Africa is undergoing a "demographic dividend". All these lead to Africa's promising developments.

4. What measures should Africa take in order to achieve further development?

   African governments should make it easier to start businesses and cut some taxes and collect honestly the ones they impose. Land needs to be taken out of communal ownership and title handed over to individual farmers so that they can get credit and expand. Above all, it is critical for politicians to recognize their position and willing to give up their power when they are not needed by their voters.

5. What are the main reasons leading to Africa rising?

   The commodities boom is the first reason for the rising of Africa. In 2000—08 around a quarter of Africa's growth came from higher revenues from natural resources. Africa, over the past decade, grows strikingly fast, six of world's ten fastest-growing countries, and faster than East Asia. Though Africa is still facing notonly a few obstacles, it surely has some favorable factors in its growth, such as its fast-growing middle class, increasing foreign investment, peaceful environment, etc.

   Favorable demography is another reason. With fertility rates crashing in Asia and Latin America, half of the increase in population over the next 40 years will be in Africa, which will bring Africa "demographic dividend". A bulge of better-educated young people of working-age is entering the job market and birth rates are beginning to decline. Clearly, having a lot of young adults is beneficial to any country if its economy is thriving.

Words to Know

agro-info, backdrop, ballot box, boom, breakneck, colonial shackle, commodities boom, corruption, demographic dividend, demography, fertility rate, oil-sodden kleptocracies, piracy, shoddy, slump, strife, tail off, tariff

Part Four

Supplementary Reading

Aspiring Africa (From The *Economist*, March 2, 2013)

Lesson Twenty

Greece as Victim

Part One

Summary

欧债危机,全称欧洲主权债务危机,是指自2009年以来在欧洲部分国家爆发的主权债务危机。欧债危机是美国次贷危机引发的金融危机和经济衰退或危机在全球的延续和深化,其本质原因是政府的债务负担超过了自身承受的能力。2009年12月,希腊主权债务问题凸显,2008年希腊的债务余额为GDP的99%;2009年该数据上升至113.4%;2010年8月以前,希腊债务的绝对额为2800亿欧元,但其国民总值只有2400亿元。从数据来看,希腊实际上已经破产。受希腊的影响,欧洲其他的国家也开始相继陷入危机。于是,很多研究者开始寻找欧债危机的症结到底在哪里。本篇评述中,保罗·克鲁格曼认为,尽管希腊本身存在各种问题,例如:腐败丛生,偷税漏税现象严重,劳动生产率低下,福利体系存在缺陷等等,但是导致这次危机的根源在于欧洲没有一个像中央政府般的单一政府实行的单一货币制度。加之欧元本身的弊端(如英国和丹麦就未加入欧元区)和欧洲官员的傲慢态度,所以希腊不过是欧元的牺牲品而已。

然而,《上海证券报》评论版主编时寒冰就否定了这一观点。他认为:欧元区内贸易给小国(希腊)带来的收益显然比给区内大国带来的收益更高。况且,滥用廉价资本投资的是希腊,享受高福利的是希腊,坐享欧洲国家救助资金的还是希腊,将一切过错归到欧元和欧洲区领导的身上是有失公允的。美国著名经济史学家查尔斯·P.金德尔伯格也不认同krugman的意见。

欧债危机的根源众说纷纭,只能见仁见智或让历史去判断。不过在全球化经济大环境下,没有一国能独善其身,这就需要各国合作共同努力应对。

The Author

Paul R. Krugman, 60, American economist, won the Nobel Prize in 2008. Now he is the professor in Princeton University. He studies International trade, international finance, monetary crisis and the theory of exchange rates.

Background Information

1. European debt crisis 欧债危机

One of the long-term worldwide consequences of the economic breakdown is the 2010 European sovereign debt crisis(欧洲主权债务危机). This crisis primarily impacted five countries: Greece, Ireland, Portugal, Italy, and Spain. The governments of these nations habitually run large government budget deficits. Other Eurozone countries include: France, Belgium, the Netherlands, Luxembourg, Germany, Finland, Austria, and Italy. Greece, which at the time of the crisis also suffered from bad governing with widespread corruption and tax evasion, was hit the hardest and was thus targeted by credit rating agencies(信用评级机构) as the weak link of the Eurozone. Fear that Greece's debt problems would cause lenders to stop lending to it, with the result that Greece would default(违约) on its sovereign debt, sparked speculation that such a default would cause lenders to stop loaning money to the other PIGS (Portugal, Ireland/Italy, Greece and Spain) as well, with the result that they would also eventually default on their sovereign debt. A sovereign default by Spain, Portugal, Italy and Greece would result in bank losses so large that almost every bank in Europe would become insolvent(破产的) due to the now uncollectible outstanding loans(未偿还的贷款) to those four countries.

On Friday, May 7, 2010 a long-desired financial aid package for Greece was constructed; however, it was obvious that other states, because of their extremely large debts, would have—or already had—financial difficulties. Therefore, the following Sunday a large group of ministers of Eurozone gathered in Brussels, decided on a mutual financial aid package of 750 billion; and the European Centre Bank announced that in the future it would support by explicit monetary help, if necessary, government bonds of the Eurozone countries (which was not allowed before, because of fears of inflation).

While this aid package has so far averted a financial panic, the PIGS continue to have difficulties.

2. Greek election

The Greeklegislative election on 17 June 2012. It was the second, and probably final election for Greece after the resignation of the last Greek Prime Minister, George Papandreou (乔治·帕潘德里欧,希腊前总理), and will probably have a critical effect on the decision whether or not Greece will stay or quit the Eurozone in the months that follow. (支持国际救助协议的希腊保守派新民主党在 2012 年 6 月 18 日的大举中以微弱优势获胜,缓解了市场对该国退出欧元区的担忧。)

Part Two

Language Points

I. New Words

accusation /ˌækjʊˈzeɪʃn/ n. a statement saying that sb is guilty of a crime or of doing sth wrong

apparent /əˈpærənt/ adj. easy to notice; obvious

automatic /ˌɔːtəˈmætɪk/ adj. acting or operating in a manner essentially independent of external influence or control

bailout /ˈbeɪlaʊt/ n. a rescue from financial difficulties 注资救助

currency /ˈkʌrənsɪ/ n. the particular type of money in use in a country

failing /ˈfeɪlɪŋ/ n. a fault or weakness

Greek /griːk/ adj. belonging or relating to Greece or its language
n. sb who comes from Greece

loan /ləʊn/ n. money that an organization such as a bank lends and sb borrows

margin /ˈmɑːdʒɪn/ n. the amount by which one thing differs from another

Mississippi /ˌmɪsɪˈsɪpɪ/ n. a U.S. state located in the southern part of the country (美国)密西西比州

paradise /ˈpærədaɪs/ n. a place that is extremely pleasant, beautiful, or enjoyable 天堂

say /seɪ/ adv. for example

sin /sɪn/ n. an offence against God or against a religious or moral law

substitute /ˈsʌbstɪtjuːt/ v. to use sth new or different instead of sth else

替代

uncompetitive /ˌʌnkəmˈpetətɪv/ adj. 无竞争力的

II. Notes

1. flawed monetary system (Par. 2)——有缺陷的货币体系 (here referring to the euro system)
2. tax evasion (Par. 3)——the crime of not paying the full amount of tax that you should pay(逃税)
3. living beyond its means (Par. 3)——spending more money than it can afford(寅吃卯粮;支出大于收入)
4. by about the same margin (Par. 3)——The difference between Mississippi and American standards is almost the same as that between Greece and European standards.
5. Nor does Greece have a runaway... the European crisis pretty well. (Par. 4)——希腊的福利体系也并非像保守派人士喜欢声称的那样已经失去控制;社会性支出占国内生产总值的比例是衡量福利国家规模的标准,而希腊的这一比例要大大低于迄今为止相当顺利地度过了欧债危机的瑞典和德国等国。

　　a runaway welfare state——a welfare system that is too large to control
6. pay its way (Par. 6)——(Greece) can yield a return on its investment sufficient to repay its expenses. (收支相抵;勉强维持)
7. come flooding in (Par. 7)——(Foreign money) come into Greece in large amounts.
8. ...but then so did everyone else...the euro bubble. (Par. 7)——Like Greece, the other countries that were affected by the euro bubble also squandered much money.

　　a. get caught up in——become involved in sth, esp. when you do not want to

　　b. the euro bubble——欧元泡沫。指欧元前期过热,强势上扬,看似根基稳固,随着欧债危机的到来,泡沫破灭,欧元大跌。
9. all too apparent (Par. 8)——very obvious
10. in effect (Par. 9)——in fact, although perhaps not appearing so(实际上)
11. come up with (Par. 10)——to find or produce a sum of money, etc.
12. Southern Europeans (Par. 11)——here referring to the Greeks

Part Three

Reference Answers to Questions

1. Are there any failings in Greece's economy? What are they?

   Yes, there are. Greece has lots of corruption and a lot of tax evasion. Besides, Greek government has had a habit of living beyond its means, and Greek labor productivity is low by European standards.

2. What happened after Greece became a member of the euro zone?

   After Greece joined the euro, a large sum of foreign money poured into the country. With the booming of the economy, inflation rose, and Greece became increasingly uncompetitive.

3. Why is the Florida housing bubble mentioned in the text?

   To show us the important role a strong central government could play in dealing with regional crisis. In the aftermath of Florida housing bubble, Florida is receiving large-scale automatic bailouts that no European nation could dream of.

4. Is it possible for the euro to be saved? How?

   Yes, according to the text, the only way for the euro to be saved is if the Germans and the European Central Bank realize that they're the ones who need to change their behavior, spending more money and accepting higher inflation.

5. According to the author, what are the causes of the Greek debt crisis?

   a. The fundamental flaws in the whole euro system;

   b. The arrogance of European officials, mostly from richer countries, who thought that they could make a single currency work without a single government;

   c. The European officials' false conception that debt crises were caused by irresponsible behavior of the Greeks;

Words to Know

bailout, Brussels, currency, EU, euro bubble/system, European Central Bank, G. D. P., governing coalition, government deficit, housing bubble, inflation, labor productivity, Medicare, monetary system, revenues, social expenditure, /security, squander, tax evasion.

Part Four

Supplementary Reading

Italy and the euro zone: That's all, folks (From The *Economist*, Nov. 12, 2011)

Lesson Twenty-one

The Coming Conflict in the Arctic

Part One

Summary

　　北冰洋，这片亿万年来被冰雪覆盖着的海洋，似乎是一片纯洁的净土，没有人在意他究竟属于谁。然而，当气候变化触发北极冰盖消融的时候，世界强国看到了前所未有的机遇，争夺航行权和北冰洋海床上自恐龙时期便已完好保存至今的自然资源。俄罗斯国家杜马副主席、北极探险家阿尔图尔·奇林加罗夫(Artur Chilingarov)大张旗鼓地在北极冰下四千米的海床插下俄罗斯国旗。瞬间俄罗斯对北极主权的声张又重新出现在地图上。奇林加罗夫先生自己则宣称："北极是我们的领土，我们必须表明自己的存在。"对此次出其不意的公然行动，加拿大立刻回以颜色。总理斯蒂芬·哈珀(Stephen Harper)宣布将在巴芬岛北端的纳尼斯维克矿场建造一个深水港。此项计划估计耗资一亿加元，哈珀总理称这些项目向世界证明了加拿大"在北极拥有实质、长期且不断巩固的存在性。"丹麦也涉足北极圈，宣称计划在 2004 到 2010 年间花费 2000 万丹麦克朗(约合 180 万英镑，360 万美元)用于收集证据，在国际上声张合法的北极领土。

　　北冰洋外围五个国家——俄罗斯、美国、挪威、丹麦和加拿大对部分边界存在争议。这些国家先前都无意解决这片不可逾越的大洋上的争端，但现在全球变暖把过去难以染指的财富送到了他们眼前。石油是让这些国家突然采取行动的原因之一。"这场竞赛表明，是资源而不是智慧主宰了当今世界，"俄罗斯隶属国防部战略技术分析中心的军事专家安德烈·约宁(Andrei Ionin)如是说。可见，无论这场争夺结果如何，其过程注定是异常激烈和残酷的。

The Author

　　Vladimir Frolov, the former director of the National Laboratory for Foreign Policy, a Moscow-based think tank, now serves as President of LEFF GROUP, his own government and public communications company. He received his first degree from the Moscow Defense Institute of Foreign Languages and earned a Ph. D. in political science from the Moscow Diplomatic Academy. Mr. Frolov had a distinguished career in the Foreign Service, including postings at the Russian Embassy in Washington D. C. before serving as the Deputy Staff Director of the State Duma Committee on Foreign Affairs and Counsel to the Deputy Chief of the Presidential Administration for Foreign Policy. Mr. Frolov coordinates the Russia Profile Experts' Panel as well as contributing comments and articles about Russia's foreign policy.

Background Information

1. Territorial Claims in the Arctic

Under international law, no country currently owns the North Pole or the region of the Arctic Ocean surrounding it. The five surrounding Arctic countries, the Russian Federation, the United States (via Alaska), Canada, Norway and Denmark (via Greenland), are limited to an exclusive economic zone (EEZ) of 200 nautical miles (370km; 230 mi) adjacent to their coasts.

Upon ratification of the United Nations Convention on the Law of the Sea (UNCLOS 联合国海洋法公约), a country has a ten-year period to make claims to an extended continental shelf which, if validated, gives it exclusive rights to resources on or below the seabed of that extended shelf area. Norway (ratified the convention in 1996), Russia (ratified in 1997), Canada (ratified in 2003 and Denmark (ratified in 2004) launched projects to provide a basis for seabed claims on extended continental shelves beyond their exclusive economic zones. The United States has signed, but not yet ratified the UNCLOS.

The status of certain portions of the Arctic sea region is in dispute for various reasons. Canada, Denmark, Norway, the Russian Federation and the United States all regard parts of the Arctic seas as "national waters" (territorial waters out to 12 nautical miles [22 km]) or "internal waters". There also are disputes regarding what passages constitute "international seaways" and rights to passage along them.

A 2008 United States Geological Survey estimates that areas north of theArctic Circle have 90 billion barrels (1.4×10^{10} m^3) of undiscovered, technically recoverable oil and 44 billion barrels (7.0×10^9 m^3) of natural gas liquids in 25 geologically defined areas thought to have potential for petroleum. This represented 13% of the expected undiscovered oil in the world. Of the estimated totals, more than half of the undiscovered oil resources were estimated to occur in just three geologic provinces—Arctic Alaska, the Amerasia Basin, and the East Greenland Rift Basins. More than 70% of the mean undiscovered oil resources was estimated to occur in five provinces: Arctic Alaska, Amerasia Basin, East Greenland Rift Basins, East Barents Basins, and West Greenland-East Canada. It was further estimated that approximately 84% of the oil and gas would occur offshore.

2. Russia's Arctic Policy

The Russian region of the Arctic is defined in the "Russian Arctic Policy" as all Russian possessions located north of theArctic Circle. (About one-fifth of Russia's landmass is north of the Arctic Circle.) Russia is one of five countries bordering theArctic Ocean. In 2011, out of 4 million inhabitants of Arctic, roughly 2 million lived in arctic Russia, making it thus the largest arctic country by population. However, in recent years Russia's Arctic population has been declining.

The main goals of Russia in its Arctic policy are to use Russia's Arctic as a resource source, protect its ecosystems, use the seas as a transportation system in Russia's interests, and ensure that it remains a zone of peace and cooperation. Russia currently maintains a military presence in the Arctic and has plans to improve it, as well as strengthen the Border Guard/Coast Guard presence there. Using the Arctic for economic gain has been done by Russia for centuries for shipping and fishing. Russia has plans to exploit the large offshore resource deposits in the Arctic. The Northern Sea Route is of particular importance to Russia for transportation, and the Russian Security Council is considering projects for its development. The Security Council also stated a need for increasing investment in Arctic infrastructure.

Russia conducts extensive research in the Arctic region, notably the manned drifting ice stationsand the Arktika 2007 expedition, which was the first to reach the seabed at the North Pole. The research is partly aimed to back up Russia's territorial claims, in particular those related to Russia's extended continental shelf in the Arctic Ocean.

3. World oil reserves

Summary of Proven Reserve Data as of 2012					
Country	Reserves 10^9 bbl	Reserves 10^9 m^3	Production 10^6 bbl/d	Production 10^3 m^3/d	Reserve/Production Ratio[1] years
Venezuela	296.5	47.14	2.1	330	387
Saudi Arabia	265.4	42.20	8.9	1,410	81
Canada	175	27.8	2.7	430	178
Iran	151.2	24.04	4.1	650	101
Iraq	143.1	22.75	2.4	380	163
Kuwait	101.5	16.14	2.3	370	121
United Arab Emirates	136.7	21.73	2.4	380	156
Russia	74.2	11.80	9.7	1,540	21
Kazakhstan	49	7.8	1.5	240	55
Libya	47	7.5	1.7	270	76
Nigeria	37	5.9	2.5	400	41
Qatar	25.41	4.040	1.1	170	63
China	20.35	3.235	4.1	650	14
United States	26.8	4.26	7.0	1,110	10
Angola	13.5	2.15	1.9	300	19
Algeria	13.42	2.134	1.7	270	22
Brazil	13.2	2.10	2.1	330	17
Total of top seventeen reserves	1,324	210.5	56.7	9,010	64

Notes:
1 Reserve to Production ratio (in years), calculated as reserves / annual production.

Part Two

Language Points

I. New Words

anticipate /æn'tɪsɪpeɪt/ *v*. to think likely to happen; expect 预期，期望

continuation /kənˌtɪnju'eɪʃn/ *n*. 1. the act of continuing 2. sth which continues from sth else 延续物，接续物

convention /kən'venʃn/ *n*. a formal agreement, esp. between countries on sth that is important to them all(尤指国际间的)公约；协定

exclusive /ɪk'sklu:sɪv/ *adj*. limited to one person, group, or organization; not shared with others 专用的，独家的

lobster /'lɒbstə(r)/ *n*. 龙虾

missile /'mɪsaɪl/ *n*. an explosive flying weapon with its own engine, which can be aimed at a distant object 导弹

mutual /'mju:tʃʊəl/ *n*. having or based on the same relationship of one towards the other 相互的，彼此的

negotiate /nɪ'gəʊʃɪeɪt/ *v*. to talk with another person or group in order to try to come to an agreement or settle an argument 谈判，协商

overt /'əʊvɜ:t/ *adj*. *fml*. (of beliefs or actions) public; not secret

press /pres/ *v*. to continue to try to gain acceptance of 坚持；竭力要求

privileged /'prɪvəlɪdʒd/ *adj*. (often *derog*.) having advantage because of wealth, social rank etc [常贬]有特权的

providing /prə'vaɪdɪŋ/ *conj*. if

tension /'tenʃn/ *n*. an anxious, untrusting, and perhaps dangerous condition in the relationship between people, countries etc(人与人，国家与国家等之间的)紧张关系，紧张局势

via /'vaɪə/ *prep*. 1. traveling or sent through (a place) on the way 取道，经由 2. by means of; using

II. Notes

1. ... getting out of hand. (Par. 1)—getting out of control
2. The media and international... a new Cold War. (Par. 1)—媒体和国际问题专家都认为，俄美之间争议最大的问题就是欧洲的导弹防御和科索沃最终地位问题。他们就"民主的标准"问题的互相指责，成为很多人预见新一轮冷战开始的背景。
3. But while this may well be... Denmark. (Par. 1)—但是，尽管现在

这种情况很可能是真的,俄美之间在不久的将来爆发愈加严峻的冲突的条件已经具备,其中还有加拿大、挪威和丹麦卷入。("this"指上句中的"the onset of a new Cold War"。)

the stage has been quietly set—preparations have been gradually made

4. ... Norway's reserves are good ... the world's energy future. (Par. 4)—挪威的石油储量还可以使用十年,英国北海石油储量维持的时间将不会超过5年。因此,虽然北极的石油储量大部分尚未开发,但是已经对未来世界的能源形式变得至关重要。

5. In 2001, Russia submitted documents ... beyond the 200 mile zone (Par. 8)—2001年,俄罗斯向联合国递交了关于大陆架边界划分问题的文件,试图将其海上边界延伸至200海里区域以外。

seeking to—trying to; making an attempt

6. The United States has been jealous of ... outside Russia's territory. (Par. 12)—俄罗斯企图扩大其在能源方面的优势地位,这使美国红了眼,因此千方百计地限制俄罗斯对出口路线及其领土之外的能源储备的控制。

7. For decades, international powers ... but no longer. (Par. 12)—几十年来,由于距离遥远和不适宜居住,国际强国对俄罗斯的北极地区没有提出所有权问题,但是现在情况不同了。

 a. press—continue to try to make sb accept a claim or statement that you are making

 b. claim—a right to sth.

8. It would certainly... energy resources. (Par. 13)—俄罗斯声称美国对俄的政策取决于美是否有得到俄能源的保障和特权,这一说法显然是对的。

driven by—inspired by

Part Three

Questions and Answers for Your Reference

1. What issues would the two heads of states discuss at the Lobster Summit at Kennebunkport?

 Putin and Bush spent most of their time at the "lobster summit" discussing how to prevent the growing tensions between their two countries caused by missile defense in Europe and the final status of Kosovo.

2. What's the real purpose of Russia's claim to the vast area of the ice-covered Arctic seabed?

The claim is not really about territory, but rather about the huge hydrocarbon reserves that are hidden on the seabed under the Arctic ice cap. Since these newly discovered energy reserves will play a crucial role in the global energy balance as the existing reserves of oil and gas will be depleted over the next 20 years. And the Russian government wants to secure Russia's long-term dominance over global energy markets.

3. Why are the Arctic reserves so attractive to Arctic-rim countries?

Because the whole world is in danger of depleting natural resources, and scientists estimate that the Arctic territory contains more than 10 billion tons of gas and oil deposits. That's why the Arctic reserves will be of such crucial importance to the world's energy future, though they are still largely unexplored.

4. Why doesn't International Law recognize Russia's right to the entire Arctic seabed north of the Russian coastline?

The U.S. government has been jealous of Russia's attempts to project its dominance in the energy sector and has sought to limit opportunities for Russia to control export routes and energy deposits outside Russia's territory. As a result, it refused to recognize Russia's claim to the entire Arctic seabed and blocked the anticipated Russian bid.

5. What is the viable scientific evidence supporting Russia's claim? What has boosted Russia's claim over the oil- and gas-rich triangle?

After a group of Russian geologists taking a six-week voyage to the Lomonosov Ridge, they claimed the ridge was linked to Russian Federation territory. Their research boosted Russia's claim over the oil- and gas-rich triangle. The latest findings are likely to prompt Russia to lodge another bid at the UN to secure its rights over the Arctic sea shelf.

6. What is the US government's attitude to the Russian claim? Why did President Bush urge the Senate to ratify the Law of the Sea Convention?

The US government refused to recognize Russia's claim and blocked the bid. President Bush urge the Senate to ratify the Law of the Sea Convention because, if the Senate ratified the Law of the Sea Convention, U.S. would have the same right to claim a 12 mile zone for territorial waters and a larger 200 mile economic zone in the Arctic territory.

7. Why did the author say that it promises to be a tough fight?

If the Russian government wants to get its Arctic claim approved, it should have a tough diplomatic fight with other countries, especially the U.S. government.

Words to Know

the Arctic ice cap, be slated to, contentious, continental platform, continental shelf, deplete, deposit, dominance, energy reserves, exploration, extract, the high seas, hydrocarbon, lobster summit, maritime, missile defense, negotiate, onset, get out of hand, privileged, project(*v.*), recrimination, ratify, seabed, sea shelf, square off, surmountable

Part Four

Supplementary Reading

Battle hots up for Arctic resources (From the *Financial Times*, July 4, 2011)

Lesson Twenty-two

Does Online Dating Makes It Harder to Find 'the One'?

Part One

Summary

　　婚恋网站的日益风靡不仅是对传统婚恋模式的颠覆，也引发了人们对其利弊影响的思考。尽管很多人认为它存在着诸多弊端，但它仍受到相当规模人群的追捧。然而，网络约会和传统约会方式同样不可预测，网络约会虽然使你能接触到更多在通常情况下结识不到的人，但你永远不知道事情会发生怎样的变化。

　　发表在美国著名学术杂志 *Psychological Science in the Public Interest* 的一项关于网络约会的研究，试图通过调查来揭示网络约会与传统约会的差异。该研究通过一系列数据说明，总的来说网络约会是一个不错的方式，对于那些因为社交接触面较窄而没有太多机会结交陌生人的单身者尤其如此。但网络约会的一些特性事实上不利于寻爱者寻找幸福的恋情，网络约会的效果并不比传统约会好。

　　网络约会的一大弊端与其主要特点之一"个人简介"有关。在现实世界中，"求偶之舞"需要数天甚至数周时间才能进入状态，人们在这段时间里了解彼此的好恶，磕磕绊绊中寻找共同语言。而在网上，这个过程被事先压缩成一份个人简介，导致单身者见面时少了神秘感和惊奇。个人简介虽然有助于人们迅速剔除明显不适合或不相配的潜在对象，但也冲淡了约会以及逐渐喜欢而建立恋爱关系的某些乐趣。同时，人们还可能不知不觉中因为错误的理由漏掉潜在的伴侣。简介上那个人并非真实的人，某人在网上的简介可能不符合你想要的类型，但你与他/她之间可能会产生的吸引力却无法预测也无法解释。在现实生活中，那种异性吸引力可能会自然而然地萌生。

　　如何解释约会网站的持久流行和成功呢？其中一个原因或许是借助于约会网站的单身男女是动机特别强的一群人。他们找伴侣并与之结婚的愿望使他们更有希望真的在网上找到或自认为找到了终身伴侣。然而，到网上寻找爱情的人有可能会遇到各种各样的雷区。令人安慰的是，网络约会也有不少成功的案例。如果拿婚恋网站与为你和"你的配偶"热心牵线的媒人或朋友们相比，它的优势就是可以为你找到大把大把的候选者。但你必须要清楚，个人简历跟你"般配"的人并非个个都是你的"意中人"。

The Author

Alice Park is a staff writer at TIME and covers health, medicine, nutrition and fitness. Since 1993, she has reported on the breaking frontiers of health and medicine in articles covering issues such as AIDS, anxiety and Alzheimer's disease.

Background Information

1. Online dating

Online dating or Internet dating is a dating system which allows individuals to make contact and communicate with each other over the Internet, usually with the objective of developing a personal, romantic, or sexual relationship. Online dating services usually provide unmoderated matchmaking over the Internet, through the use of personal computers or cell phones.

2. eHarmony, Perfect Match and Chemistry

eHarmony is an online dating website designed specifically to match single men and women for long-term relationships, launched on August, 2000, based in Santa Monica, California. It has members in more than 150 countries and maintains operations in the United States, Australia, Canada, the United Kingdom, and Brazil.

Perfect Match is an online dating and relationship service based in Seattle, Washington. The company reports "it is the best approach for adults seeking successful, lasting relationships." The company offers the Duet Total Compatibility System (Duet), which analyzes and takes into account each member's personality, values and ideals, life and love-style and preferences to identify and help them find the person right for them.

Chemistry. com is an online dating service. This online dating process begins with the Chemistry Profile, which helps you to get to know you on a deeper personal level, to predict which single men or women you'll have relationship and dating chemistry with. Today, more than 10 million people across the world have taken the Chemistry. com personality test. The website became notable after several ads portrayed online daters who were rejected by eHarmony, highlighting the fact that eHarmony will not match people with individuals of the same gender.

Part Two

Language Points

I. New Words

access /'ækses/ n. the way by which you can enter a building or a place 入口

artificial /ˌɑːtɪ'fɪʃl/ adj. made or produced to copy sth natural, not real 人造的；人工的

evolve /ɪ'vɒlv/ v. to change and develop gradually into different forms 进化；演变

extensive /ɪk'stensɪv/ adj. covering a large area, great in amount 广泛的；广阔的

illuminate /ɪ'luːmɪneɪt/ v. to make sth much clearer and easier to understand 阐释；说明

irrelevant /ɪ'reləvənt/ adj. not important or connected with a situation cf. relevant

navigate /'nævɪgeɪt/ v. to go all the way across or along 通过；穿越

notoriously /nəʊ'tɔːrɪəsli/ adv. well known for being bad 臭名昭著地；众所周知

realm /relm/ n. an aera of activity, interest or knowledge 领域

sheer /ʃɪə(r)/ adj. pure, large

spouse /spaʊs/ n. a husband or a wife 配偶

superficial /ˌsuːpə'fɪʃl/ adj. not studying or looking at sth carefully and only the most obvious thing 表面的；肤浅的

translate /træns'leɪt/ v. to change sth from one form into another 转化为……

undermine /ˌʌndə'maɪn/ v. to gradually make someone or something less strong or effective 破坏；削弱

II. Notes
1. he was full of himself... (Par. 2)—he only thought about himself... 自以为是
2. ...dating online gives you access to a lot more people... (Par. 3)—...online dating offers you a lot of opportunities to know many people
3. it takes days or even weeks for the mating dance to unfold (Par. 8)—"求偶之舞"需要数天甚至数周时间才能进入状态
4. stumble through the awkward... finding common ground (Par. 8)—在磕磕绊绊中……寻找共同语言
5. skip button (Par. 9)—"跳过"键
6. physical appeal (Par. 11)—physical attraction, consisting of beauty, sex appeal, self-presentation, social skills, liveliness and sexual competence 外在吸引力
7. take precedence over (Par. 11)—to be considered more important than sb or sth else and therefore come or be done before them

Part Three

Reference Answers to Questions

1. Is online matching a better way than traditional dating according to the writer's friend who met her husband online?

    No, she doesn't think so. She couldn't bear her husband when she first met him online. She thought he only thought about himself and rude during their first encounter. It definitely wasn't love at first sight. So, online dating is just as unpredictable as traditional face-to-face dating.

2. What benefits does online dating create?

    Online dating gives singles access to a lot more people than they'd ordinarily get to meet. It is good for those love-seekers who don't have many opportunities to meet people. Now it is the second most common way that couples get together, after meeting through friends.

3. Does online dating lead to more successful romantic relationships?

    No, because there are certain characteristics of online dating that actually work against love-seekers, making it no more effective

than traditional dating for a happy relationship. There is no reason to believe that online dating improves romantic outcomes. There is no evidence to that right now.
4. How to understand that one of the disadvantages of online dating is the profile?

Although online dating offers people great opportunity to know about a likely mate and the profile helps them quickly remove those who do not suit their tastes, after the love-seekers look at the profiles, they may feel less interested in the pleasure of dating and also they may unknowingly skip over potential mates for the wrong reasons.
5. Although there are many pitfalls occurring in the online dating websites, why does its popularity keep rising?

One reason is that singles who use online dating sites are a particularly motivated lot. Their desire to find a spouse and get married may make them more likely to actually find a life partner on the site. Another is that the matchmaking algorithms that power so many sites really can find them that person who is meant to be.
6. Why does online dating appeal so much to people delaying their marriage?

People delay their marriage either for financial or professional reasons, and they may move around to find a better job, so their social networks may not be so fixed and even disrupted. Thus the easily accessed digital dating will undoubtedly attract these people so much.

Words to Know

Account for, blind date, chemistry, dating site, formula, industry, inflated, online or internet dating/matchmaking, over time, physical appeal, profile, property, skip button, superficial, tenor, traditional, face to face dating, vested interest

Part Four

Supplementary Reading

Psychologists Highlight Pitfalls of Online Dating (From *http://edition.cnn.com*, Feb 6, 2012)

Lesson Twenty-three

Yawns: A generation of the young, rich and frugal

Part One

Summary

　　Yawns 这个词来源于英国伦敦的《星期日电讯报》,是年轻(young)、富有(wealth)、普通(normal)几个英文单词的首字母缩写。它的意思是"富有但过着普通日子的年轻人(young and wealth but normal)"。他们是社会上一批有高学历高背景的年轻富人阶层,但是他们的生活方式简朴、低调、重视环保、低碳。相对于出现在 20 世纪 80 年代崇尚享乐主义的雅皮士(Yuppies),YAWNS 更重视家庭生活和关心慈善。

　　上世纪 80 年代,年轻"雅皮士"的标志性动作就是抱着大砖头手机一通狂打,而电影《华尔街》中的台词"贪婪就是美德"更成为这一阶层的宣言;到了 90 年代,富人们通常狂饮香槟酒,开豪华跑车。不过,时代已经不同了,如今 Yawns 一族不再喜欢卖弄财富,他们为人低调,将更多钱投入慈善事业中。本文作者伊夫琳·尼弗斯指出,Yawns 一族是"生态社会发展意识在全球逐渐觉醒的重要元素。自 20 世纪 70 年代《小的是美好的》一书的出版以及生态运动被开展以来,目前的经济状况和地球状况都会促使人们在消费时,更多地考虑'买什么'和'如何以新方式消费'的问题。"

　　其中一个代表就是 2004 年从西雅图搬到印度的 32 岁的肖恩·布拉格斯维德。他当时为微软在当地设立研究中心,但当看到印度街头充斥着乞讨孩童时,他深有感触,于是辞去微软职位,创建了两个求职网站,在用人单位和失业人群之间架起了沟通的桥梁。另一名 Yawns 的代表是 37 岁的里克·怀布林。虽然他早已因在多家网络公司任职而成百万富翁,但他限制自己每年开支在 5 万美元内;他没有电视机;他的 MP3 音乐播放器才花了 20 美元;他只开低档车;购物只去农贸市场。

　　也许 Yawns 就是一种风尚。但是"自己花费节俭,捐出大量金钱"的 Yawns 一族,的确为环保及可持续发展做出了重要贡献。他们的生活方式表明了后物质主义时期的到来。

The Author

Evelyn Nieves is a freelance writer living in San Francisco. She has been a reporter for both the *New York Times* and the *Washington Post*.

Background Information

Post-materialism

In sociology, post-materialism is the transformation of individual values from materialist, physical and economic to new individual values of autonomy and self-expression. Post-materialism is a tool in developing an understanding of modern culture. It refers to materialism as a value-system relating to the desire for fulfillment of material needs (such as security, sustenance and shelter) and an emphasis on material luxuries in a consumerist society.

The sociological theory of *post-materialism* was developed in the 1970s by Ronald Inglehart. After extensive survey research, Inglehart postulated that the Western societies under the scope of his survey were undergoing transformation of individual values, switching from materialist values, emphasizing economic and physical security, to a new set of post-materialist values, which instead emphasized autonomy and self-expression. Inglehart argued that rising prosperity was gradually liberating the publics of advanced industrial societies from the stress of basic acquisitive or materialistic needs.

Observing that the younger people were much more likely to embrace post-materialist values, Inglehart speculated that this silent revolution was not merely a case of a life-cycle change, with people becoming more materialist as they aged, but a genuine example of intergenerational value change.

The so-called "Inglehart-index" has been included in several surveys (e.g. General Social Survey, World Values Survey, Eurobarometer, ALLBUS, Turning Points of the Life-Course). The time series in ALLBUS (German General Social Survey) is particularly comprehensive. From 1980 to 1990 the share of "pure post-materialists" increased from 13 to 31 percent in West Germany. After the economic and social stress caused by German reunification in 1990 it dropped to 23 percent in 1992 and stayed on that level afterwards (Terwey 2000: 155; ZA and ZUMA 2005). The ALLBUS sample from the less affluent population in East Germany show much lower portions of post-materialists (1991: 15%, 1992: 10%, 1998: 12%). International data from the 2000 World Values Survey show the highest percentage of post-materialists in Australia (35%) followed by Austria (30%), Canada (29%), Italy (28%), Argentina (25%), United States (25%), Sweden (22%), Netherlands (22%), Puerto Rico (22%) etc. (Inglehart et al. 2004: 384). In spite of some questions raised by these and other data, measurements of post-materialism have *prima facie* proven to be statistically important variables in many analyses.

As increasing post-materialism is based on the abundance of material possessions or resources, it should not be mixed indiscriminately with asceticism or general denial of consumption. In some way post-materialism may be criticized as super-materialism. German data show that there is a tendency towards this orientation among young people, in the economically rather secure public service, and in the managerial middle class (Pappi and Terwey 1982).

Recently, the issue of a "second generation of postmateralism" appearing on the scene of worldwide civil society, to a large extent conceived as their "positive ideological embodiment", has been brought up by cultural scientist Roland Benedikter in his seven-volume book series *Postmaterialismus* (2001—2005).

Part Two

Language Points

I. New Words

breed /briːd/ *n*. a kind or class of animal or plant, usu. developed under human influence

cause /kɔːz/ *n*. a principle, aim, or movement that is strongly defended or supported 事业;原则目标

charity /ˈtʃærəti/ *n*. an organization that helps people who are poor, sick, in difficulties etc 慈善机构

headquarter /'hed'kwɔːtə/ n. the central office or place where the people work who control a large organization, such as the people or army or a private company 司令部,大本营,指挥部

quit /kwɪt/ v. infml. to stop (doing sth) and leave

stuff /stʌf/ n. infml. things in a mass, esp. one's possessions or things needed to do sth (尤指个人的)东西,所有物；做某事所需要的东西

track /træk/ n. a course, esp. prepared for racing(比赛用的)跑道

II. Notes

1. Moved by young children begging on streets ... the people who need labor. (Par. 6)—When he saw young children begging on the streets, Blagsvedt decided to do something for them. So he quit his job in Microsoft and built two websites to help India's numerous potential workers find jobs.

2. The state of the economy ... ecology movement of the 1970s. (Par. 9)—目前的经济形式和地球的状况激发人们去思考买什么和怎么样消费。自从《小的就是美的》出版和20世纪70年代的生态运动以来,当时推崇的这种消费方式一直没有像现在这样受到青睐。

3. The upshot, he said, is that "a cultural ... the coming period." (Par. 11)—He said that the result is that the violent changes in cultural and demographic trends may urge us to live in an extreme form of post-materialism in the future, i.e. in a green and frugal way.

4. be sick to death (Par. 15)—be extremely sick
   to death—beyond all acceptable limits; extremely

5. dry their clothes on a line, (Par. 24)—dry their clothes in the sun not by machine

6. Marshland offsets his family's ... environmental groups online. (Par. 26)—Marshland makes up for the energy his family consumes by donating money to environmental organizations online.

7. ... have to rely on private transportation to get to and from work (Par. 29)—... have to drive their private cars to get to work and back

8. to keep it around and try to improve it (Par. 33)—to protect this world and try to improve it.

keep sth. around—*infml* keep sth. which may seem to have no value because it may be useful later 将……保留(以备日后使用)

Part Three

Questions and Answers for Your Reference

1. What are the main characteristics of Yawns?

    They are socially aware, concerned about the environment and given less to consuming than to giving money to charity.
2. What is their dream?

    Their dream is to change the world and save the planet.
3. What social-economic background has given rise to the consumer trends of Yawns?

    The fast development of the economy and the damage done to the natural environment of the planet have inspired them to consider what they buy and how they spend.
4. How do you understand "post-materialism?"

    It means that people are no longer interested in or desire material possessions, money etc. They pay more attention to spiritual matters than the material.
5. What does "freecycling" mean? What's the most important reason for freecycling?

    It means offering items for free. The most important reason for freecycling is environmental—reusing and recycling instead of helping create more waste.
6. What do you think of the Yawns' life style?

    (Open.)

Words to Know

acronym, anti-materialist, binge, carbon footprint, charity, chump change, disposable income, donate, dot-com, environmentally friendly, frugal, frugality, garage sale, grapple with, guilt trip, high-tech, hippie movement, hybrid car, offset, ostentation, pet (*adj.*), post-materialism, pro-materialist, spawn, sprout, startup, stock options, subset, upshot, the yuppie period

Part Four

Supplementary Reading

Millennials: The Me Me Me Generation (From *Time*, May. 20, 2013)

Lesson Twenty-four

Ahead-of-the-Curve Careers

Part One

Summary

随着社会的发展和科技的进步，人们的需求也在发生着变化。这篇刊登在《美国新闻与世界报道》的文章详细介绍了美国当今最时尚前沿的六种新的职业需求：(1)医疗保健。随着美国"婴儿潮"时期出生的人步入老年，对医疗保健的需求日益增长。(2)世界步入数字化时代。人们对网上购物和数字化娱乐产品的需求在增长，数字化信息也成了人们主要的信息来源。在这方面有两个最有前途的行业：数据分析师和模拟软件开发人员。(3)全球化趋势。由于经济的全球化，特别是亚洲的崛起，美国需要大量懂外语和具有跨文化交际技能的管理人才。同时，向美国移民的人数也在增加，因此具有各方面知识的移民专家也有很大的需求量。(4)基因图谱学的临床应用。基因图谱学进入临床应用阶段将为医学、心理学和教育学带来一场新的革命，这场革命的主力军将包括计算生物学家和行为遗传学佳。(5)保护环境。地球变暖的趋势给全世界的人们敲响了警钟，人们在保护环境方面的努力将创造大量就业机会，包括环境管理、检测以及技术人员在开发环保产品方面的工作。(6)反恐。"9·11"恐怖袭击之后，许多人认为美国将再次遭到恐怖分子的袭击，因此，美国加强了情报、安全和计算机安全方面的工作。

The Author

Martin Nathan Nemko (born June 30, 1950) is an American career coach, author, columnist, and radio host specializing in career/workplace issues and higher education reform. In 2011 — 2012, Dr. Nemko wrote The Big Idea column in *The Washington Post* and the Working it Out column in *The Atlantic*. He has written over 1,000 published articles including six years of columns in the *San Francisco Chronicle*. He writes weekly at AOL.com and at *USNews.com*, where as Contributing Editor, he created and directed its annual *Best Careers rankings*. He has written six books including in 2012, *How to Do Life: What they didn't teach you in school* and *What's the Big Idea? 39 Disruptive Proposals for a Better Society*. The *San Francisco Bay Guardian* named Nemko "The Bay Area's Best Career Coach." *U.S. News* described him as "job coach extraordinaire." In its summit on education, ABC-TV called him "The Ralph Nader of Education." He was selected by Toastmasters International as the non-member Northern California Speaker of the Year.

Background Information

1. U.S. healthcare system

Health care in the United States is provided by many distinct organizations. Health care facilities are largely owned and operated by private sectorbusinesses. 62% of the hospitals are non-profit, 20% are government owned, 18% are for-profit.

60—65% of healthcare provision and spending comes from programs such as Medicare, Medicaid, TRICARE, the Children's Health Insurance Program, and the Veterans Health Administration. Most of the population under 67 is insured by their or a family member's employer, some buy health insurance on their own, and the remainder are uninsured. Health insurance for public sector employees is primarily provided by the government.

The United States life expectancy of 78.4 years at birth, up from 75.2 years in 1990, ranks it 50th among 221 nations, and 27th out of the 34 industrialized OECD countries, down from 20th in 1990. Of 17 high-income countries studied by the National Institutes of Health in 2013, the United States had the highest or near-highest prevalence of infant mortality, heart and lung disease, sexually transmitted infections, adolescent pregnancies, injuries, homicides, and disability. Together, such issues place the U.S. at the bottom of the list for life expectancy. On average, a U.S. male can be expected to live almost four fewer years than those in the top-ranked country.

According to the World Health Organization (WHO), the United States spent more on health care per capita ($8,608), and more on health care as percentage of its GDP (17.9%), than any other nation in 2011. The Commonwealth Fund ranked the United States last in the quality of health care among similar countries, and notes U.S. care costs the most. In a 2013 Bloomberg ranking of nations with the most efficient health care systems, the United States ranks 46th among the 48 countries included in the study.

The U.S. Census Bureau reported that 49.9 million residents, 16.3% of the population, were uninsured in 2010 (up from 49.0 million residents, 16.1% of the population, in 2009). A 2004Institute of Medicine (IOM) report said: "The United States is among the few industrialized nations in the world that *does not guarantee access* to health care for its population." A 2004 OECD report said: "With the exception of Mexico, Turkey, and the United States, all OECD countries had achieved universal or near-universal (at least 98.4% insured) coverage of their populations by 1990." Recent evidence demonstrates that lack of health insurance causes some 45,000 to 48,000 unnecessary deaths every year in the United States. In 2007, 62.1% of filers for bankruptcies claimed high medical expenses. A 2013 study found that about 25% of all senior citizens declare bankruptcy due to medical expenses, and 43% are forced to mortgage or sell their primary residence.

On March 23, 2010, the Patient Protection and Affordable Care Act (PPACA) became law, providing for major changes in health insurance.

Intergovernmental Panel on Climate Change

The Intergovernmental Panel on Climate Change (IPCC) is a scientific intergovernmental body, set up at the request of member governments. It was first established in 1988 by two United Nations organizations, the World Meteorological Organization (WMO) and the United Nations Environment Programme (UNEP), and later endorsed by theUnited Nations General Assembly through Resolution 43/53. Its mission is to provide comprehensive scientific assessments of current scientific, technical and socio-economic information worldwide about the risk of climate change caused by human activity, its potential environmental and socio-economic consequences, and possible options for adapting to these consequences or mitigating the effects. It is chaired by Rajendra K. Pachauri.

Thousands of scientists and other experts contribute (on a voluntary basis, without payment from the IPCC) to writing and reviewing reports, which are reviewed by representatives from all the governments, with a Summary for Policymakers being subject to line-by-line approval by all participating governments. Typically this involves the governments of more than 120 countries.

The IPCC does not carry out its own original research, nor does it do the work of monitoring climate or related phenomena itself. A main activity of the IPCC is publishing special reports on topics relevant to the implementation of the United Nations Framework Convention on Climate Change (UNFCCC), an international treaty that acknowledges the possibility of harmful climate change. Implementation of the UNFCCC led eventually to the Kyoto Protocol. The IPCC bases its assessment mainly on peer reviewed and published scientific literature. Membership of the IPCC is open to all members of the WMO and UNEP.

The IPCC provides an internationally accepted authority on climate change, producing reports which have the agreement of leading climate scientists and the consensus of participating governments. It has provided authoritative policy advice with far-reaching implications for economics and lifestyles. Governments have been slow to implement the advice. The 2007 Nobel Peace Prize was shared, in two equal parts, between the IPCC and Al Gore.

Part Two

Language Points

I. New Words

advocate /'ædvəkeɪt/ v. to spread in favor of; support (an idea or plan), publicly 拥护,提倡,主张 n. 提倡者,拥护者,鼓吹者

dawn /dɔːn/ n. the beginning or first appearance of a new period, idea, feeling etc 开端,萌芽

deem /diːm/ v. fml. to think of sth. in a particular way; consider 认为,视为

diagnose /ˈdaɪəgnəʊz/ v. to discover the nature of (a disease or fault) by making a careful examination 诊断 **diagnosis** /ˌdaɪəgˈnəʊsɪs/ n. pl. diagnoses

implication /ˌɪmplɪˈkeɪʃn/ n. a possible later effect of an action, decision etc（行动、决定等）可能产生的影响

initiative /ɪˈnɪʃətɪv/ n. the first movement or action which starts sth happening 创始，发端；主动的行动

generate /ˈdʒenəreɪt/ v. fml. to cause (esp. feelings or ideas) to exist; produce [正式]使存在；引起，导致；招来

genius /ˈdʒiːnɪəs/ n. great and rare powers of thought, skill, or imagination 天才

longevity /lɒnˈdʒevətɪ/ n. 1. fml. long life [正式]长寿 2. tech length of life [术语]寿命

mushroom /ˈmʌʃrʊm/ v. to grow and develop fast

navigate /ˈnævɪgeɪt/ v. to direct the course of (a ship, plane, etc.) 给（船舶、飞机等）指引航向；导航

resistant /rɪˈzɪstənt/ adj. having or showing resistance 有抵抗力的，抵抗的

specialty /ˈspeʃəltɪ/ n. a special field of work or study 专业，专门研究，专长

view /vjuː/ v. to watch (esp. television) 观看（尤指电视）

II. Notes

1. The already overtaxed U. S. healthcare system ... in the next president's administration. (Par. 2)—由于婴儿潮出生的人们已经开始上了年纪、大量移民的涌入以及数以百万的没有保险的美国人将要纳入国家医疗规划，开支过大的美国医疗系统将不得不接受更多的病人。下一届总统任职期间有可能颁布新的医疗方案。

   take on—accept (work, responsibility etc) 接受（工作等）；承担（责任等）

2. Hospitals, insurers, and... healthcare system. (Par. 2)—Hospitals, insurers, and patient families will hire patient advocates to guide them in the complicated and ever tighter healthcare system.

3. On the prevention side... in an experiment. (Par. 2)—在预防方面，人们从原来请私人教练到现在请健康教练，因为他们意识到，如果吸烟、饮酒或承受巨大压力，即使多做一百个俯卧撑也不会对身体有帮助。

4. Quietly, companies are offshoring ... market research, for example.

(Par. 4)—以前认为十分依赖美国文化而不能外包的工作如研发和市场调查,慢慢地也开始外包。
5. So, immigration specialists of all types... the unprecedented in-migration. (Par. 4)—All types of immigration specialists majoring in marketing, education and criminal justice will be needed to deal with the unprecedented immigration.
6. Within a decade... retardation to genius. (Par. 5)—十年里,我们将弄清人类的方方面面是由哪些基因决定的:如性格方面是消沉还是狂暴,长寿还是短命,迟钝还是有天赋。
7. encourage those in which we'd delight (Par. 5)—encourage the predispositions which we like

  delight in—take great pleasure in (esp. sth unpleasant) 对……很喜欢,以……为乐(尤指不愉快的事情)
8. The expertconsensus is that the United Stated will again fall victim to a major terrorist attack. (Par. 7)—Most experts agree that the U.S. will be the aim of another major terrorist attack in the future.

Part Three

Questions and Answers for Your Reference

1. What are the causes of the growth in healthcare demand?
  They are the aging baby boomers, the influx of immigrants, and the millions of now uninsured Americans who would be covered under a national healthcare plan.
2. Why do patient families hire patient advocates?
  They hire patient advocates to navigate the labyrinthine and ever more parsimonious healthcare system.
3. What are the characteristics of a digitized world?
  People do most of their shopping on the Net. They obtain most of their entertainment digitally: Computer games are no longer just for teenage boys; billions are spent by people of all ages and both sexes. Increasingly, they get information from online publications, increasingly viewed on iPhones and BlackBerrys.
4. What effects will globalization have on the U.S. job market?
  It will create great demand for business development specialists,

helping U.S. companies create joint ventures with foreign firms. And offshoring managers are needed to oversee those collaborations as well as the growing number of offshored jobs. Conversely, large numbers of people from impoverished countries will immigrate to the United States. So, immigration specialists of all types will be needed to attempt to accommodate the unprecedented in-migration.

4. What clinical implications will genomics start to yield?

It will be less expensive to decode a person's genome, which, indicates whether a person is at increased risk of diseases. We will probably understand which genes predispose humans. And such discoveries will most likely give rise to ways to prevent or cure our dreaded predispositions and encourage those in which we'd delight.

5. What are the main elements that contribute to the creation of cutting-edge careers?

People's growing need for healthcare services, the development of science and technology, the development of our economy and society, and the need to protect our environment and to fight terrorism.

Words to Know

accommodate, ascendancy, baby boomers, booze, cutting-edge, diagnose, diagnosis, green careers, implication, impoverished, influx, initiative, joint venture, longevity, megatrend, mushroom, navigate, novelty, offshore, overtax, panel, simulation, specialty, take on, ubiquity, unsung hero, venture, viable, wellness

Part Four

Supplementary Reading

What the Hell is the Meaning of Life (http://www.martynemko.com Revised, June 1, 2013)

Lesson Twenty-Five

Model economies: The beauty business

Part One

Summary

　　模特行业一直对漂亮的年轻人颇有吸引力,它总是让人联想到高贵的气质和辉煌的场面。然而,跻身此行并非易事,真正能攀上顶峰者更是凤毛麟角。仅凭漂亮脸蛋和魔鬼身材及其吃苦耐劳的精神远远不够,模特行业也不像寻梦者想象的那么光鲜。

　　模特的职业生涯通常很短暂,且经纪公司抽成往往较多,模特实际拿到的薪水少得可怜。为了保持身材,大多模特都选择少进食,身体健康受到严重影响。不过这一行业正在慢慢发生变化,一些超级名模跻身高收入人群,受过良好教育的年轻女性纷纷进入行业,头脑聪明、举止端庄的模特成为经纪公司青睐的对象。模特的0号身材一直受到追捧,如今在全球化的风潮中,多数模特公司在世界范围内寻求形象更为健康的模特。模特的收入也出现了两级分化的趋势,名模给其代言产品带来巨大的利润,也让他们自己的收入剧增;而普通模特则只能忍受日趋下降的收入。全球化使更多新兴国家人才辈出,电视的发展也使得时装表演的利润日趋下降。毕竟模特那么多,而镜头就那么几个。

　　在时尚界,名气决定实力,面对如此竞争激烈的模特行业,如何站稳脚跟不仅由时尚大牌和艺术总监说了算,还要靠模特自身的智慧。有的名模被授权推出了自己的服装品牌,成功转行。时尚界瞬息万变,谁也琢磨不透下一个流行潮流会走向何方,谁也无法预测下一个超级名模会是谁。这也许正是这一职业的诱惑所在,难怪无数少女争相恐后地涌入这一行当。

　　本文是一篇述评,探讨了欧美模特行业近年来所产生的变化,主要关注了人才需求的变化以及模特行业全球化发展的趋势。该文分析了模特行业的现状,产生的原因以及未来的走向。文中虽然提到了模特经济状况,但避开了任何专业的经济学理论或术语,分析简洁明了。文中出现了大量专有名词,包括人名、地名、品牌名称、书名、电影名、电视节目名,可能会给不熟悉这个行业的读者带来障碍。这也正体现了报刊英语词汇的一大特点。作者举出了不少实例，并且提供了一些具体数据，报道还配有表格，力图全方位客观地展现模特行业的整体状况，体现了新闻报道用事实说话的特点。

Background Information

1. Different Types of Modelling

a. High Fashion Modelling

High Fashion Modeling is the modeling for famous fashion houses and designer, either at fashion shows or in publications. The pay rate is the highest among all modeling jobs. Of course, the advertisers' expectations also run high. To get this kind of job you must be experienced and known model with a proven track record for this type of modeling.

b. Runway Modelling

Runway Models works in Fashion Shows, where clothes designers present their upcoming designs or Fashion Shows, run by a store, mall, club etc. All runway models must meet special requirements and have measurements that fit an actual standard clothing size. Almost all modeling agencies works with Runway Models.

c. Editorial Modelling

Editorial Modeling is similar to High Fashion Modeling, except that the model works for a particular publication. The readers of that publication make up a target audience for the photographs taken. Images in the non-advertisement sections of the fashion magazines are good examples of this type of modeling. Even the pay rate is considerably low, Editorial modeling is a great way to open the door to High Fashion Modeling. （硬照模特，专指那些因为广告和杂志拍摄平面照片的专业模特。所谓硬照，是一种摄影术语，是指为广告和杂志拍的平面照。）

d. Clamour Modeling

There are no established physical requirements for Glamour Models, other than the model must be beautiful and sexy in the photographs. An elegant lady in an evening dress, the eye-catching face of a beautiful girl, a shapely woman in casual dress, swim-wear, or lingerie can all become subjects for glamour photography. Most of the nude photography also falls into this category. Pay rates can be very good for Glamour Modeling. Usually, the pay rate doubles for posing in lingerie or in the nude. Some Figure and Art Modeling, typically artistic nude photography, is also included in the Glamour Modeling category.

    e. Catalogue Modelling

While some Catalogue Modeling involves posing with products, most is done wearing store-brand clothes. Pay rates are considerably lower than for High Fashion Modeling. Look through some mail-order catalogs to get an idea of what is involved. Several years ago it was absolutely impossible to see the Top Models in any catalogue. But everything is changing. Even famous models are modeling for catalogues now.

    f. Specialty Modelling

There are numerous other Specialty Modeling opportunities.

Models (male and female) with beautiful hands have opportunities to display their hands demonstrating different products. For men, it could be masculine hand, or alternatively the more elegant, long-fingered hand. Women with well-proportioned feet are needed for shoe advertisements. Advertisements of stockings, pantyhose, and razors require women with nicely shaped legs. Hair products call for female and male models with good hair.

    g. Character Modelling

Some jobs require models with an everyday look, such as a truck driver, mechanic, grocery clerk, schoolteacher, cleaning person, appliance repair person, and so on. All models in television commercials are character models.

    h. Convention and Trade Show Modelling

These shows use many female models to demonstrate products, hand out leaflets or brochures, and answer questions.

    i. Commercial Print Modelling

When models are photographed to promote a product. Photographs can appear on buses, magazines, newspapers and billboards.

    j. Modelling in TV Commercials

TV Commercials offer a growing area of opportunities to models with some acting background. Many modeling agencies now include a TV Commercial Department. editorial models and catalogue models.

Part Two

Language Points

I. New Words

boyish /'bɔɪʃ/ *adj.* of or like a boy, esp. in appearance

campaign /kæm'peɪn/ *v.* to engage in an operation planned to achieve a certain goal

clutch /klʌtʃ/ *n.* a group; a bunch 一群；一束

commercial /kə'mɜːʃəl/ *n.* an advertisement on television or radio 在电视或无线电上的广告

courtesy /'kɜːtəsɪ/ *n.* willingness or generosity in providing something needed 恩惠，好心

distinctiveness /dɪ'stɪŋktɪvnɪs/ *n.* the status of being clearly making a person or thing as different from others 有特色，与众不同 distinctive *adj.*

distract /dɪ'strækt/ *v.* to cause to turn away from the original focus of attention or interest; divert 分散；使分心

disorder /dɪs'ɔːdə(r)/ *n.* an ailment that affects the function of mind or body

elite /eɪ'liːt/ *n.* a group that is of higher level or rank, e.g. professionally, socially, or in ability or that has a great deal of power or influence in relation to its size

foster /'fɒstə(r)/ *v.* to promote the growth and development of; cultivate 促进，培养

halve /hɑːv/ *v.* to lessen or reduce by half 减少至一半

lens /lenz/ *n.* 镜头，透镜，镜片

lucrative /'luːkrətɪv/ *adj.* producing wealth; profitable 获利的；产生财富的；有利润的

one-off /'wʌnˌɒf, -ˌɔːf/ *adj.* done of made only once 一次性的

play-fight *v.* fight for fun 打打闹闹

portray /pɔː'treɪ/ *v.* to depict or describe in words 用语言描绘或描述

prominent /'prɒmɪnənt/ *adj.* widely known; eminent 著名的

promote /prə'məʊt/ *v.* to attempt to sell or popularize by advertising or publicity 促销

propel /prə'pel/ *v.* to move, drive, or push forward

reign /reɪn/ *v.* to be predominant or prevalent 占统治地位或盛行的

shrink /ʃrɪŋk/ v. to (cause to) become smaller (as if) from the effect of heat or water

signify /ˈsɪgnɪfaɪ/ v. fml to be a sign of; represent; mean 表示,代表,象征

slim /slɪm/ adj. small in quantity or amount; meager 微小的,微薄的

II. Notes

1. models were showing up to photo-shoots hours late or drug-addled (Par. 6)—models were late for photo-shoots or became addicted to drugs.
2. America reigned supreme (Par. 7)—America absolutely dominated the field.
3. They never woke up for less than $10,000. (Par. 7)—You can have them work only when the payment is more than $10,000
4. shoot up (Par. 9)—to increase greatly and rapidly
5. lesser models (Par. 10)—less famous or renowned models
6. Too many faces are chasing too few lenses. (Par. 12)—Too many models are seeking the few jobs. (模特那么多,镜头就那么几个。)
7. not least (Par. 13)—especially, particularly
8. And agencies must find models… artistic directors. (Par. 16)—经纪公司还必须去寻找那些多多少少体现"时代潮流"的面孔,而什么是"时代潮流"则是由大品牌以及他们那些捉摸不透的艺术总监们说了算。
9. Ms Mears adds that the industry keeps models thin to "signify elite luxury distinctiveness". (Par. 19)—米尔斯女士补充说,这个行业让模特保持骨瘦如柴是为了"表明该行的精英层对服装与模特怎样搭配变得最为华丽有着与众不同的眼光"。
10. detain some prospective bookings in New York (Par. 21)—to prevent the reserved model from leaving for New York

Part Three

Reference Answers to Questions

1. What are the changes in the modeling business?

    a. More educated models are in the business. There has been a shift away from the "very young, impressionable models", who were popular in the past ten years, to "more aspirational young women". There is an appetite now for models to be intelligent, well-mannered and educated.

  b. International agencies now scout for talent in emerging economies instead of the US alone. In the 1990s they hired hordes of high-cheeked Slav teenagers. Now the hottest hunting-ground is Brazil, which produces Amazonian height and athletic looks. Size 0 is not as popular as before.

  c. Average models are making less money because the business is getting competitive. But supermodels can make a lot more by starting their own business.

2. What kind of models is preferred now by fashion houses?

  Fashion houses prefer intelligent, well-mannered and educated models because they don't show up late or take drug and they don't go doolally as often.

3. Why do models make less money?

  a. This is partly because the labor pool has globalised and therefore grown much bigger. International agencies now scout for talent in emerging economies. Although the industry has grown in the past decade, individual contracts have shrunk. Too many faces are chasing too few lenses.

  b. With the development of technology, television fees have fallen. The rate for fashion show have roughly halved in recent years.

4. What are the reasons for skinny models to be preferred by designers?

  Because designers think clothes look better when there is no distracting flesh beneath them. And the industry keeps models thin to "signify elite luxury distinctiveness"—to show something different from the normal women.

5. Who have more say in fashion business, supermodels or super-brands?

  Surely super-brands have more say in the business. Such famous brands as Gucci, Burberry and Marc Jacobs can require supermodels to attend or not attend the fashion shows at will.

Words to Know

antitrust case, Burberry, camaraderie, catwalk, Chanel, courtesy, cover-shoot, cultural icon, Dior, doughnut, economics of modeling, emerging economics, fashion house, financial crash, Gucci, have/get sth under one's belt, Hermes, impressionable, last year, mega-girls, one-off deal, obscurity, peanuts, Procter & Gamble, rags-to-riches, size 0, spring fashion week, stardom, superbrand, supermodel, Vivienne Westwood

Part Four

Supplementary Reading

Pots of promise (From http://fifty2ninety.com Aug 30, 2013)

Lesson Twenty-six

Nanospheres leave cancer no place to hide

Part One

Summary

癌症是目前威胁人类生命安全最大的顽症之一,癌症治疗也是世界性难题。即使在发达国家,癌症占总死亡原因也高达 20%。目前,癌症的临床治疗主要是通过手术、放疗、化疗等方法。幸运的是,科学家已经找到了治疗癌症的新希望,纳米技术有望在这一方面取得突破。纳米粒子可以发现肿瘤的位置,并发出热量迅速杀死癌细胞。这种疗法最大的优点就在于它能够"欺骗"人体免疫系统,不会对其展开攻击,从而大大提高了疗效,并能缓解患者因服药或化疗而产生的不适,因为它可以直接杀死癌细胞而不会损害到其周围的健康组织。纳米技术的发展为诸多癌症患者带来了福音,为人类最终战胜癌症带来了希望。

The Author

Celeste Biever is physical sciences news editor of *New Scientist*. She edits stories about physics, chemistry and mathematics and writes stories about AI, robots and the brain.

Background Information

1. nanometer

The nanometre or nanometer (American spelling) is a unit of length in the metric system, equal to one billionth of a metre. The name combines the prefix *nano-* (from the Ancient Greek νάνονς, *nanos*, "dwarf") with the parent unit name *metre* (from Greek μέτρον, *metron*, "unit of measurement"). It can be written in scientific notation as 1×10^{-9} m, in engineering notation as 1 E−9 m, and is simply 1 m / 1,000,000,000.

2. Nanotechnology

Nanotechnology (sometimes shortened to "nanotech") is the manipulation of matter on an atomic and molecular scale. The earliest, widespread description of nanotechnology referred to the particular technological goal of precisely manipulating atoms and molecules for fabrication of macroscale (宏观尺度的) products, also now referred to as molecular nanotechnology. A more generalized description of nanotechnology was subsequently established by the National Nanotechnology Initiative, which defines nanotechnology as the manipulation of matter with at least one dimension sized from 1 to 100 nanometers. This definition reflects the fact that quantum (量子的) mechanical effects are important at this quantum-realm scale, and so the definition shifted from a particular technological goal to a research category inclusive of all types of research and technologies that deal with the special properties of matter that occur below the given size threshold. It is therefore common to see the plural form "nanotechnologies" as well as "nanoscale technologies" to refer to the broad range of research and applications whose common trait is size. Because of the variety of potential applications (including industrial and military), governments have invested billions of dollars in nanotechnology research. Through its National Nanotechnology Initiative, the USA has invested 3.7 billion dollars. The European Union has invested 1.2 billion and Japan 750 million dollars.

Nanotechnology as defined by size is naturally very broad, including fields of science as diverse as surface science, organic chemistry, molecular biology, semiconductor physics, microfabrication, etc. The associated research and applications are equally diverse, ranging from extensions of conventional device physics to completely new approaches based upon molecular self-assembly, from developing new materials with dimensions on the nanoscale to direct control of matter on the atomic scale.

Scientists currently debate the future implications of nanotechnology. Nanotechnology may be able to create many new materials and devices with a vast range of applications, such as in medicine, electronics, biomaterials and energy production. On the other hand, nanotechnology raises many of the same issues as any new technology, including concerns about the toxicity (毒性) and environmental impact of nanomaterials, and their potential effects on global economics, as well as speculation about various doomsday scenarios. These concerns have led to a debate among advocacy groups and governments on whether special regulation of nanotechnology is warranted.

Part Two

Language Points

I. New Words
incorporate /ɪnˈkɔːpəreɪt/ v. to include sth. as part of a group, system, plan etc 把某物并入,包括;吸收
inject /ɪnˈdʒekt/ v. to part (liquid) into sb with a special needle 注射
leaky /ˈliːkɪ/ adj. letting things leak in or out 漏的,有漏洞的;有裂缝的
nanospectra /ɪnˈspektəz/ n. 纳米光谱
penetrate /ˈpenətreɪt/ v. to enter, pass, cut, or force a way (into or through) 穿透;渗入
reveal /rɪˈviːl/ v. to make known (sth previously secret or unknown)
vital (for) /ˈvaɪtl/ adj. 1. very necessary; of the greatest importance 2. necessary in order to stay alive 维持生命所必需的;生死攸关的

II. Notes
1. This extra stage can mean multiple hospital visits and more drugs for the patient. (Par. 4)—In order to find all the tumour sites, patients have to go to hospital many times and take more medicine.
2. That means any cancer sites... be zapped with the laser. (Par. 5)—那就意味着,任何癌症病灶在低强度红外线照射下都会变亮,因而很容易用激光消除掉。
   light up—to make or become bright with light or color
   infrared—红外线
3. the imaging stage (Par. 6)—造影阶段

4. an imaging agent (Par. 7)—a thing that works to produce an image

Part Three

Questions and Answers for Your Reference

1. In the author's view, can gold-coated glass nanoshells be used to cure cancer? How can they?

    Yes, they can, though they are still trying various experiments on mice. The nanoshells can expose the sites of tumours and then kill them with heat.

2. Which of them are better for the treatment of cancer—nanoparticles or drugs? Why?

    Particles are better because patients can recover faster and suffer less side effects during their treatment.

3. What does plasmon resonance produce, and can it serve the purpose of destroying cancer cells?

    Plasmon resonance can create heat. Yes. The heat can destroy all the nearby cancer cells.

4. What purpose do MRI and CT serve in the treatment of some diseases before nanoshells can be used to cure cancer?

    If doctors want to find the sites of some diseases like tumours before treatment, they must rely on MRI or CT to examine patients closely.

5. Do the different sizes of nanospheres work differently? Why?

    Yes. Smaller ones can change more radiation into heat, which make them better at zapping cancers, but larger ones emit more radiation, which is vital for the imaging stage. Therefore, they have different functions.

6. What animal and technique did the West's team use for its experiment? Did its experiment succeed?

    The team used mice with colon carcinoma tumours into whomthey injected the new particles, and used optical coherence tomography to test the particles' ability to act as an imaging agent. Yes, it did. 80% of the mice treated lived longer than the control ones.

Words to Know

accumulate, bounce back, convert, delicate, illuminate, imaging, incorporate, infrared, inject, intact, intensity, leaky, light up, nanosphere, optical, particle, resonance, scan, scatter, sphere, tissue, toxic, tumour, zap

Part Four

Supplementary Reading

10 common scientific misconceptions (From *The Christian Science Monitor*)

Lesson Twenty-seven

Why Bilinguals Are Smarter

Part One

Summary

　　在日益全球化的世界里,懂两种语言的人显然比只会一种语言的人更有优势。近年来,科学家们通过实验发现,通双语不仅仅能够使你和更多的人进行交流,还能使你更聪明。懂双语对大脑有着深刻的影响,激发大脑潜力,改善认知能力,甚至有助于防止老年痴呆。

　　2004年,心理学家艾伦·拜厄利斯托克和米歇尔·马丁瑞对学习双语的学龄前儿童和只会讲母语的同龄儿童进行对比研究,运用著名的斯特鲁测验(Stroop Test)得出结论,学习双语的孩子对大脑中的行为控制系统运用自如,在智力方面优势突出。研究证明,懂双语者大脑中有两种语言系统,即便他们在某个时间只使用一种语言,两种语言系统都是活跃的,这就造成了其中一种语言系统会压抑另一种语言系统的现象,而两种同时作用的语言系统能够提高人的认知能力。正是这种现象使通双语者在语言系统的长期受压抑中得到训练,使他们大脑中的认知活动区域得到完善,帮助他们在不同的环境下集中注意力,在处理信息时更加专注。

　　西班牙庞培法布拉大学的阿尔伯特·科斯塔认为,双语者与单语者的最根本区别是对环境的监测程度能力不同。"双语者需要不断地在两种语言之间进行转换,这就要求双语者必须随时观察环境的变化,这和在开车时需要随时观察周围情况是一个道理。"无疑,懂双语者在监测环境方面的能力相对强大。在一项对德意双语者和意大利单语者监测事物的对比研究中,科斯塔及其同事们发现,接受测试的双语者任务完成得更好,而且大脑用于监测事物的区域活动量更小,表明他们完成任务的效率更高。

　　2009年,意大利国际高等研究院的艾格尼丝·科瓦克斯主导了一项研究,将双语环境中成长的7个月幼儿与和单语环境下成长的幼儿进行对比测试。在最初的几组实验中,研究人员提示幼儿在屏幕的一端将闪现出一个木偶,两组幼儿都关注到了预期出现的木偶。但在接下来的几组试验中,当木偶出现在屏幕的另一端时,双语环境中成长的幼儿能够很快地转移他们的预期目光,而单语环境下的孩子则没有这样的动作。

双语效应同样影响着人们的晚年。最近,在加州大学圣地亚哥分校的神经心理学家塔玛·高兰的领导下,科学家们对44位使用西班牙语和英语两种语言者进行了调查,发现双语能够减少老年痴呆症的发作。双语的水平越高,发病年龄就越晚。

从另一方面说,语言是文化的载体,能运用两种或更多语言者必将更多了解异国风情和世事的发展,思维更活跃,知识面更广。在全球化时代,这种人才不可或缺。

The Author

Yudhijit has been a staff writer(本报或本刊撰稿者) at *Science*s since 2003. He has written stories on different topics related to research and policy, such as the fight over teaching evolution in U.S. classrooms and the neuroscience of time perception, and has profiled scientists with different interests and backgrounds, such as an astrophysicist(天体物理学家) who discovered dark energy and a fisherman-scientist who is working to protect fisheries in the Gulf of Maine. Yudhijit now spends most of his time covering astronomy, along with science and security and a few other areas of science policy. Yudhijit spent the first 26 years of his life in India, receiving an undergraduate degree in chemical engineering from the Indian Institute of Technology, Bombay. He has a master's degree in journalism from Ohio State University in Columbus, and nothing to show for a semester's worth of classes as a Ph. D. student in the history and philosophy of science at the University of Chicago, which he left to join *Science*. His work has appeared in *The New York Times*, *The Atlantic*, *The New York Times Magazine*, *Time*, *Wired*, and *Discover*.

Background Information

1. cognitive skill

Cognitive skill/ability/functioning is a term referring to a human's ability to process thoughts that should not deplete(衰竭) on a large scale in healthy individuals. Cognition mainly refers to things like memory, the ability to learn new information, speech, and the understanding of written material. The brain is usually capable of learning new skills in the aforementioned areas, typically in early childhood, and of developing personal thoughts and beliefs about the world. Old age and disease may affect cognitive function, causing memory loss and trouble thinking of the right words while speaking or writing ("drawing a blank"). Multiple sclerosis (MS)（硬化症）, for example, can eventually cause memory loss, an inability to grasp new concepts or information, and depleted verbal fluency. Not all with the condition will experience this side effect, and most will retain their general intellect and the ability.

Humans generally have a capacity for cognitive function once born, so almost every person is capable of learning or remembering. However, this is tested using tests like the IQ test, although these have issues with accuracy and completeness. In these tests, the patient will be asked a series of questions or to perform tasks, with each measuring a cognitive skill, such as level of consciousness, memory, awareness, problem-solving, motor skills, analytical abilities, or other similar concepts. Early childhood is when most people are best able to absorb and use new information. In this period, children learn new words, concepts, and various methods to express themselves.

Part Two

Language Points

I. New Words

demanding /dɪˈmɑːndɪŋ/ *adj*. calling for intensive effort or attention. 要求高的

executive /ɪɡˈzekjətɪv/ *n*. a person or group of persons having administrative or supervisory authority in an organization 行政

fundamental /ˌfʌndəˈmentl/ *adj*. serving as, or being an essential part of, a foundation or basis; basic; underlying: fundamental principles; the fundamental structure

heighten /ˈhaɪtn/ *v*. to make high or higher; to raise

inadequate /ɪnˈædɪkwət/ *adj*. not good enough; not enough

monitor /ˈmɒnɪtə(r)/ *v*. to watch or check sth over a period of time in order to see how it develops 监视;检查;跟踪调查

onset /ˈɒnset/ *v*. the beginning of sth, esp. sth unpleasant 开端;发生

primarily /praɪˈmerəli/ *adv.* essentially; mostly; chiefly; principally
hinder /ˈhɪndə(r)/ *v.* to make it difficult to do and to happen 阻碍
initial /ɪˈnɪʃl/ *adj.* happening at the beginning; first
intellectual /ˌɪntəˈlektʃuəl/ *adj.* connected with or using a person's ability to think in a logical way and understandings 智力的;脑力的
peer /pɪə(r)/ *n.* people of the same age 同龄人
preschooler /ˌpriːˈskuːlə/ *n.* children in preschool.
proficiency /prəˈfɪʃnsi/ *n.* a high standard of ability and skill 熟练;精通 proficient *adj.*
profound /prəˈfaʊnd/ *adj.* very deep; felt or experienced very strongly
puppet /ˈpʌpɪt/ *n.* a model of a person or an animal that can be made to move. 木偶
remarkable /rɪˈmɑːkəbl/ *adj.* unusual or surprising in a way that causes people to take notice.
resistant /rɪˈzɪstənt/ *adj.* not affected by sth 抵抗的;有抵抗力的
symptom /ˈsɪmptəm/ *n.* a change in your body or mind that shows you are not healthy 症状
thread /red/ *v.* to join small objects onto a string or thread by pushing the string through them 将……穿/串起来

II. Notes

1. But this interference, researchers are finding out, isn't so much a handicap as a blessing in disguise. It forces the brain to resolve internal conflict, giving the mind a workout that strengthens its cognitive muscles. (Par. 3)——如今,研究人员发现,这种干扰作用并非是一种不利的障碍,反而是一件因祸得福的事情,它强迫大脑去解决内部冲突,从而让思维得到更多的锻炼,增强人的认知能力。

2. so-called executive function—a command system that directs the attention processes that we use for planning, solving problems and performing various other mentally demanding tasks. (Par. 6)——所谓执行功能——即大脑的指挥系统,在我们制定计划、解决问题和完成其他各种思维任务时,它一直指挥着我们的注意力。

3. the bilingual advantage stemmed primarily from the ability for inhibition... (Par. 7)——双语的优势最初源于一种抑制的能力……
   stem from—to originate from

4. threading a line through an ascending series of numbers scattered randomly on a page. (Par. 7)——将一系列随机散布于纸上的数字按数

值大小的顺序串联起来。
5. The bilingual experience appears to influence the brain from infancy to old age (and there is reason to believe that it may also apply to those who learn a second language later in life). (Par. 9)—从婴儿时期到老年,双语经历似乎一直都会影响着我们大脑(我们有理由相信这也适用于那些后天学习第二语言的人)。

Part three

Reference Answers to Questions

1. What practical benefits can you get by being bilingual except conversing with various people?

    Being bilingual can make us smart and have a profound effect on our brain, improving cognitive skills not related tolanguage and even shielding against dementia in old age.

2. Some researchers claim that bilingualism can be interference, but in what way does the interference influence our brain system?

    The interference forces the brain to resolve internal conflict, giving the mind a workout that strengthens its cognitive muscles.

3. According toa study in 2004, bilingual experience improves the brain's executive function that directs the attention processes we can use for difficult tasks, what do the processes refer to?

    These processes include ignoring distractions to stay focused, switching attention willfully from one thing to another and holding information in mind.

4. What is the major difference between bilinguals and monolinguals?

    Bilinguals have to switch languages quite often, so they are inclined to have a strong ability to monitor the environment. Their mind is more sensitive than monolinguals.

5. How bilingualism affect people in their old age?

    People in their old age with bilingualism will be more resistant to the onset of dementia and othersymptoms of Alzheimer's disease: the higher the degree of bilingualism, the later the age of onset.

Words to Know

Alzheimer's disease, bilingual, bilingualism, cognitive skill/ability/functioning/muscle, dementia, inhibition, monolingual, neuropsychologist, preschool, proficiency, random

Part Four

Supplementary Reading

An Infant's Refined Tongue (From *http://news.sciencemag.org* February 18, 2011)

Lesson Twenty-eight

Basketball: The incredible story of Jeremy Lin, the new superstar of the NBA

Part One

Summary

林书豪是美国职业篮球联赛(NBA)中第一个美籍华裔球员。他有篮球天赋,头脑聪明,技术全面,身体条件也不错,但在非洲裔和白种人球星"黑白双煞"占据绝对统治地位的NBA世界里,黄皮肤的林书豪就像童话中的"灰姑娘",起初很难得到应有的重视。种族偏见、华裔身份推迟了他展示才能的机会。高中毕业时,他没有拿到美国大学体育总会的一级篮球奖学金;大学毕业后,这位哈佛大学的篮球明星又在2010年NBA选秀中落选。金州勇士队虽然与他签约,签下的却是一个无保障的合同,将他"定义"为随时可以转会的自由球员。随后,他又两次经历过被NBA球队裁员的痛苦。2012年2月,他终于迎来了一展身手的机会,纽约尼克斯队在打入季后赛无望的情况下,教练突发奇想,让替补席上处于第三次被裁员边缘的控球后卫林书豪上场。他如猛虎下山,锐不可挡,在两周之内带领球队取得六战全胜的记录。这位不起眼的华裔球员,凭借其精湛的球技在短时间内震惊四座,体坛为之侧目,世人更为之震惊。他横空出世的传奇故事让世人认识到,华裔球员也有成为超级球星的潜质。这位多才多艺的球员向NBA世界证明了自己的实力,盼望他能笑到最后。

Background Information

1. Jeremy Lin

Jeremy Lin is an American professional basketball player for the National Basketball Association (NBA), one of the few Asian Americans in NBA history, and the first American of Chinese or Taiwanese descent to play in the league. Lin was born in 1988 in Los

Angeles and grew up near San Francisco. His parents had moved to the US from Taiwan in the mid-1970s. After receiving no athletic scholarship offers out of high school and being undrafted out of Harvard University, Lin reached a partially guaranteed contract deal in 2010 with his hometown Golden State Warriors. He seldom played in his rookie (新手) season and was assigned to the NBA Development League (NBA 发展联盟,简称 D-League) three times. He was released by the Warriors and the Rockets the following preseason before joining the New York Knicks early in the 2011—12 season. He continued to play sparingly and again spent time in the D-League. In February 2012, he unexpectedly led a winning streak(连胜) by New York Knicks while being promoted to the starting lineup(首发阵容), which generated a global following known as "Linsanity." In the summer of 2012, Lin signed a three-year contract with the Rockets.

2. NBA

The National Basketball Association, the pre-eminent men's professional basketball league and one of the Big Four major sports leagues in North America. With thirty franchised (加盟的) member clubs (29 in the United States and 1 in Canada), the NBA is widely considered to be the premier men's professional basketball league in the world. It is an active member of USA Basketball (USAB,美国篮球联合会), which is recognized by FIBA (also known as the International Basketball Federation) as the national governing body for basketball in the United States. The NBA is one of the four major North American professional sports leagues. NBA players are the world's best paid sportsmen, by average annual salary per player. The league was founded in New York City on June 6, 1946, as the Basketball Association of America (BAA).

3. Division I(D-I)

The highest level of intercollegiate athletics sanctioned(制裁) by the National Collegiate Athletic Association (NCAA 美国大学体育总会) in the United States. D-I schools include the major collegiate athletic powers, with larger budgets, more elaborate facilities, and more athletic scholarships than Divisions II and III as well as many smaller schools committed to the highest level of intercollegiate competition.

Part Two

Language Points

I. New Words

assist /ə'sɪst/ *n*. (sports) the act of enabling another player to make a good play（篮球）助攻

cut /kʌt/ *v*. to discharge from a group 裁员

descent /dɪ'sent/ *n*. a person's family background such as his or her nationality or social status 血统

foreseeable /fɔː'siːəbl/ *adj*. knowing that it will happen or that it can happen 可以预见的

minimal /'mɪnɪməl/ *adj*. very small in quantity, value, or degree 极少的，最小的

obscure /əb'skjʊə(r)/ *adj*. unknown, unclear 不清楚的，模糊的

recruit /rɪ'kruːt/ *v*. to find new people to work in a team, do a work or join the army etc. 招募

release /rɪ'liːs/ *n*. the termination of someone's employment (leaving them free to depart) 解约（根据上下文此处意为林成为自由身，可自由交换了。）这里与本文的 cut 义同。release *v*.

span /spæn/ *n*. the complete duration of sth. 期间

stun /stʌn/ *v*. to surprise sb. so much that they do not react immediately （使）大吃一惊

surpass /sə'pɑːs/ *v*. to be better than

third-string *adj*. third-rate 三流的

tweet /twiːt/ *v*. to make micro blog on Twitter （在"推特"网站）发微博

II. Notes

1. He was the last player ... this season. (Par. 4)—他曾是尼克斯队替补席末端的球员，在本赛季面临第三次被裁员危险的三流控球后卫。

   on the verge of—to be about to do sth 处于……边缘

2. After receiving ... in all of sports. (Par. 6)—林书豪高中毕业时没有拿到美国大学体育总会的一级篮球奖学金，在 NBA 选秀中也落选了，后来又曾经被两支 NBA 球队裁掉，但现在他是所有体育赛事中最知名的运动员之一。

3. But in a sport... to show off his talent. (Par. 7)—然而毫无疑问，在 NBA 这一大多数球星都是非洲裔美国人或者白人的篮球赛事中，种

族的偏见推迟了林书豪展示才华的机会。

show off—to bring forward

4. paved an obscure path (Par. 9)—made it difficult for him to pursue his career

5. Harvard—Harvard University(哈佛大学)

6. "…gets you offers,…"—此处 offers 为直接宾语,you 为间接宾语,等于…get offers for you.（给你机会）

7. "I think … treated differently."(Par. 12) 此句用虚拟语气,表示他并没有受到这种对待。

8. "I think if I were a different race, I would've been treated differently."此句用虚拟语气,表示他并没有受到这种对待。

9. But excelling at Harvard … NBA scouts. (Par. 13)—Though Lin starred excellently in the basketball team at Harvard, his performance did not attract the attention of NBA scouts,

10. … that has now awarded him the chance to start for the foreseeable future. (Par. 14)"that"为关系代词,引导定语从句,修饰前文中的 performance。

11. … Daryl Morey tweeted on 9 February (Par 15)—…Daryl Morey released a micro blog on Twitter on 9 February

12. His pure basketball talents … more opportunities to play last season. (Par 17)—Now sports experts around the world are praising his pure basketball talents, which should have earned him a Division I scholarship, a draft pick in the NBA and more opportunities to play in the last season. But he had not received any opportunities before.

draft pick—选秀 A draft is a system in which the exclusive rights to new players are distributed among professional teams. In a draft, teams take turns selecting from a pool of eligible(合格的) players. When a team selects a player, the team receives exclusive rights to sign that player to a contract, and no other team in the league may sign the player.

Part Three

Reference Answers to Questions

1. How does Jeremy Lin become Cinderrella or Lin-derella?

Just two weeks ago, Jeremy Lin was not a household name. He was the last player on the Knicks bench and a third-string point guard on the verge of being cut, but now he has made NBA history by scoring 136 points in his first five career starts thus become very famous.
2. What has Lin changed in two weeks? What has unchanged?

   Jeremy Lin was from an unknown basketball player two weeks ago, now it has become a household name. But he is still the same, versatile basketball player as he has always been.
3. How does racial stereotyping affect Lin?

   In high school, Lin failed to receive a single scholarship offer from Division I collegiate basketball programs across America. He went undrafted by NBA in 2010, received minimal playing time in the Golden State Warriors. He had hardly received opportunities to show his basketball talent those days.
4. What does Jeremy mean when Houston Rockets G. M. Daryl Morey tweeted "Anyone who says they knew misleading U"?

   In his micro blog, Daryl Morey implied the meaning that he shouldn't believe other persons' words.
5. Do you think Lin breaks the stereotype? Why?

   Yes, he breaksthe stereotype. He has done something that will forever change the landscape of not only Asian Americans in the NBA, but racial stereotyping in all of sports, for his excellent performance.

Words to Know

   free agent, assist, break the stereotype, descent, on the bench, point guard, racial stereotyping, rebound, recruit, release, have the last laugh, scout, steal, the NBA draft, (first/second-) third-string, tweet

Part Four

Supplementary Reading

   Just Lin, Baby! 10 Lessons Jeremy Lin Can Teach Us Before We Go To Work Monday Morning (From *Forbes*, Feb. 2, 2012)

Lesson Twenty-nine

He's Back All Right, Now with a Memoir

Part One

Summary

施瓦辛格的人生无论怎么说都堪称传奇,他一路走来,一路风光无限。1947年出生于奥地利的一个警察家庭,从少年时期起就志存高远,喜欢冒险和品味大大小小的胜利。1968年,这位已经在健美运动领域取得不凡成就的21岁奥地利小子来到美国,从健美界起步开始了他追逐美国梦的奋斗。他获得了空前的成功,攀上健美运动的巅峰。接着,在没有接受过专门的表演训练的情况下,半路出家闯入好莱坞,历经摸爬滚打,在电影银幕上跻身于主流影星之列,在一系列动作片中塑造了一个又一个超级"硬汉"的银幕形象,成为美国一个最受欢迎的电影明星,国际影坛娱乐片领域里人人皆知的"硬汉"巨星。然而,施瓦辛格是一个永不止步的"硬汉",好莱坞的辉煌成就并没有让他满足。2003年,他开始从政,出任加州州长达7年之久。

从健美明星到电影演员又到政治家,施瓦辛格以一个个漂亮的转身,完成了一次又一次成功的转型。在个人生活方面,施瓦辛格也是活得有声有色。他娶了肯尼迪总统的外甥女玛丽亚·施莱弗,与肯尼迪家族联姻,使他的传奇人生又增添了几分色彩。他也有过多段婚外情,甚至与管家生了一个私生子,最终导致与施莱弗的婚姻破裂。

本文是一篇书评,就施瓦辛格的名人效应而言,足以引起读者的强烈兴趣。作者在报道的一开头就用施瓦辛格接受采访的几笔定格了施瓦辛格自信执拗的形象,然后把他的职业生涯、政治生涯和家庭生活状况穿插在书评当中做了评论性介绍。很明显作者对于施瓦辛格本人不乏负面看法,措辞略带有嘲讽,比如 scandalous, puffy, master conniver, atypically keeps the crowing minimal 等,甚至用施瓦辛格出演的同名电影中的台词来影射他本人是"a thief, a reaver, a slayer"等,就连施瓦辛格在自传中总结的人生准则也被评价为 big on denial, not-great, borderline helpful,颠覆了施瓦辛格在很多人眼中美国梦典范的形象。

而在语言风格上,句式简洁,较口语化,大量运用了通俗易懂的合成词和复合词。

The Author

Janet Maslin, (1949—) an American journalist, best known as a film and literary critic for *The New York Times*. She was the long-time film critic for *The New York Times*, serving from 1977—1999.

Background Information

1. Arnold Schwarzenegger 阿诺德·施瓦辛格

Arnold Alois Schwarzenegger (1947 —) is an Austrian and American former professional bodybuilder, actor, businessman, investor, and politician. Schwarzenegger served two terms as the 38th Governor of California from 2003 until 2011. Schwarzenegger was born in Austria in 1947. His father was a local police chief. He grew up in a Roman Catholic family who attended Mass(弥撒) every Sunday. He won the Mr. Universe (环球先生:世界业余健美大赛冠军) title at age 20 and went on to win the Mr. Olympia contest(奥林匹亚先生健美大赛) seven times. Schwarzenegger has remained a prominent presence in bodybuilding and has written many books and articles on the sport. Schwarzenegger moved from bodybuilding into acting in 1970's and gained worldwide fame as a Hollywood action film icon in 1980's.

As a Republican, he was first elected on October 7, 2003, in a special recall election(罢免选举) to replace then-Governor Gray Davis. Schwarzenegger was sworn in on November 17, 2003, to serve the remainder of Davis's term. Schwarzenegger was then re-elected in California's 2006 gubernatorial(州长的) election, to serve a full term as governor. He was sworn in for his second term on January 5, 2007. In 2011, Schwarzenegger completed his second term as governor, and it was announced that he had separated from Maria Shriver, his wife for the last 25 years, and a member of the influential Kennedy family, as a niece of the late Democrat US President John F. Kennedy.

Schwarzenegger has had a highly successful business career. Following his move to the United States, Schwarzenegger became a "prolific goal setter" and would write his objectives at the start of the year on index cards, like starting a mail order business or buying a new car-and succeed in doing so. By the age of 30, Schwarzenegger was a millionaire, well before his career inHollywood. His financial independence came from his success as a budding entrepreneur with a series of successful business ventures and investments including bricklaying business, real estate investing, restaurant and planet Hollywood investment.

Schwarzenegger's selected notable roles:

- 1970: *Hercules in New York* as Hercules; 1973: *The Long Goodbye* as Hood in Augustine's office; 1974: *Happy Anniversary and Goodbye* as Rico; 1976: *Stay Hungry* as Joe Santo; 1977: *Pumping Iron* as Himself; 1979: *The Villain* as Handsome Stranger; 1979: *Scavenger Hunt* as Lars; 1980: *The Jayne Mansfield Story* as Mickey Hargitay; 1981: *Conan the Barbarian* as Conan; 1984: *Conan the Destroyer* as Conan; 1984: *The Terminator* as The Terminator/T-800; 1985: *Red Sonja* as Kalidor; 1985: *Commando* as John Matrix; 1986: *Raw Deal* as Mark Kaminsky, aka Joseph P. Brenner; 1987: *Predator* as Major Alan "Dutch" Schaeffer; 1987: *The Running Man* as Ben Richards; 1988: *Red Heat* as Captain Ivan Danko; 1988: *Twins* as Julius Benedict; 1990: *Total Recall* as Douglas Quaid/Hauser; 1990: *Kindergarten Cop* as Detective John Kimble; 1991: *Terminator 2: Judgment Day* as The Terminator/T-800; 1993: *Last Action Hero* as Jack Slater / Himself; 1993: *Dave* as Cameo; 1994: *True Lies* as Harry Tasker; 1994: *Junior* as Dr. Alex Hesse; 1996: *Eraser* as U. S. Marshal John "The Eraser" Kruger; 1996: *Jingle All the Way* as Howard Langston; 1997: *Batman and Robin* as Mr. Freeze; 1999: *End of Days* as Jericho Cane; 2000: *The 6th Day* as Adam Gibson/Adam Gibson Clone; 2001: *Dr. Dolittle 2* as White Wolf; 2001: *Collateral Damage* as Gordy Brewer; 2003: *Terminator 3: Rise of the Machines* as The Terminator/T-800; 2003: *The Rundown* as Cameo; 2004: *Around the World in 80 Days* as Prince Hapi; 2010: *The Expendables* as Trench; 2012: *The Expendables 2* as Trench; 2013: *The Last*

Stand as Sheriff Ray Owens; 2013: *Escape Plan* as Rottmayer; 2014: *Sabotage* as John "Breacher" Wharton; 2014: *The Expendables* 3 as Trench Mauser

Part Two

Language Points

I. New Words

buddy /'bʌdɪ/ *n.* friend
commission /kə'mɪʃn/ *v.* to place an order for 委托做某事
cultivate /'kʌltɪveɪt/ *v.* to develop a friendship with
enthusiastic /ɪn,θjuːzɪ'æstɪk/ *adj.* showing how much you like or enjoy sth the way that you behave and talk 热心的; 热情的
guesthouse /'gesthaʊs/ *n.* a private house where visitors can stay and have meals for payment, a small hotel 宾馆, 小旅馆
helpmate /'helpmeɪt/ *n.* a helper and companion, esp. a spouse 帮手, 尤指配偶
innocent /'ɪnəsnt/ *adj.* not guilty of a crime 无罪的
minimal /'mɪnɪməl/ *adj.* smallest in amount or degree (在程度或数量上) 最小的
nonstop /nɒn'stɒp/ *adj.* made or done without stops 不间断的
pin /pɪn/ *v.* (up) to fasten or secure with or as if with a pin or pin 用大头针或钉子固定住
public-employee *adj.* 公职人员的
red-blooded /'red'blʌdɪd/ *adj.* strong and highly spirited 健壮的, 精力充沛的
savor /'seɪvə/ *v.* to taste or smell, esp. with pleasure 品尝, 品味
stem /stem/ *n.* 茎; 干
summon /'sʌmən/ *v.* to call forth, to make an effort to use strength, courage energy etc 唤起, 使出 (力气), 鼓起 (勇气), 振作 (精神)
tell-all *n.* the act of admitting that you have done sth 告白
throne /θrəʊn/ *n.* a special chair used by a king or queen at important ceremonies (君王的) 宝座
triumph /'traɪʌmf/ *n.* a complete victory or success

II. Notes

1. Nothing in his upward progress seems to have happened in an

innocent way. (Par. 5)—Everything in his course of career seems to have designed with much calculation.
2. ... there was nothing "wrong" with her red-blooded, heterosexual boy. (Par. 6)—... her son was normal, healthy in body and in mind, as well as in sexual orientation.
3. This earned him an early release from service. (Par. 7)—This led to his dismissal from the army ahead of his service.
4. land the Hollywood acting role... (Par. 7)—to get the Hollywood acting role
5. from pedestal to pedestal (Par. 9)—to him from one ordinary film to another, which were not his breakthrough ones.
6. come to light (Par. 10)—become known(暴露;为众人所知)
7. a buddy's pre-wedding quip (Par. 10)—a guy's joke before wedding
8. He does not appear to be joking. (Par. 10)—He seems to be serious.
9. He's dead tired (Par. 11)—He's extremely tired。
10. But he atypically keeps the crowing minimal (Par. 12)—But not as usual, he tries to keep his triumphant manner under control.

Part Three

Reference Answers to Questions

1. What is "Total Recall?"

   In one sense, "Total Recall" is a 1990 American dystopian science fiction action film starring Arnold Schwarzenegger. In another, "Total Recall" is a 646-page memoir written by Arnold Schwarzenegger and his co-writer Peter Petre. The full name of the book is "Total Recall: My Unbelievably True Life Story." It was a New York Times bestseller published in October 2012.

2. What does the book "Total Recall" contain?

   The book is an account of the personal experiences of Arnold Schwarzenegger. As a memoir, the book is full of descriptions about Schwarzenegger's life from his childhood to the time when he retired from his governorship. It contains illustrations of how he aims high, tramples on competitors, breaks barriers and savors every victory, and his politic career, his marriage life and his relationships with

some other women.
3. What happened to Mr Schwarzenegger with his housekeeper Mildred Baena?

   Schwarzenegger had an affair with his housekeeper Mildred Baena who gave birth to their son in 1996. This directly led to the separation of Schwarzenegger and his wife Maria Shriver after 25 years of marriage.
4. What information can you get from the book about Arnold Schwarzenegger's childhood?

   Schwarzenegger was born in a strict family in Austria. In his childhood, he and his brother were forced to do situps to earn their breakfast. He admired the successful bodybuilders very much and pinned up their photos in his room. His mother worried about this for a time, for she was afraid of his sexual orientation. After seeking a doctor's advice, she was assured that there was nothing "wrong" with her red-blooded, heterosexual boy.
5. Can you name some films starring Arnold Schwarzenegger?

   a. *Stay Hungry*, a film in 1976, for which Arnold Schwarzenegger was awarded a Golden Globe for New Male Star of the Year in 1977.

   b. *Conan the Barbarian*, Schwarzenegger's breakthrough film in 1982, which was a box-office hit.

   c. *Commando*, a 1985 American action-comedy film.

   d. *True Lies*, a 1994 American action spy film.

   e. *The Terminator*, a 1984 film, a number of fictional characters portrayed by Arnold Schwarzenegger. The first film in the series features only one cyborg.

   f. *Terminator 3: Rise of the Machines*, a 2003 science fiction action film. This film was Schwarzenegger's final starring role before becoming Governor of California.
6. How did Mr Schwarzenegger start his political career?

   As a Republican, Schwarzenegger announced his candidacy in the 2003 California recall election for Governor of California—a special recall election to replace then-Governor Gray Davis. He was elected on October 7, 2003 and sworn in on November 17, 2003, to serve the remainder of Davis's term. In California's 2006 gubernatorial election, Schwarzenegger was re-elected on November

7, 2006, to serve a full term as governor. He was sworn in for his second term on January 5, 2007 and completed his second term in 2011.
7. What is Peter Petre's attitude towards Schwarzenegger and his book?

(Open.)

Words to Know

accentuate, bodybuilder, be big on sth, brush up on, centrist credentials, come to light, commission, Condoleezza Rice, crowing, encapsulation, fool around, from pedestal to pedestal, garner the attention of, George Bush (老布什), George W. Bush (小布什), Golden Globe, governor of California, grapple with, groom, helpmate, heterosexual, Karl Rove master conniver, Mr. Olympia, one's strong suit, personable, public-employee unions, quip, recall election, red-blooded, regimen, stem cell, summon, tell-all

Part Four

Supplementary Reading

Chinese fiction writer Mo Yan wins Nobel Prize in Literature (From *The Washington Post*, October 11, 2012)

Lesson Thirty

The reality-television business:
Entertainers to the world

Part One

Summary

好莱坞可以制作出世界上最好的电视剧,但在无脚本电视节目的全球贸易中,占据主导地位的却是英国。如今世界上广受欢迎的电视节目,包括智力竞猜、歌唱比赛和其他形式的真人秀,大多首创于英国。2011年上半年,在全球的电视娱乐节目中,出自英国的节目模式就占了43%。例如,初创于2006年的"英国达人秀",已在世界各地衍生出44种版本。

英国电视节目之所以能走向全球原因有二:一是政府支持,20世纪90年代,政府相关机构就要求电视台节目至少有1/4要从独立制片公司定制。2004年,行业规章又确定电视节目大部分权利属于制作方而非播出方,使制作公司有了向海外推销节目的动力。以Shed Media公司为例,该公司的利润中有70%—80%来自知识产权,即向其他国家出售真人秀节目或节目制作权。二是许多电视台管理层并不看重国内电视台商业上的盈利,他们判断成功的标准是创造性和新颖性。英国的电视台因此而在实践中涌现出大量的奇妙构想。

然而,在无脚本娱乐节目领域中,竞争正在全球范围内日趋白热化。英国的"创意"出口大国的地位并非不可动摇的。在一年一度的法国戛纳世界视听内容交易会上,节目买家可以看到来自各国的真人秀节目剪辑。英国广播公司(BBC)计划削减真人秀节目制作费用,也给制作公司带来极大的挑战。此外,节目定制方的口味也正在发生变化,现在流行的是直面现实、拍摄手法逼真的纪实片,如《忙碌的产房》、《急诊室的24小时》等。

总的来说,这些趋势并没有对规模庞大的制作公司巨头产生太大的威胁,尽管这些公司的总部设在伦敦,但其运营方式已经日益全球化,能够适应这种不断的变化。这些制作商在世界各地的分支机构,也有了更多的尝试新节目、完善老节目的机会。

英国仍然是最受关注的市场,也是原创真人秀节目的大熔炉。从事电视节目制作、出口的公司遍布伦敦,虽然它们在财力上不能与金融业攀比,在对政治家的魅力上不如高新技术企业抢眼,但它们对全球的娱乐方式仍然能够产生巨大的影响。在经济增长缓慢的环境下,英国将以举国之力抢夺发展的制高点。

Background Information

1. reality television

Reality television, also known as reality shows, is a television programming genre (类型) that presents unscripted situations, documents actual events and usually features unknowns instead of professional actors. Such shows usually have various standard tropes (殊质), including frequent interviews with participants that double as the show's narration, and sometimes an emphasis on drama and personal conflict. Competition-based reality shows, a notable subset, often have additional common elements such as one participant being eliminated per episode, a panel of judges, and the concept of immunity (豁免) from elimination.

The genre began in the early to mid-1990s with shows such as *Nummer 28*, *The Real World* and *Changing Rooms*, then exploded as a phenomenon in the late 1990s and early 2000s with the global success of the series *Survivor* and *Big Brother*. These shows and a number of others became global franchises, mutating local versions in dozens of countries. Reality television as a whole has become a fixture of television programming.

There are grey areas around what is classified as reality television. Documentaries, television news, sports television, talk shows and traditional game shows are usually not classified as reality television, even though they also feature non-actors in unscripted situations. There has been controversy over the extent to which reality television truly reflects reality. In many cases the entire premise of the show is a contrived one, based around a competition or another unusual situation. However, various shows have additionally been accused of using fakery in order to create more compelling television, such as having premeditated storylines and in some cases feeding participants lines of dialogue, focusing only on participants' most outlandish behavior, and altering events through editing and re-shoots.

Nowadays, reality television has become more and more popular all around the world. Many of the world's most popular television show were invented in Britain, so its programs such as quiz shows, singing competitions and other forms of reality television dominate the global trade. But now competition is growing. Other countries have learned how to create reality television formats and are selling them aggressively.

2. MIPCOM

MIPCOM is a TV and entertainment market held in Cannes once every year, normally in October. It is essentially a content event for co-producing, buying, selling, financing and distributing entertainment content. It provides the people involved in the TV, film, digital and audiovisual content, production and distribution industry a market and networking forum to discover future trends and trade content rights on a global level.

Part Two

Language Points

I. New Words

arm /ɑːm/ *n.* an administrative division of some larger or more complex organization 分部,分支,某一职能部门

clone /kləʊn/ *v.* to produce a copy of 复制;模仿

consultancy /kənˈsʌltənsɪ/ *n.* a company that gives advice and training in a particular area to people in other companies 咨询公司;顾问公司

format /ˈfɔːmæt/ *n.* general plan of organization, arrangement, or choice of material, the size, shape, design etc. in which sth is produced; the way or order in which sth is arranged and presented (电视节目)总体安排,设计

outfit /ˈaʊtfɪt/ *n.* any organization or company 机构;组织

prime-time *n.* golden hour

showcase /'ʃəʊkeɪs/ n. a setting in which sth can be displayed in its best 展示平台

slot /slɒt/ n. the time assigned on a schedule or agenda（名单、日程安排或广播节目表中的）位置,时间（时段）

sophisticated /sə'fɪstɪkeɪtɪd/ adj. more advanced or complex than others 熟练的；富有经验的

swap /swɒp/ v. to exchange or give sth in exchange for 交换

ware /weə(r)/ n. products 商品；货物

II. Notes

1. "Britain's Got Talent"... into 44 national versions... (Par. 2)— "Britain's Got Talent" which was a format invented in 2006 has developed into different versions in 44 nations...

2. If a show is a hit in Britain... in production companies' offices. (Par. 3)—Production companies may receive many phones asking for more services if a show made by them is successfully presented or performs unusually well in its time slot.

3. Foreign broadcasters... a version for them. (Par. 3)—Foreign broadcasters are eager for excellent entertainment materials and thus may hire the producers of a British show to make a correspondent version for them.

4. ... hawking their wares overseas. (Par. 4)—... marketing their products overseas in high spirits.（雄心勃勃地向海外推销节目。）

5. The BBC is funded almost entirely by a licence fee on television-owning households. (Par. 6)—英国广播公司的资金来源几乎全部是百姓家庭缴纳的电视收看费。

6. At such outfits ... that everyone talks about. (Par. 6)—在这些机构,成功的判断标准主要是创造性和新颖性,所播节目要成为公众话题。

7. The rather tacky BBC3 will be pruned hard... (Par. 8)—The budget for the showy and tasteless BBC3 will be reduced sharply...

8. Perhaps most dangerously for the independents ... its own programming. (Par. 8)—Perhaps the most dangerous thing for the independents is that Britain's biggest free commercial broadcaster Independent Television aims to produce more programmes itself.

12. And, in a slow-moving economy ... it can get. (Par. 12)—Though the economy develops slowly, Britain will use all the national

powers to seize the commanding height. （在经济增长缓慢的情况下，英国将以举国之力抢夺发展的制高点。）

Part Three

Reference Answers to Questions

1. Why does the author say "The risk of putting prime-time entertainment on your schedule has been outsourced to the UK?"

    Because oreign broadcasters hire British producers to make a British show into a local version for them. If the entertainment programmes fail, the British producers may shoulder the responsibility of making the programme.

2. What are the effects when broadcasters were told to commission at least one-quarter of their programmes from independent producers?

    Independent producers have a high motivation to sell their products.

3. What are the reasons for creativity in British programmes?

    There are two reasons. One is the result of government action; the other is the assessment by many domestic television executives. They do not prize commercial success. Success is measured largely in terms of creativity and innovation.

4. What happens at MIPCOM held in France this year?

    Many other countries have shown excellent reality programmes. British status as the world's pre-eminent inventor of unscripted entertainment is not assured.

5. What kind of challengesdoes Britain face?

    Mainly there are twochallenges. One is that other countries have learned how to create reality television formats and are selling them hard. The other is that British economy develops slowly and the commissioning budgets are ever-shrinking.

Words to Know

BBC, broadcaster, commissioner, contestant, creativity, documentary, prime-time, format, hit (n.), Hollywood, independent producer, intellectual producer, programme, property, innovation, international revenues, licence fee, quiz show, reality television/show, showcase, soft-scripted show, Sony, Time Warner, time slot, unscripted programmes

Part four

Supplementary Reading

China's Death-Row Reality Show (From *The New York Review of Books*, March 27, 2012)

附 录

I 美国政府
U. S. Government

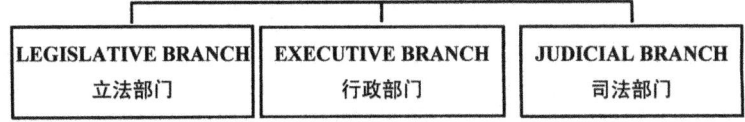

President 总统
Vice President 副总统
Presidents 总统（见Ⅲ"美国历任总统一览表"）

Congress 国会
Members of Congress 国会议员
Senate 参议院
    President 主席（副总统兼）
    President Pro Tempore 临时主席
    Standing Committees of the Senate 参议院常设委员会
House of Representatives 众议院
    Speaker 议长
    (Senate/House) Majority Leader （参议院/众议院）多数党领袖
    (Senate/House) Minority Leader （参议院/众议院）少数党领袖
    (Senate/House) Majority Whip （参议院/众议院）多数党督导
    (Senate/House) Minority Whip （参议院/众议院）少数党督导
    Standing Committees of the House 众议院常设委员会
    House Special Committees 众议院特别委员会
Congressional Joint Committees 国会联合委员会
General Accounting Office 总审计局
Copyright Royalty Tribunal 版权裁判所

The Cabinet 内阁
    Secretary of State 国务卿
    Secretary of the Interior 内政部长

Secretary of Labor 劳工部长
Secretary of Agriculture 农业部长
Secretary of Defence 国防部长
Attorney General 司法部长
Secretary of the Treasury 财政部长
Secretary of Energy 能源部长
Secretary of Health and Human Services 卫生与公众服务部长
Secretary of Transportation 运输部长
Secretary of Housing and Urban Development 住房和城市发展部长
Secretary of Commerce 商务部长
Secretary of Education 教育部长
Secretary of Veterans Affairs 退伍军人事务部长
Secretary of Homeland Security 国土安全部长

Executive Office of the President 总统办事机构
White House Office 白宫办公厅
Office of Management and Budget 行政管理和预算局
Council of Economic Advisers 经济顾问委员会
National Economic Council 国家经济委员会
National Security Council 国家安全委员会
Office of Policy Development 政策制定办公室
Office of the U. S. Trade Representative 美国贸易代表办公室
Council on Environmental Quality 环境质量委员会
Office of Science and Technology Policy 科技政策办公室
Office of Administration 行政管理办公室
Office of National Drug Control Policy 国家药品政策管制办公室
National Critical Materials Council 国家重要物资委员会
National Space Council 国家空间委员会

White House Office 白宫办公厅
Chief of Staff 主任
Assistants to the President for：
　　Economic & Domestic Affairs 负责经济和国内事务的总统助理
　　National Security 负责国家安全事务的总统助理

Executive Departments 行政各部
  Department of State 国务院
    Secretary of State 国务卿
      Deputy Secretary 第一或常务副国务卿
      Under Secretary for Political Affairs 负责政治事务的副国务卿
      Under Secretary for Management 负责管理工作的副国务卿
      Under Secretary for Global Affairs 负责全球事务的副国务卿
      Legal Advisor 法律顾问
      Assistant Secretaries for：
        East Asian & Pacific Affairs 负责东亚和太平洋事务的助理国务卿
        Human Rights & Humanitarian Affairs 负责人权和人道主义事务的助理国务卿等
      Senior Deputy Assistant Secretary 助理国务卿高级帮办
      Deputy Assistant Secretary 助理国务卿帮办
  Department of the Treasury 财政部
    Secretary of the Treasury 财政部长
    Deputy Secretary 第一或常务副部长
    Under Secretary for Domestic Finance 负责国内财政事务的副部长
    Under Secretary for International Affairs 负责国际财政事务的副部长
    General counsel 总顾问
    Assistant Secretaries for：
      Economic Policy 负责经济政策的助理部长等
  Department of Defense 国防部
    Secretary of Defense 国防部长
    Deputy Secretary 第一或常务副部长
    Under Secretary for Acquisition 负责武器采购的副部长
    Under Secretary for Policy 负责政策的副部长
    Assistant Secretaries for：
      International Security Policy 负责国防安全政策的助理部长
    Chairman of the Joint Chiefs of Staff 参谋长联席会议主席
    Secretary of the Army 陆军部长
    Secretary of the Navy 海军部长
    Secretary of the Air Force 空军部长
  Department of Justice 司法部
    Attorney General 司法部长

Deputy Attorney General 第一或常务副部长
   Associate Attorney General 副部长
   Solicitor General 副总检察长
   Federal Bureau of Investigation 联邦调查局
   Office of Inspector General 督察长办公室
   Executive Office for U.S. Attorneys 联邦检察官办公室
   U.S. Parole Commission 美国假释委员会
   U.S. Marshals Service 美国执法官局
   U.S. National Central Bureau of International Criminal
      Police Organization 国际刑事警察组织美国全国中心局
Department of Commerce 商务部
   Secretary of Commerce 商务部长
   Deputy Secretary 副部长
   Chief of Staff 参事室主任
   General Counsel 总顾问
   Assistant Secretaries for:
      Import Administration 负责进口管理的助理部长等
Department of the Interior 内政部
Department of Labor 劳工部
Department of Agriculture 农业部
Department of Energy 能源部
Department of Health and Human Services 卫生与公众服务部
Department of Housing and Urban Development 住房和城市发展部
Department of Transportation 运输部
Department of Education 教育部
Department of Veterans Affairs 退伍军人事务部
Department of Homeland Security 国土安全部

Local Government 地方政府
   State Legislature 州议会
   State Government 州政府
      Governor 州长
      Lieutenant-Governor 副州长
   District of Columbia = Washington, D.C. 哥伦比亚（或华盛顿哥伦比亚）特区

County 县
City，Township，Village 市、镇、村
School District 学区
Territory and Trust Territory 美国属地和托管地

Judiciary 司法机构

II 英国政府
British Government

Queen 女王
 Queen Elizabeth Ⅱ (1952—) 伊丽莎白二世女王

Parliament 议会
 Upper House (House of Lords) 上议院(贵族院)
  Lord High Chancellor 议长
  Deputy Speaker 副议长
  Member 议员
 Lower House (House of Commons) 下议院(平民院)
  Speaker 议长
  Deputy Speaker 副议长
  Member 议员

Government 政府
 Prime Minister,/& First Lord of the Treasury (and Minister for the Civil Service) 首相兼首席财政大臣(和文官部大臣)
 Prime Ministers 首相(见"英国历任首相一览表")

Ministers in the Cabinet 内阁大臣(包括首相在内)
 Secretary of State for the Home Department 内政大臣
 Lord High Chancellor 大法官
 Secretary of State for Foreign and Commonwealth Affairs 外交和联邦事务大臣
 Chancellor of the Exchequer 财政大臣
 Secretary of State for Trade and Industry and President of the Board of Trade 贸易和工业大臣兼贸易委员会主席
 Secretary of State for Defence 国防大臣
 Lord Privy Seal and Leader of the House of Commons 掌玺大臣兼下院领袖(有时兼上院领袖)
 Secretary of State for Employment 就业大臣

Lord President of the Council and Leader of the House of Lords 枢密院长兼上院领袖（有时兼下院领袖）
Minister of Agriculture, Fisheries and Food 农业、渔业和粮食大臣
Secretary of State for the Environment 环境事务大臣
Secretary of State for Scotland 苏格兰事务大臣
Secretary of State for Wales 威尔士事务大臣
Secretary of State for Northern Ireland 北爱尔兰事务大臣
Secretary of State for Social Service 社会事务大臣
Secretary of State for Energy 能源大臣
Secretary of State for Education and Science 教育和科学大臣
Chief Secretary to the Treasury 财政部常务大臣
Secretary of State for Transport 运输大臣
Chancellor of the Duchy of Lancaster 兰开斯特公爵郡大臣

Ministers not in the Cabinet 非内阁大臣

Attorney-General 检察总长
Solicitor-General 副检察长
Lord Advocate 苏格兰检察长
Solicitor-General for Scotland 苏格兰副检察长
Parliamentary Secretary to the Treasury 财政部政务次官
Economic Secretary to the Treasury 财政部经济次官
Financial Secretary to the Treasury 财政部财务次官
Ministers of State 国务部长
Parliamentary Under Secretaries 政务次官
Permanent Undersecretary/Secretary 常务次官

Foreign and Commonwealth Office 外交和联邦事务部

Secretary of State 大臣
Minister of State 国务大臣
Parliamentary Under Secretary of State 政务次官
Inspector 监察长
Legal Advisor 法律顾问

Political Party 政党

Conservative and Unionist Party (Conservative Party) 保守统一党（保守党）

    Leader 领袖
    Chairman 主席
    Annual Session 年会
    Chief Whip 总督导，督导长
    National Executive Committee 全国执行委员会
    Conservatives' 1992 Committee 保守党后座议员委员会
  Labour Party 工党
    Leader 领袖
    Deputy Leader 副领袖
    National Executive Committee 全国执行委员会
    General Secretary 总书记
    Chairman of Parliamentary Group 议会党团主席

Local Government 地方政府
    County 郡
    District 区
    Region 大区
    Parish (Community, Town)（农村最小的行政单位）村（乡、镇）
    Metropolitan District 城市区
    Metropolitan County 城市郡
    Borough (District) Council 自治区议会
    City of London 伦敦城
    Council of London Borough 伦敦自治区议会
    Greater London Council 大伦敦议会
    Lord Mayor 大市长

Judiciary 司法机构

III 二战以来美国历任总统一览
U. S. Presidents

顺序	总统	任期	届别	政党
1	George Washington 乔治·华盛顿	1789—1797	1—2	联邦党
2	John Adams 约翰·亚当斯	1797—1801	3	联邦党
3	Thomas Jefferson 托马斯·杰斐逊	1801—1809	4—5	民主共和党
4	James Madison 詹姆斯·麦迪逊	1809—1817	6—7	民主共和党
5	James Monroe 詹姆斯·门罗	1817—1825	8—9	民主共和党
6	John Quincy Adams 约翰·昆西·亚当斯	1825—1829	10	先"无党派"后"民主共和党"
7	Andrew Johnson 安德鲁·杰克逊	1829—1837	11—12	民主党
8	Martin Van Buren 马丁·范布伦	1837—1841	13	民主党
9	William Harrison 威廉·哈里森	1841	14	辉格党(任内病逝)
10	John Tyler 约翰·泰勒	1841—1845	14	辉格党
11	James Knox Polk 詹姆斯·K.波尔克	1845—1849	15	民主党
12	Zachary Taylor 扎卡里·泰勒	1849—1850	16	辉格党(任内病逝)
13	Millard Fillmore 米拉德·菲尔莫	1850—1853	16	辉格党
14	Franklin Pierce 富兰克林·皮尔斯	1853—1857	17	民主党
15	James Buchanan 詹姆斯·布坎南	1857—1861	18	民主党

续表

顺序	总统	任期	届别	政党
16	Abraham Lincoln 亚伯拉罕·林肯	1861—1865	19—20	共和党(任内遇刺)
17	Andrew Johnson 安德鲁·约翰逊①	1865—1869	20	共和党
18	Ulysses Grant 尤利西斯·格兰特	1869—1877	21—22	共和党
19	Rutherford Hayes 卢瑟福·海斯	1877—1881	23	共和党
20	James Abram Garfield 詹姆斯·A.加斐尔德	1881	24	共和党(任内遇刺)
21	Chester Arthur 切斯特·亚瑟	1881—1885	24	共和党
22	Grover Cleveland 格洛弗·克利夫兰	1885—1889	25	民主党
23	Benjamin Harrison 本杰明·哈里森	1889—1893	26	共和党
24	Grover Cleveland 格洛弗·克利夫兰	1893—1897	27	民主党
25	William McKinley 威廉·麦金利	1897—1901	28—29	共和党(任内遇刺)
26	Theodore Roosevelt 西奥多·罗斯福	1901—1909	29—30	共和党
27	William Taft 威廉·塔夫脱	1909—1913	31	共和党
28	Woodrow Wilson 伍德罗·威尔逊	1913—1921	32—33	民主党
29	Warren Harding 沃伦·哈定	1921—1923	34	共和党(任内病逝)
30	Calvin Coolidge 卡尔文·柯立芝	1923—1929	34—35	共和党
31	Hubert Hoover 赫伯特·胡佛	1929—1933	36	共和党
32	Franklin Roosevelt 富兰克林·罗斯福	1933—1945	37—40	民主党(任内病逝)

续表

顺序	总统	任期	届别	政党
33	Harry Truman 哈里·杜鲁门	1945—1953	40—41	民主党
34	Dwight Eisenhower 德怀特·艾森豪威尔	1953—1961	42—43	共和党
35	John Kennedy 约翰·肯尼迪	1961—1963	44	民主党(任内遇刺)
36	Lyndon Johnson 林登·约翰逊	1963—1969	44—45	民主党
37	Richard Nixon 理查德·尼克松	1969—1974	46—47	共和党
38	Gerald Ford 杰拉尔德·福特	1974—1977	47	共和党
39	James Carter 詹姆斯·卡特	1977—1981	48	民主党
40	Ronald Reagan 罗纳德·里根	1981—1989	49—50	共和党
41	George Bush 乔治·布什	1989—1993	51	共和党
42	William Clinton 威廉·克林顿	1993—2001	52—53	民主党
43	George Walker Bush 乔治·W.布什	2001—2009	54—55	共和党
44	Barack Obama 贝拉克·奥巴马②	2009—	56	民主党

① 安德鲁·约翰逊(Andrew Johnson)是民主党人,被共和党提名为林肯(Abraham Lincoln)的副总统候选人。竞选获胜后,他成为副总统,1865年林肯被刺后接任总统。

② 奥巴马是第44任总统,但不是第44位总统,因为Grover Cleveland分别担任过第22任和24任总统。

IV 二战以来英国历任首相一览
British Prime Ministers

顺序	首相	译名	任期	政党
1	Sir Robert Walpole	罗伯特·沃波尔爵士	[1721]—1742	辉格党
2	Earl of Wilmington	威尔明顿伯爵	1742—1743	辉格党
3	Henry Pelham	亨利·佩尔汉姆	1743—1754	辉格党
4	Duke of Newcastle	纽卡斯尔公爵	1754—1756	辉格党
5	Duke of Devonshire	德文郡公爵	1756—1757	辉格党
6	Duke of Newcastle	纽卡斯尔公爵	1757—1762	辉格党
7	Earl of Bute	比特伯爵	1762—1763	托利党
8	George Grenville	乔治·格兰维尔	1763—1765	辉格党
9	Marquis of Rockingham	罗金厄姆侯爵	1765—1766	辉格党
10	Earl of Chatham	查塔姆伯爵	1766—1768	辉格党
11	Duke of Grafton	格拉夫顿公爵	1768—1770	辉格党
12	Lord North	诺斯勋爵	1770—1782	托利党
13	Marquis of Rockingham	罗金厄姆侯爵	1782—1782	辉格党
14	Earl of Shelburne	谢尔本伯爵	1782—1783	辉格党
15	Duke of Portland	波特兰公爵	1783—1783	联合内阁
16	William Pitt	威廉·皮特	1783—1801	托利党
17	Henry Addington	亨利·埃丁顿	1801—1804	托利党
18	William Pitt	威廉·皮特	1804—1806	托利党
19	Lord William Grenville	威廉·格伦维尔勋爵	1806—1807	辉格党
20	Duke of Portland	波特兰公爵	1807—1809	托利党
21	Spencer Perceval	斯潘塞·帕西瓦尔	1809—1812	托利党
22	Earl of Liverpool	利物浦伯爵	1812—1827	托利党
23	George Canning	乔治·坎宁	1827	托利党
24	Viscount Goderich	戈德里奇子爵	1827—1828	托利党
25	Duke of Wellington	威灵顿公爵	1828—1830	托利党
26	Earl Grey	格雷伯爵	1830—1834	辉格党

续表

顺序	首相	译名	任期	政党
27	Viscount Melbourne	墨尔本子爵	1834—1834	辉格党
28	Duke of Wellington	威灵顿公爵	1834—1834	托利党
29	Sir Robert Peel	罗伯特·皮尔爵士	1834—1835	保守党
30	Viscount Melbourne	墨尔本子爵	1835—1841	辉格党
31	Sir Robert Peel	罗伯特·皮尔爵士	1841—1846	保守党
32	Lord John Russell	约翰·罗素勋爵	1846—1852	辉格党
33	Earl of Derby	德比伯爵	1852	保守党
34	Earl of Aberdeen	阿伯丁伯爵	1852—1855	联合内阁
35	Viscount Palmerston	帕尔姆斯顿子爵	1855—1858	自由党
36	Earl of Derby	德比伯爵	1858—1859	保守党
37	Viscount Palmerston	帕尔姆斯顿子爵	1859—1865	自由党
38	Earl Russell	罗素伯爵	1865—1866	自由党
39	Earl of Derby	德比伯爵	1866—1868	保守党
40	Benjamin Disraeli	本杰明·迪斯雷利	1868—1868	保守党
41	William Ewart Gladstone	威廉·E.格莱斯顿	1868—1874	自由党
42	Benjamin Disraeli	本杰明·迪斯雷利	1874—1880	保守党
43	William Ewart Gladstone	威廉·E.格莱斯顿	1880—1885	自由党
44	Marquess of Salisbury	索尔兹伯里侯爵	1885—1886	保守党
45	William Ewart Gladstone	威廉·E.格莱斯顿	1886—1886	自由党
46	Marquess of Salisbury	索尔兹伯里侯爵	1886—1892	保守党
47	William Ewart Gladstone	威廉·E.格莱斯顿	1892—1894	自由党
48	Earl of Rosebery	罗斯贝利伯爵	1894—1895	自由党
49	Marquess of Salisbury	索尔兹伯里侯爵	1895—1902	保守党
50	Arthur James Balfour	亚瑟·J.贝尔福	1902—1905	保守党
51	Sir Henry Campbell-Bannerman	H.坎贝尔—班内南爵士	1905—1908	自由党
52	Herbert Henry Asquith	赫伯特·H.阿斯奎斯	1908—1916	自由党
53	David Lloyd George	大卫·L.乔治	1916—1922	联合内阁
54	Andrew Bonar Law	安德鲁·B.劳	1922—1923	保守党
55	Stanley Baldwin	斯坦利·鲍德温	1923—1924	保守党
56	James Ramsay MacDonald	詹姆斯·R.麦克唐纳	1924	工党

续表

顺序	首相	译名	任期	政党
57	Stanley Baldwin	斯坦利·鲍德温	1924—1929	保守党
58	James Ramsay MacDonald	詹姆斯·R.麦克唐纳	1929—1935	联合内阁
59	Stanley Baldwin	斯坦利·鲍德温	1935—1937	联合内阁
60	Neville Chamberlain	尼维尔·张伯伦	1937—1940	联合内阁
61	Winston Churchill	温斯顿·丘吉尔	1940—1945	联合内阁
62	Clement Attlee	克莱门特·艾德礼	1945—1951	工党
63	Sir Winston Churchill	温斯顿·丘吉尔爵士	1951—1955	保守党
64	Sir Anthony Eden	安东尼·艾登爵士	1955—1957	保守党
65	Harold Macmillan	哈罗德·麦克米伦	1957—1963	保守党
66	Sir Alec Douglas-Home	亚历克·道格拉斯—霍姆爵士	1963—1964	保守党
67	Harold Wilson	哈罗德·威尔逊	1964—1970	工党
68	Edward Heath	爱德华·希思	1970—1974	保守党
69	Harold Wilson	哈罗德·威尔逊	1974—1976	工党
70	James Callaghan	詹姆斯·卡拉汉	1976—1979	工党
71	Margaret Thatcher	玛格丽特·撒切尔	1979—1990	保守党
72	John Major	约翰·梅杰	1990—1997	保守党
73	Tony Blair	托尼·布莱尔	1997—2007	工党
74	Gordon Brown	戈登·布朗	2007—2010	工党
75	David Cameron*	戴维·卡梅伦	2010—	保守党

* 从 Robert Walpole 至 David Cameron,共有 53 位首相。从这份表中可以看出,有的首相如 Winston Churchill 担任过不连续的两任首相,还有的担任过三任甚至四任。

V 值得注意的几个词缀
New Meanings of Some Affixes

anti-，-Aid，-friendly，-wise 等词缀已衍生出新义，其中的-Aid，现在一般词典尚未收入。是否出自 Band-Aid（创可贴）这个商标，有待研究。

anti-（前缀）①反传统的，反正统的：这是该前缀的新义。如 anticulture 反传统文化的/antihero 反对以传统手法塑造主角的　②关于反物质（一般物质的对应物）构成的假设世界的，如 anti-quark（反夸克）/antibaryon 反重子，指重子的反粒子，如反质子或反中子等

-Aid（后缀）救助，赞助；尤指义赛或义演性的，与其构成的词有：
Fashion-Aid 慈善时装表演
Kurd-Aid 为救济库尔德难民而进行的如音乐会等的义演
Sport-Aid 体育义演

-friendly（后缀）有助于……的；有利于……的；对……无污染或保护的；支持或同情的：customer-friendly 考虑客户需要的/environment-friendly 环保的/Labor-friendly 支持工党的/Thatcher-friendly 支持撒切尔（夫人）的

-ism（后缀）歧视：ageism 年龄歧视，lookism 容貌歧视

-wise（后缀）讲到……（speaking of）；在某方面（with regard to）；从某观点上看（from the standpoint of）；至于……（when it comes to）：在现代英语中，它几乎可以在任何名词后加上-wise 而组成形容词或副词，如 strategywise/weatherwise/rentwise/caloriewise 等。现在已被语言专家认为用得太滥而不够优雅。一位美国共和党资深议员在下面所说的话便是典型用得太滥的例句：

　　Timewise, I've reached the age of 70, but ideawise or outlookwise, I'm still 50 or less.

　　（按年纪，我已经到了 70 岁，但思想和人生观方面，我不过还 50 岁不到。）

VI 报刊标题常用词汇
The Vocabulary of Headlines

读者一定见过下列这些词汇，但用在标题时，或许不一定知道其中如 accord, bid, gut 和 man 等的意思。事实上，这类短字不但用于标题，正文里也是常用词。对我们而言，记住这些词汇，犹如添砖加瓦，对读报是大有裨益的。

Headline Word	Common Headline Meaning	Example
accord	agreement	Wages **Accord** Reached
aid	to help	Man **Aids** Police
air	to make known	TV **Airs** "Facts" on Arms Delivery
assail	to criticize strongly	Soviets **Assail** US on A-tests
axe	to dismiss from a job	Governor to **Axe** Aide?
	to cut, destroy, take away	Labour **Axes** Colleges in Tory Towns
back	to support	Unions **Back** Peace Move
balk	to refuse to accept	Union **Balks** at Court Order
ban	prohibition	Bus **Ban** on Pupils after Attack on Crew
bar	not to allow, exclude	Club Faces Shutdown for **Barring** Women
bid	attempt	New Peace **Bid** in Rhodesia
	offer	Union Rejects Latest **Bid**
bilk	to cheat	Clerk **Bilks** City of $1 m.
blast *n.*	explosion; strong criticism	Tanker **Blast** near Manila
v.	to criticize strongly; strike with explosives	Heagan **Blasts** Democrats
blaze	fire	**Blaze** Destroys Factory
blow	injury/disappointment suffered	Carter Poll **Blow**
boost	help, incentive	Industry Gets **Boost**
cite	to mention	Management **Cites** Labor Unrest for Shutdown
claim	to declare to be true	Man **Claims** Ghost sighting

Headline Word	Common Headline Meaning	Example
claim (claim the life of)	to kill	Bombs **Claim** 40
clash *n.*	dispute, violent argument Battle	Strikers in **Clash** With Police Marine Dies in **Clash**
v.	to disagree strongly; fight	Mayor **Clashes** with City Council
cool	uninterested; unfriendly	Hanoi **Cool** to Aid Offer
coup	revolution, change in government	Generals Ousted in **Coup**
curb	restraint, limit	New **Curbs** on Immigration
cut	reduction	Big **Cuts** in Air Fares
deadlock	a disagreement that cannot be settled	Jury **Deadlock** in Kidnap Trial
deal	agreement	Pay Pits **Deal** Hope
drive	campaign, effort	Peace **Drive** Succeeds
due	expected	Greek FM **Due** Today
ease	to reduce or loosen	1000 Freed as Poland **Eases** Martial Law
envoy	diplomat	American **Envoy** Taken Hostage
exit	to leave	**Exit** Envoys in Race Storm
eye	to watch with interest	Women's Groups **Eye** Court Vote
eve	the day before	Violence on **Eve** of Independence
fault	to find in the wrong	Study **Faults** Police
feud	dispute; strong disagree-ment	Border **Feud** Danger to Regional Peace
flay	to accuse; criticize strongly	US **Flays** Soviet Block
foe	opponent; enemy	Reagan Talks with Congressional **Foes**
foil	to prevent from succeeding	FBI **Foils** Bid to Hijack Plane to Iran
Gems	jewels	Actress Loses **Gems**
go-ahead	approval	**Go-Ahead** for Dearer Gas
grip	to take hold of	Cholera Fear **Grips** Japan
gunman	man with gun	**Gunman** Raids 3 Banks
gut	to destroy completely by fire	Year's Biggest Fire **Guts** 178 Homes
halt	stop	Channel Tunnel **Halt**
haul	large quantity which has been stolen and later discovered	Cannabis **Haul**
head	to lead, direct	Buchanan to **Head** Peace Mission
head off	to prevent	President **Heads off** Rail Strike

续表

Headline Word	Common Headline Meaning	Example
heist	theft	Jewel **Heist** Foiled
hit	to affect badly	Fuel Strike **Hits** Hospitals
hold	to keep in police control; detain	7 **Hold** for Gambling
ink	to sign	Thailand, Malaysia **Ink** Sea Treaty
jet	aeroplane	Three Killed in **Jet** Plunge
jobless	unemployed	Number of **Jobless** Increases
key	essential, vital, very important	**Key** Witness Dies
kick off	to begin	Fiery Speech **Kicks off** Campaign
lash out	to criticize strongly; accuse	Warsaw Pact **Lashes out** at Nato Missile Plan
laud	to praise	PM **Lauds** Community Spirit
launch	to begin	Police **Launch** Anti-crime Drive
line	position; demand	Israel Softens **Line**
link *v.*	to connect	Fungus **Linked** to Mystery Disease
n.	connection	Mafia **Link** Scandal Breaks
loom	expected in the near future	Treaty Dispute **Looming**
loot *n.*	stolen money or goods	Police Recover **Loot**
v.	to take away of valuable goods unlawfully	Rioters **Loot** Stores
man	representative	Carter **Man** in China
nab	to capture	Gang Leader **Nabbed**
net	to total	Drug Raid **Nets** £1 M
	to capture	Patrol **Nets** 2 Prisoners
nod	approval	Ministry Seeks **Nod** for Oil Saving Plan
ordeal	painful experience, drama	Jail **Ordeal** Ends
office	an important government position	Minister Quits: Tired of **Office**
opt	choose; decide	Swiss **Opt** to Back Tax for Churches
oust	to take power away from, push out, drive out, replace	Voters **Oust** Incumbents Argentina **Ousts** Union Leaders
output	production	Industrial **Output** Increases in Italy
pact	agreement, treaty	Warsaw **Pact** Ends
pay	wages, salary	**Pay** Rise for Miners
pit	coal mine	**Pit** Talks End

Headline Word	Common Headline Meaning	Example
plea	request for help	"Free Children" **Plea**
	a statement in court indicating guilt or innocence	Guilty **Pleas** Expected
pledge	promise	Labour **Pledges** Higher Pensions
plunge	steep fall	Dollar **Plunges**
poised	ready for action	Bolivian Workers **Poised** to Strike
poll	election, public opinion survey	Swedish **Poll** Shows Swing to Right
	voting station	Voters Go to the **Polls** in Japan
post	position in government, business, etc.	Unknown Gets Key Cabinet **Post**
press for	to demand, ask for	Teachers **Press for** Pay Rise
probe v.	to investigate	New Vaccine to Be **Probed**
n.	investigation	Mayor Orders Fire **Probe**
prompt	to cause	Court Decision **Prompts** Public Anger
quit	to leave, resign	Will Carter **Quit**?
rage	to burn out of control	Forest Fire **Rages**
raid	attack, robbery	£23 M Drug **Raid**
rap n.	accusation; charge	Corruption **Rap** Unfair Says Senator
v.	to criticize	Safety Commission **Raps** Auto Companies.
riddle	mystery	Girl in Shotgun Death **Riddle**
rock	to shock; to surprise	Gov't. Report **Rocks** Stock market
rout	to defeat completely	Rebels **Routed**, Leave 70 Dead
row	a quarrel, argument, dispute	Oil Price **Row** May Bring Down Gov't.
rule	to decide (especially in court)	Court **Rules** Today in Corruption Case
rule out	to not consider as a possibility	Israel **Rules Out** PLO Talks
sack	dismiss from a job	Jail Chief **Sacked**
sack (from "ransack")	to search thoroughly and rob	14 Held for US Embassy **Sacking**
scare	public alarm	Rabies **Scare** Hits Britain
set	decided on, ready	Peace Talks **Set** for April
slay	to kill or murder	2 **Slain** in Family Row
snag	problem; difficulty	Last Minute **Snag** Hits Arms Talks
snub	to pay no attention to	Protestants **Snub** Ulster Peace Bid
soar	to rise rapidly	Inflation Rate **Soars**

续表

Headline Word	Common Headline Meaning	Example
spark	to cause; to lead to action	Frontier Feuding **Sparks** Attack
split	to divide	Nationalisation **Splits** Party at Conference
squeeze	shortage, scarcity	Petrol **Squeeze** Ahead
stalemate	a disagreement that cannot be settled	New Bid to Break Hostage **Stalemate**
stall	making no progress	Peace Effort in Lebanon **Stalled**
stance	attitude; way of thinking	New **Stance** Toward Power Cuts
stem	to prevent or stop	Rainy Season **Stems** Refugee Exit
storm	angry reaction, dispute	MP's Racist Speech **Storm** Grows
strife	conflict	Inter-Union **Strife** Threatens Peace Deal
sway	to influence or persuade	President Fails to **Sway** Union Strike
swindle	an unlawful way of getting money	Stock **Swindle** in NY
switch	change, deviation	Dramatic **Switch** in Incomes Policy Announced
swoop	sudden attack or raid	Drug **Swoop** in Mayfair
talks	discussions	Peace **Talks** Threatened
thwart	to prevent from being successful	Honduras Attack **Thwarted**
ties	relations	Cuba **Ties** Soon?
top	to exceed	Post Office Profits **Top** £40 M
trim	to cut	Senate **Trims** Budget
trigger	to cause	Killing **Triggers** Riot
vie	to compete	Irish Top Ranks **Vie** for Office
void	to determine to be invalid	Voting Law **Voided** by Court
vow	to promise	Woman **Vows** Vengeance
walkout	strike (often unofficial)	Factory **Walkout** Threat over Sacking
wed	to marry	Financier Free to **Wed**
weigh	to consider	Reagan **Weighs** Tax Increase

VII 标题自我测试
Self-Tests in Comprehension of Headlines

Below you will find a set of 9 headlines from *Financial Times* and the *Washington Post*. Following these are the articles which appeared with the headlines. Match the headlines and the articles.

1. **Hong Kong's Cheng quits over company disclosure**
2. **Thailand and Vietnam agree to form rice pool**
3. **Rupee sinks against dollar**
4. **Indian workers plan strike**
5. **Kyrgyz Troops Free 4 U.S. Hostages**
6. **U.S. to Close Its Seoul Firing Range**
7. **Colombian Sent to U.S. for Drug Trial**
8. **3 Freed in Philippines, Rebels Say**
9. **Iran seeks foreign tea buyers**

A   **JOLO, Philippines**—Muslim rebels in the southern Philippines apparently released three Malaysian hostages from nearly four months of captivity, but not before bargaining for $1 million more in ransom, negotiators said. Chief negotiator Robert Aventajado said he expects that the Abu Sayyaf rebels will free their remaining 25 hostages, including 12 Westerners, today.

    Aventajado said he received information from another negotiator "that the Malaysian hostages have been released and are now . . . on the way to Jolo." There was no independent confirmation of their release.

Negotiators working for the Malaysians' freedom said they had reached an agreement on the rebels' demand for an additional $1 million ransom payment. An estimated $5.5 million was paid last month to the rebels for the release of six other Malaysians, and a German woman was supposed to cover the three remaining Malaysians, military officials said.

(Associated Press)

B   **SEOUL**—The United States has agreed to stop using a firing range in South Korea following complaints from local residents, South Korea's Defense Ministry said.

Anti-U.S. protesters have held rallies demanding the closure of a strafing area and a nearby bombing range since May, when a U.S. Air Force pilot with engine trouble was forced to drop six 500-pound bombs near a village.

Residents said the bombs shattered windows and caused other damage in Maehyang-ri village, on the Yellow Sea southwest of Seoul. They have been demanding compensation and the closure of both the strafing and bombing ranges.

Gen. Lee Han Ho, deputy director of the South Korean air force, said in a news conference that the U.S. air force would close the strafing range and would stop using live bombs at the bombing range. Lee also said approach paths for jets would be moved offshore, residents would be notified of exercises and the special area for emergency bomb drops would be moved 700 yards further offshore.

(Reuters)

C   Iran said yesterday it was seeking foreign buyers for more than 77,000 tonnes of surplus tea. The tea had piled up in warehouses over the years and was being withheld from a saturated domestic market, said Mohammad Hassan Ammari Allahyari, a member of the management board of the State Tea Organisation of Iran (STOI). STOI, which once held a monopoly on production and trade, has been largely stripped of its responsibilities under a government plan to liberalise the industry.

Mr Allahyari said the organisation had already exported 20,000 tonnes of tea in the past year. Until recently, STOI bought from farmers and sold in Iran at subsidised prices. The organisation has now pulled out of the tea business.

Mr Allahyari said Iranian traders were interested in buying the surplus at subsidised rates, but STOI planned to sell at market rates and only for export.

Reuters, Tehran

D   Workers at India's two main state-owned telephone companies last night intensified their campaign against liberalisation of the telecommunications industry, which has as part of its final goal privatisation of the two state-owned telephone companies, MTNL and VSNL.

Telephone communications inside the country and abroad have been disrupted by a work to rule since late last week as MTNL employees in particular stepped up their agitation. They now plan to launch a three-day strike from today.

The government of Atal Behari Vaypayee this year opened up national long-distance telephony to private investors and ended VSNL's monopoly on access to international bandwidth links to the internet. The government also recently said that the state monopoly on international calls would end by 2002, two years ahead of schedule. **David Gardner, New Delhi**

E   The Indian rupee sank to an all-time low against the US dollar yesterday after concerns over the rising price of oil, the country's costliest import. Oil prices have touched 10-year highs in recent days. The Nepali rupee, which is fixed against the Indian currency, also fell to a fresh low against the dollar.

The Indian rupee has weakened by about 6.6 per cent since January. The Reserve Bank of India (RBI) tried to calm the markets but as in last month's bout of rupee nervousness, the impact of the central bank's attempts to reassure markets was short-lived. After a brief spurt, the rupee weakened following the RBI's assurances that domestic oil companies' foreign exchanges needs would be fully met. **Khozem Merchant, Bombay**

F   **BISHKEK, Kyrgyzstan**—Government troops battling Islamic fighters have freed four U.S. mountaineers held hostage by rebels in this Central Asian country, a presidential spokesman said.

The spokesman gave no information about the climbers' names, or where or when they were released, and the U.S. Embassy said it had no information. The State Department warned Americans on Thursday to avoid travel to embattled parts of Kyrgyzstan, saying the security situation was "fluid and potentially dangerous."

The rebels are thought to be members of the Islamic Movement of Uzbekistan, which opposes Uzbek President Islam Karimov, who swept across a remote, mountainous area where all three countries share frontiers.

(Reuters)

G   **BOGOTA, Colombia**—The alleged leader of one of Colombia's most powerful drug cartels was sent yesterday to the United States to stand trial, days after drug dealers threatened violence if authorities carried out the extradition.

Security forces escorted Alberto Orlandez Gamboa onto the tarmac at Bogota's international airport, where he boarded a U.S. Drug Enforcement Administration plane, said President Andres Pastrana.

U.S. authorities say Gamboa, 44, is the head of an international drug trafficking and money laundering organization headquartered in Barranquilla on Colombia's Caribbean coast. He faces charges in U.S. District Court in Manhattan that he conspired to import and distribute thousands of pounds of cocaine from Colombia to New York and other U.S. destinations. He is also accused of **smuggling cocaine to Europe and conspiring to launder millions of dollars in drug profits.**

Gamboa is the third Colombian Pastrana has extradited to the United States to face drug charges in the past nine months, following a 10-year moratorium. Gamboa's extradition comes three days after a newspaper ad paid for by a band of drug dealers known as the Our Country Movement threatened to assassinate judges and government officials unless authorities reversed their decision.

Meanwhile, the U.S. government yesterday added two other Colombians to its list of 524 individuals and companies suspected of drug trafficking and banned from doing business in the United States. Arcangel de Jesus Henao Montoya and Juan Carlos Ramirez Abadia are responsible for huge volumes of drugs that have entered the United States, the Treasury Department said.

(Associated Press)

H   Thailand and Vietnam, the world's two largest rice exporters, agreed yesterday to form a limited rice pool that will attempt to support sagging rice prices in key sales. According to a memorandum of understanding signed in Bangkok, each of the two countries will sell 100,000 tonnes of 25 per cent broken rice for $152/tonne, slightly over the current market price.

Niphon Wongtrangan, director of Thailand's Public Warehouse Organisation, said **Manila was expected** to buy bulk rice from the newly formed pool. The Philippines had been hoping to buy 200,000 tonnes of rice from Vietnam at $140/tonne, but Bangkok persuaded Hanoi to form a pool for the sale to stop price-cutting. Mr Niphon said that if successful, the pool sale could be the foundation of an Organisation of Rice Exporting Countries, which he said could work together to support rice prices, just as the Organisation of Petroleum Exporting Countries controls petroleum prices.

However, agricultural analysts said they were sceptical that Thailand and Vietnam – normally competitors in the world rice market – would be able to sustain and deepen their co-operation when it came to sales of higher-quality rice.

The signing of the deal comes at a time when both Thailand and Vietnam are still trying to assess the impact of recent severe flooding in key rice-growing areas. Around 20 per cent of Thailand's rice-growing area has been affected by the floods.

Although both Thailand and Vietnam are estimated to have lost at least 1m tonnes of rice due to the monsoon flooding, Bamroong Krichphaporn, president of the Thai Rice Miller's Association, said he expected only a slight increase in the low market prices for rice, which is in oversupply.

Thailand grows about 22m-23m tonnes of rice annually and sells 6-6.5 tonnes abroad. Vietnam produces an average 33m tonnes of rice a year. **Amy Kazmin, Bangkok**
Additional reporting by Panwadee Uraisin

I   A prominent Hong Kong political party's deputy leader yesterday stepped down from the legislative seat he won in last week's election in response to a public outcry over his failure to disclose ownership of a company to the legislature.

Gary Cheng had also come under fire after a local daily revealed that he passed on confidential government information to a client.

Despite the scandal, Mr Cheng's party, the pro-Beijing Democratic Alliance for the Betterment of Hong Kong, increased its share of the popular vote in last week's election to nearly 30 per cent from 25 per cent in the 1998 election. The party is expected to benefit politically from Mr Cheng's resignation, but observers said it was too early to say that a culture of accountability was taking root in Hong Kong.

Earlier this summer, the head of the local housing authority resigned after revelations of a series of scandals at the authority. Then, this month, the head of the University of Hong Kong resigned following allegations that he sought to interfere with opinion polls conducted by a university professor that tracked the popularity of Hong Kong's chief executive, Tung Chee-hwa, who was hand-picked by Beijing. **Rahul Jacob, Hong Kong**

Key：1—I,2—H,3—E,4—D,5—F,6—B,7—G,8—A,9—C

VIII 报刊课考试的若干建议
A Brief Introduction to Tests in Reading Comprehension of English Newspapers & Magazines

由高等学校外语专业教学指导委员会英语组 2000 年制定的《高等学校英语专业英语教学大纲》,只将外国报刊选读作为选修课,而六级考试的要求却是"能读懂难度相当于英国[The] *Times* 或[美国][The] *New York Times* 的社论和政论文章",对八级要求"能读懂一般英文报章杂志上的社论和书评"。这么高的要求表明,大纲制定者并未征求报刊教学第一线老师的意见,因而也没有多少学生能达到那么高的水平。

1985 年,编者根据以前出考试题的经验,订出这个外刊选读课考试提纲,供授课教师和读者参考。

1. 考试的目的和要求

考试的目的是使学生通过学习,了解美英的政治、外交、军事、经济、社会、文教和科技及其它当今世界大事,牢牢掌握好有关这方面的核心词语和报刊语言主要特点及读报的核心知识。对美英几大报刊的背景、立场、影响等情况也应有所了解。此外,还要求在阅读理解考试中分析外刊的政治倾向,提高判断能力。

通过 15 或 30 课报刊文选的学习、复习和考试,要求学生大大提高英语报刊阅读理解能力,初步掌握阅读美英报刊必备基本知识,从而为独立阅读打下基础。

2. 考试范围

考试以语言和读报知识基本功为主。具体讲,以课文中出现的政治、经济、外交、军事、文教、宗教、科技、国名、地名等词语为主,如 community, interest, presence, story, the White House, Whitehall, Capitol, Speaker, spokesman, G. N. P. , recession, Patriot law/missile, the House of Windsor, Protestant, launch window, Black Africa 等,并了解其中有些词的喻义。学生只要掌握课文内容并将课文后的注释(Notes)、《学习辅导》书里"**Words to Know**"及"新闻写作""语言解说""读报知识"和"学习方法"中介绍的词语和知识掌握好,及格应不成问题。不要求学生去记忆应该在中学或大学一二年级掌握的基本词语,如 byproduct, contract, prolong 等,更不能作为考试范围。阅读理解试题应结合课文中的上述内容,不宜太难。(参见《导读》"语言"和"读报知识")

3. 题型

考试题分三大部分：一是词语翻译：尤其要课文中各种题材如政治、经济、社会、宗教、科技等内容的词语，特别是一讲再讲，仍会混淆的词语。例如：the Capitol(美国国会大厦，喻"国会")与 capital 和小写的 capitol(州议会大厦，喻"州议会")不同；the Hill(国会山，也喻"国会")与 hill 不同；Speaker(议长)与 speaker 和 spokesman(发言人，不用 speaker)不同。同一名词作抽象名词与可数名词时词义不同，如 combat fatigue 与 combat fatigues 不同，democracy 与 a democracy 不同等。此外，学生尚需掌握一些习惯性翻译，如 Secretary of State 译为（美国）"国务卿"，Foreign Secretary（英国）"外交大臣"，Foreign Minister（我国）"外交部长"等。再如 Prime Minister，是王国政府的如英国、荷兰和挪威等按惯例都译为"首相"。但也有例外，如泰国虽是王国，却称"总理"。又如英国外交（和联邦事务）部的"部"，既不是"Ministry"也不是"Department"，而是"Office"。翻译党派也应注意，如德国 Christian Democratic Union 是"**基督教**民主联盟"，而意大利的 Christian Democratic Party 则指"**天主教**民主党"。此外，还应掌握其他一些用作借喻法、提喻法和隐语等的词语。二是选择题：要测试根据上下文判断词义及掌握同义词和反义词等词汇量；三是阅读 passage 或 article 后回答若干问题。passage 或 article 可考虑用要求学生自学的课文。如是课外的，文字应比课文容易些。试题内容与所学课文尽可能有联系。自考生和专科生试题应比在校本科生要浅显些，但第一部分的试题基本相同。

4. 时限

考试时间限定为两小时。考试第一部分的 20—35 个词语翻译需约 20 分钟，第二部分约 40 分钟，第三部分约一小时。

5. 复习方法和建议

复习时一定要读懂课文内容，结合有关文化背景知识重点讲解，使学生掌握上述有关方面的词语，尤其要学会辨析易混淆的词和掌握报刊语言中常见的多义词和喻词。使学生语言和知识双丰收。

以上选自《导读》第七章第五节，部分内容做了修改。

IX 考试样题
Sample Test

Part One (共 30 分)

Translate the following terms into Chinese. (Note: the complete form is REQUIRED if the term is an abbreviation.)

Ⅰ. (共 10 分, 每小题 2 分)

1. Yawn
2. GOP
3. NATO
4. CIA
5. FIFA

Ⅱ. (共 20 分, 每小题 1 分)

6. The Pulitzer Prize
7. The Pentagon (fig.)
8. Times Square
9. geopolitics
10. Silicon Valley (fig.)
11. guru
12. op-ed
13. classified ads
14. The Ivy League
15. Hispanic
16. The physically challenged
17. the Capitol (fig.)
18. House Speaker
19. the House of Lords/Commons
20. perjury and obstruction of justice
21. the Senate/the House of Representatives
22. checks and balances
23. Attorney General (U.S.)
24. recession
25. private sector

Part Two (共 10 分)

Answer the following questions briefly.

1. List the dominant British newspapers and magazines. (at least three for each)

2. List the four major news agencies in the world.

Part Three (共 10 分, 每小题 2 分)

Paraphrase the underlined parts in the following sentences.

1. Hebert Wang worked for six months at Nortel in Toronto, but he quickly returned to Beijing to found Prient, a start-up that <u>helps old-line companies go online</u>.

2. We're proving that raising standards and <u>holding schools and students accountable for results</u> can lead to dramatic improvements in student achievement.

3. <u>Such frugality seems to run in his circle.</u>

4. The government has also been <u>going after</u> employers who hire undocumented workers.

5. When consumers stop spending, <u>the companies that cater to them idle and lay off</u>.

Part Four: Reading Comprehension (共 40 分)

In this part there are four passages, each of which is followed by several questions. Answer the questions after you finish reading the passages.

Passage One (共 10 分, 每小题 5 分)

The dragon tucks in

Chinese companies are becoming aggressive buyers of overseas assets. It will take longer for them to become smarter ones.

"To spread the 'China Threat' and try to curb China's progress and starve its energy needs is not in the interest of world stability and development. Such attempts are doomed to fail." These feisty words were uttered this week by Zhang Guobao, vice-chairman of China's National Development and Reform Commission, during a visit to an energy conference in New Orleans. He was responding to efforts by American politicians to block an $18.5 billion cash bid made on June 22nd by the China National Offshore Oil Company (CNOOC) for

Unocal, a mid-sized American oil firm.

The spat (*verbal fight*) over CNOOC is a symptom of the growing unease felt in developed economies, but especially in America, as more and more Chinese companies have looked abroad for expansion and technological know-how. Just days before the CNOOC bid, Haier, a white-goods maker, bid \$2.25 billion for Maytag, a troubled American rival. In May IBM finalised the sale of its personal-computer arm to Lenovo, a deal that also raised political hackles in America.

Americans remember a similar period in the 1980s when Japan was accused of seeking global economic domination as its companies bought everything from Hollywood studios to paintings by Van Gogh. They seem to have forgotten that that threat proved transient, indeed was never really a threat at all. Now comes an increasingly assertive China, its companies flush with cheap cash and its government desperate to maintain its phenomenal economic momentum. As so often when politicians are involved, the truth about the overseas expansion of China's companies is much more complex than hot rhetoric suggests.

Even before the latest row over the CNOOC bid, there were clear signs of China's mounting interest in acquiring real assets abroad aside from oil and gas. The volume of transactions involving a Chinese buyer and an international target has jumped from \$2 billion – 3 billion in previous years to almost \$23 billion for 2005. Late last year Baosteel, China's largest steelmaker, made a big investment in Brazil, while in 2004 TCL, its leading television producer, bought most of the TV-manufacturing business of France's Thomson plus a mobile handset-making business from Alcatel. Other deals have been less visible, but no less important.

Does this amount to a carefully planned assault on global assets? For all its appearance as a communist-directed monolith, China is ultimately too fragmented for that. Unlike Japan's fabled Ministry of International Trade and Industry in the 1960s and 1970s, China does not have a single agency powerful enough to be an effective co-ordinator. Nevertheless, China's acquisition spree has clear political backing. The leadership in Beijing is determined to create its own set of "global champions"—30 – 50 internationally competitive, yet still state-controlled, firms.

To foster rapid growth and create jobs, China deliberately opened its domestic market to foreign competition relatively early in its economic development. But the quid pro quo (Latin: compensation) implicit in this strategy was that the government would support, both diplomatically and financially, Chinese companies overseas.

Questions:

1. What are the latest bids made by the Chinese enterprises to purchase overseas assets?
2. Will China succeed in its acquisition of foreign estates in the near future? Why?

Passage Two (共 15 分, 每小题 3 分)

America frets as only the rich get richer

"THE top fifth of American households claimed 50.4% of all income last year, the largest slice since the Census Bureau (人口统计局) started tracking the data in 1967." So reported *The Wall Street Journal* just one day before the Commerce Department announced that second-quarter corporate profits were 20.5% higher than a year ago and accounted for 12.2% of gross domestic product (GDP), the highest level in 40 years.

Throw in reports of layoffs at Ford, GM, Intel, and decisions in the nation's boardrooms to reduce the value of workers' pensions while preserving the generous pensions of top executives, and you have some reason to wonder if the famous American dream has turned into a nightmare.

Something is definitely going on that is worrying many observers. Since the 2001 recession year, the economy has grown by almost 12% while the income of the median household — the point at which half of American households have more, and half less — has declined by 0.5%. Last year earnings for full-time workers actually declined — by 1.8% for men, and 1.3% for women.

That said, there is no question that income distribution is becoming a matter of concern — and a political issue — in a country in which calls to man the barricades (防御工事) of the class struggle have historically fallen on deaf ears. When Al Gore played the class card in his 2000 presidential campaign, he was trumped by George Bush's call for tax cuts, even though those reductions benefited wealthy as well as lower-income families.

That was then, and this is now. Centre-left think tanks and opposition politicians are not alone in expressing concern about trends in income distribution. Federal Reserve Board chairman Ben Bernanke recently told a congressional committee: "We want everybody in this society to participate in the American dream. And to the extent that incomes and wealth are spreading apart, I think that is not a good trend."

Two developments are causing observers such as Bernanke some concern. The first is the growing sense that the rich are getting richer, something that nobody save a few hardline lefties ever objected to in America, so long as the poor were also getting richer. Now it seems they aren't. Or, at least, so far in the recent recovery they haven't been.

The second problem relates to the core of the American Dream — social mobility. An oft-told joke in America is that a European (in pre-Thatcher days, we would have said British) worker, seeing his boss drive through the gates in a Rolls-Royce, would want to scratch it, whereas an American worker would think: "Some day I will own one of those".

That worker might be re-examining his position. More and more American workers are coming to believe they and their children are no more likely to rise above their current station than are their European counterparts.

Writing in the *Financial Times*, economics professor Jacques Mistral, of the Conseil d'Analyse Economique and a senior fellow at Harvard's Kennedy School of Government, summaries recent studies as follows: "The situation of a son is more than ever likely to be dictated by his father's social position than by his own merits. If your parents are rich, the likelihood of your being rich is as high as the probability of your being tall if your parents are tall."

So what is going on in America? One thing is huge immigration by poor, unskilled workers. As they enter the workforce, taking on menial jobs at wages too low to attract American workers but a king's ransom by the standards of the clapped-out Mexican economy, they pull average wages down. Some of these workers and their children eventually move up the income ladder, witness the mowers and hoers we know in Colorado who now own their own nurseries. But many never do, partly because, unlike previous waves of immigrants, they return home after accumulating enough money to buy a home or farm or business in their native land.

Another fundamental force at work is globalisation. In recent years more than one billion unskilled, low-paid workers have entered the international workforce — good news for consumers, bad news for Americans sewing shirts and turning out trainers. Meanwhile, globalisation has opened an international market for talented managers, driving up the demand for such executives and, hence, their salaries. The result is downward pressure on wages of the unskilled, upward pressures on executive compensation, and a widening income gap, and one that government-operated retraining programmes have failed to narrow.

All is not lost, however. Ed Lazear, chairman of the president's Council of Economic Advisers, says that hourly earnings have recently begun to grow. Bernanke agrees: "I do think wages will rise. I'm a little surprised they haven't risen more already."

Equally important, Americans are taking steps to reduce the so-called education premium that accounts for some of the increased inequality. Diana Furchtgott-Roth, a colleague at the Hudson Institute since leaving the Labor Department, where she served as chief economist, says: "Our challenge is to get more people to take advantage of educational opportunities ranging from apprenticeships to universities." One million more Americans are now enrolled in institutions offering two-year programmes of advanced education and training than was the case a decade ago.

To borrow from the title of a popular sitcom about the rising black middle class, they will soon be "Movin' on Up".

Irwin Stelzer is a business adviser and director of economic policy studies at the Hudson Institute

Questions:

1. Paraphrase the underlined sentence in the fourth paragraph.

2. The core of the American dream is social mobility. Explain what is social mobility.

3. What is the function of inserting the anecdote about the

American worker and European worker in the seventh paragraph?

4. What are the reasons for the problems in America?

5. What measures has America taken to narrow the widening income gap?

Passage Three (共 5 分)

Americans honor parks at Capitol Rotunda

WASHINGTON (AP) — In hushed reverence, Americans paid tribute Monday to Rosa Parks, with more than 30,000 filing silently by her casket in the Capitol Rotunda and a military honor guard saluting the woman whose defiant act on a city bus inspired the modern civil rights movement.

"I rejoice that my country recognizes that this woman changed the course of American history, that this woman became a cure for the cancer of segregation," said the Rev. Vernon Shannon, 68, pastor of John Wesley African-Methodist-Episcopal Zion in Washington, one of many who rose before dawn to see the casket.

Senate Majority Leader Bill Frist, R-Tenn., accompanied new Supreme Court nominee Samuel Alito and his family to the Rotunda, where they paused in silent remembrance. Several senators joined the procession.

Elderly women carrying purses, young couples holding hands and small children in the arms of their parents reverently proceeded around the raised wooden casket. A Capitol Police spokeswoman, Sgt. Jessica Gissubel, said more than 30,000 passed through the Rotunda since Sunday evening, when the viewing began.

Many were overcome by emotion. Monica Grady, 47, of Greenbelt, Md., was moved to tears, she said, that Parks was "so brave at the time without really knowing the consequences" of her actions.

Parks, a former seamstress, became the first woman to lie in honor in the Rotunda, sharing the tribute bestowed upon Abraham Lincoln, John F. Kennedy and other national leaders.

Parks also was being remembered Monday at a memorial service at the Metropolitan A. M. E. Church in Washington and was then to lie in repose at the Charles H. Wright Museum of African American History in Detroit. The program at the Washington memorial service included tributes by Oprah Winfrey, NAACP chairman Julian Bond, Sen. Sam Brownback, R-Kan., and Conyers.

Bush, who presented a wreath but did not speak at the ceremony, issued a proclamation ordering the U.S. flag to be flown at half-staff over all public buildings Wednesday, the day of Parks' funeral and burial in Detroit.

"She was a citizen in the best sense of the word," said Sen. Tom Harkin, D-Iowa. "She caused things to happen in our society that made us a better, more caring, more just society."

Question:

Who was Rosa Parks? And why was she honored by the Americans at Capitol Rotunda at her death?

Passage Four (共 10 分,每小题 5 分)

Editorial: The Bra Wars

The Bush administration, ignoring the lesson offered by a similarly ill-advised move across the Atlantic, has announced more restrictions on imports of bras and some fabrics made in China. The European Union has shown quite ably just how ridiculous this strategy is. Some 80 million garments have been held up in European ports because of complaints by European textile manufacturers about the flood of cheaper Chinese-made goods since the World Trade Organization abolished the quota system on Jan. 1. Most of those shipments have already been paid for, but arrived after E.U. quotas went into effect. The E.U.'s trade chief, Peter Mandelson, has asked the group's member nations to let the bras and other items in. He recently warned that not doing so could lead to "severe economic pain for many smaller retailers and medium-sized businesses." European officials and China are still negotiating over the quota issue.

The real indication of how bankrupt the restrictions are can be seen in the emptying shelves at stores catering to low-income people. No European products can fill the breach; European manufacturers make high-end lingerie (女贴身内衣), not the cheap stuff.

This isn't the way free trade is supposed to work. For all the talk on both sides of the Atlantic about the benefits of a global market unfettered by protectionism, the wealthy developed countries seem to want free trade only when it benefits their chosen big corporations. Meanwhile, poor consumers suffer the most. The Progressive Policy Institute, a research group in Washington, estimates that shoes and clothing — particularly cheap shoes and cheap clothes — have far higher import duties, relatively speaking, than most other products.

None of this politically expedient protectionism will change a single thing about the way the future is shaping up. Trade experts are unanimous in their belief that China, with its huge modern factories and inexhaustible pool of cheap labor, will continue to dominate the world market for mass-market textiles and apparel. Instead of trying to fight the inevitable, policy leaders in America and Europe should be focusing on developing industries in which their countries can remain competitive and on retraining the textile workers whose jobs migrate. Punishing lower-income consumers in the name of protecting jobs in a dying industry is not the way to go.

Questions:

1. Why did the US and EU exert restrictions on imports of bras and some fabrics made in China?

2. What strategy does the reporter suggest the American and European governments adopt in face of a China which will inevitably dominate the world market for textiles and apparel?

Part Five: Translation (共 10 分)

Saddam verdict may be delayed, prosecutor said

A court trying Saddam Hussein for crimes against humanity could delay its verdict by a few days, the chief prosecutor said on Sunday, in a move that would shift the announcement until after US midterm elections.

The US-backed court had been due to deliver a Verdict on November 5, two days before the US elections in which President George W. Bush's Republicans fear they could lose control of Congress.

The chief prosecutor, Jaafa al-Moussawi, said the Iraqi High Tribunal was still working on the judgment. "We will know a day or two before the trial if they are ready to announce the verdict." Moussawi said.

Saddam could go to the gallows if he is found guilty over his role in the killing of 148 Shi'ite Muslims in the village of Dujail.

参考答案

Part One (共 30 分)

1. Young and Wealthy but normal (年轻而富裕但又节俭[的一代])
2. Grand Old Party (a nickname for the Republicans) 老大党(美国共和党别称)
3. North Atlantic Treaty Organization (北大西洋公约组织)
4. Central Intelligence Agency (中央情报局)
5. Federation Internationale de Football Association (国际足球联合会)
6. 普利策奖
7. 五角大楼；美国国防部
8. 时报广场
9. 地缘政治学
10. 硅谷；高科技集中地
11. 可信赖的顾问、导师
12. 社论对面版，时论专栏版
13. 分类广告
14. 常青藤联合会
15. 居住在美国说西班牙语的拉美人(的)
16. 身体有缺陷者，残疾人
17. 国会或州议会大厦；美国国会或州议会
18. 议长
19. 贵族院(英国上院)/平民院(英国下院)
20. 伪证和妨碍司法执行
21. 参议院/众议院
22. (权力)制衡
23. 司法部长(美国)
24. (经济)衰退
25. 私营部门

Part Two (共 10 分)

1. British newspapers: *The Times*, *The Financial Times*, *The*

Guardian, *The Daily Telegraph*

British magazines: *The Economist*, *The Spectator*, *New Statesman*

2. AP (Associated Press); UPI (United Press International); Reuters; PA (Press Association)

Part Three (共 10 分,每小题 2 分)

1. helps traditional companies advertise or do business through the Internet.

2. making schools and students take the responsibility for results

3. It seems that such frugality is popular among his friends.

4. trying to arrest or punish

5. the companies that provide consumers with what they need now have nothing to do and have to stop their business and dismiss their employees

Part Four (共 40 分)
Passage One (共 10 分,每小题 5 分)

1. CNOOC's ＄18.5 billion bid for Unocal (aborted); Haier's ＄2.25 billion bid for Maytag; Lenovo's purchase of IBM personal computer department; Baosteel's investment in Brazil last year; and TCL's purchase of France's Thomson plus a mobile handset-making business from Alcatel.

2. No. China is too fragmented; she does not have a single agency powerful enough to be an effective co-ordinator as Japan did in the 60s and 70s.

Passage Two (共 15 分,每小题 3 分)

1. During the 2000 presidential election the Democratic candidate Al Gore's campaign slogan is social class, while the Republican candidate George W. Bush's is tax cuts. In the end Al Gore was defeated by Bush, even though Bush's tax cut benefited the wealthy more than the middle-lower-income families.

2. Social mobility means that people can move from one social group or status to another, often higher than the original. Or moving upward to a better social group.

3. To explain the American dream, which means that a common citizen can achieve success through hard work.

4. One is the huge immigration by poor, unskilled workers. The other is globalisation which drives up the demand for talented executives and hence their salaries and the consequent downward pressure on wages of the unskilled workers.

5. To provide educational opportunities ranging from apprenticeships to universities.

Passage Three (共 5 分)

Rosa Parks was a black woman who refused to give up her seat for a white man on a city bus in Montgomery in 1955, which touched off the bus boycott and later the civil rights movement in the 1960s in the US.

Passage Four (共 10 分,每小题 5 分)

1. Because the flood of cheaper Chinese-made goods since the World Trade Organization abolished the quota system on Jan. 1 hurt their textile manufacturers.

2. Instead of trying to fight the inevitable, policy leaders in America and Europe should, instead of practising protectionism, be focusing on developing industries in which their countries can remain competitive and on retraining the textile workers whose jobs migrate.

Part Five (共 10 分)

检察官称,萨达姆判决可能被推迟

正以反人类罪审判萨达姆·侯赛因的法庭首席检察官周日表示,法庭可能推迟几天宣布判决结果。此举意味着宣判将推迟到美国中期选举以后。

这家美国支持的法庭原定的宣判日期是 11 月 5 日,也就是美国中期选举前两天。总统乔治·W. 布什领导的共和党人担心他们将在此次选举中失去对国会的控制权。

首席检察官贾法尔·穆萨维说,伊拉克高级法庭还在研究如何进行判决。他说:"我们会在审判前一两天获悉他们是否准备宣判。"

如果被判对杜贾尔村 148 名什叶派穆斯林遇害事件负有罪责,萨达姆可能被判绞刑。

以上试题和答案均由一编委提供。特此说明。

《美英报刊文章阅读(精选本)(第五版)》

尊敬的老师:

您好!

为了方便您更好地使用本教材,获得最佳教学效果,我们特向使用该书作为教材的教师赠送本教材配套课件资料。如有需要,请完整填写"教师联系表"并加盖所在单位系(院)公章,免费向出版社索取。

北京大学出版社

教 师 联 系 表

教材名称	《美英报刊文章阅读(精选本)(第五版)》					
姓名:		性别:		职务:		职称:
E-mail:		联系电话:		邮政编码:		
供职学校:			所在院系:			(章)
学校地址:						
教学科目与年级:			班级人数:			
通信地址:						

填写完毕后,请将此表邮寄给我们,我们将为您免费寄送本教材配套资料,谢谢!

北京市海淀区成府路205号
北京大学出版社外语编辑部 李 颖
邮政编码:100871
电子邮箱:evalee1770@sina.com

邮购部电话:010-62534449
市场营销部电话:010-62750672
外语编辑部电话:010-62754382